D1664279

Remaking Home

RECONSTRUCTING LIFE, PLACE AND IDENTITY IN ROME AND AMSTERDAM

Maja Korac

Berghahn Books

NEW YORK · OXFORD

First published in 2009 by

Berghahn Books

www.BerghahnBooks.com

© 2009 Maja Korac

Library of Congress Cataloging-in-Publication Data

A C.I.P. record for this title is available at the Library of Congress

British Library Cataloguing in Publication Data

A catalogue record for this book is available from the British Library

Printed in the United States on acid-free paper

ISBN: 978-1-84545-391-6 (hardback)

In memory of my father
Miladin Miša Korać

Contents

Acknowledgements

There are many people without whose generosity, encouragement, and support my research and this book would have not been possible. First and foremost, I am indebted to the people who graciously agreed to talk about their exile experiences with me, and who were unfailingly generous with their time and support for my research whilst I lived among them in Rome and Amsterdam. This opportunity to thank them in writing gives me a great pleasure.

I am also indebted to numerous people who worked in different governmental and non-governmental organisations and academic institutions in Rome, Amsterdam and the Netherlands. Without their support and generosity in providing me with essential information I would have not been able to find my way through the labyrinth of the institutional systems, policies, practices and data concerning refugees in the two cities and countries. My research benefited greatly from being able to share ideas with them.

Vela Todorvić, in Rome, and Ava Mirković, in Amsterdam, were much more than my research assistants, without whose work, knowledge and skill my research and life in these two cities would have been very different and much more difficult. I also want to thank Tanja Zvekić for being such an excellent interpreter for some of the interviews with officials in Rome.

Doing this research project was not a problem free experience and it felt at times a heavy burden to carry alone on my shoulders. We, social scientists, are not specifically trained to deal with (emotionally) difficult research experiences, which often occur during prolonged periods of fieldwork when we are continuously communicating and dealing with people who are in precarious situations and distress, as refugees often are. The friendships I developed with Grazia Curalli and Lucia Falchetti in Rome, and with Pieter Thoenes and Jolien van der Mee in Amsterdam, helped me ease the burden of the stories and situations I witnessed, some of which were not easy to take. I am also grateful for having the opportunity to discuss with them their work with refugees. These exchanges of ideas and experiences were invaluable to my research and to this book. The *joie de vivre* and friendliness of Grazia and Lucia made me also feel very much at 'home' in Rome. The insistence of Pieter and Jolien that I cannot leave Amsterdam without ever riding a bike, even if only by sitting at the back of one of theirs, made me feel that I 'belong' to that city and its distinctive way of life.

I have benefited greatly from being able to share ideas with researchers at the Refugee Studies Centre (RSC), University of Oxford, during my tenure at RSC as a Senior Researcher, between 1999 and 2001. I also want to thank the members of the Research Advisory Committee: Cathie Lloyd, Areti Siani, David Turton, and Sandra Wallman for giving me valuable advice on aspects of the project as I carried out the fieldwork.

I wish to thank the *Lisa Gilad Initiative* for funding this complex research project. The Lisa Gilad Initiative is a charitable trust, set up in 1998, to commemorate the life and work of the late Lisa Gilad, an anthropologist and a founding member of Canada Immigration and Refugee Board.

Since I joined the University of East London, in 2002, I benefited greatly from numerous fruitful exchanges of ideas with my colleagues, the members of the Refugee Studies team and the Refugee Research Centre, as well as with numerous students who have taken this MA course in the past years. I would also like to thank Peter Loizos for his thoughtful comments on an earlier version of this manuscript as well as two anonymous reviewers for their valuable suggestions and constructive critical remarks. This book has taken far too long to write and I am grateful to Dawn Chatty and Jo Boyden of RSC and Berghahn Books for their patience, support, and understanding.

My special gratitude goes to my family back 'home', who have supported me unfailingly over many years of our transnational family life, and who have always been there for me, although not necessarily physically present. And last but not least, a very special 'thank you' to my husband Mark Sanderson for his loving support, understanding, and patience while I was 'otherwise engaged'.

Introduction:
Reconstructing Life, Place
and Identity

This book focuses on the process of reconstructing life, place and identity. It examines how refugees, understood as social actors, make and remake their lives in new sociocultural environments. In this book, I explore the lived-in worlds of refugees by focusing on the different types of connection, emerging forms of interaction, and networks of social relations through which they forge a place for themselves in a new society, create meaning and form attachments. Discussion in this book is embedded in the understanding that a sense of place is developed through various forms of social relations and tied through the interaction of structure and agency. In the following pages, I uncover and examine how real people navigate through the difficulties of their *dis*placement as well as through numerous barriers to and scenarios of their *em*placement, the intersection of which is central to our understanding of what it is to be a refugee.

The term refugee here signifies forced migrants, understood as people forced into decisions to leave their homes and continue their lives elsewhere, irrespective of the legal label they may carry. Because labels such as 'refugee' or 'asylum seeker' relate to the legal processes of granting or denying certain aspects of citizenship rights, they indeed affect how and under what circumstances the lives of individual people or entire groups originating from the same country will unfold. This book examines the relationship between specific contexts of reception and how people go about their lives in new sociocultural settings. It explores how they set up priorities and develop strategies to overcome their predicament. My analysis therefore acknowledges the role of dominant institutional structures in determining one's rights to establish a home. My interest is however to uncover how people organize their experiences in different contexts and in relation to their individual biographies and life circumstances in order to negotiate a place for themselves in the new society.

This book is based upon my empirical research in Amsterdam and Rome exploring the experiences of refugees from the successor states of Yugoslavia who were struggling to make a new place for themselves in the Netherlands and in Italy.[1] It is also inspired and generated by other types of encounters I have had with people who are struggling to 'nest' themselves in new socioeconomic and cultural environments. For the past two decades I have been involved, both professionally and personally, with people who were forced by political upheavals and socioeconomic turmoil to make decisions to leave their places of origin.

In Toronto, where I lived, studied and worked for a period of time, I met many people who, like myself, left Yugoslavia and went into 'voluntary' exile in the early 1990s. Dissatisfied with the political, social, and economic situation in the country, which was caught in the turmoil of rising militant ethnonationalism, we went in search of a place which would offer 'a minimal condition for some kind of democracy of selves' (Cockburn 1997). Unlike us, who still had our family, friends and physical homes to return to, there were also many who fled to save their lives in a literal sense of the word, whose loved ones might have been killed, and homes destroyed. Their choices about when, how and where to go, and decisions to stay or leave, were of a different character, much more limited and coerced. This firsthand experience of displacement and of the struggle to emplace myself professionally, socially, culturally, and legally, prompted me to question many of the concepts and much of the knowledge produced about refugees. It made me aware, for example, how the notion of 'community', to which, somehow, all people coming from the same country naturally belong, or for which they strive, can straightjacket our understanding of the processes of nesting of refugees who may have, and often do, different ideas about connecting and belonging. In the case of people coming from Yugoslavia and its successor states, the understanding of community also had specific connotations. The conflict brought to the attention of the international media, public, political, and academic realms the issue of ethnic difference, the grievances, and animosities within the region. As a consequence, interpreting and understanding these differences and constructing the 'identity' and the 'community' of those labelled by their ethnicity became central to approaching people from the war-torn country as well as to creating knowledge about them. This experience made me also particularly sensitive to the processes and consequences of labelling people who were forced into decisions to flee their homes, the processes associated with institutional and legal systems, as well as those relating to public discourses and professional/academic settings.[2]

In Belgrade, where I did my research with and about refugee women and various autonomous women's groups, working with them in the mid 1990s, I met women who became refugees in a place and country that not long before their flight they had considered their homeland. At the time of my research however it had become a contested place for many of them.[3] This experience made me aware that displacement and emplacement are equally complex and challenging experiences, even in contexts in which there is hardly any cultural or language difference to speak of.[4]

In London, where I teach in the Refugee Studies MA Programme at the University of East London, I continue to have close contacts with students who are also refugees. Witnessing and often actively supporting their struggles in learning to live with their experiences of displacement and how to emplace themselves is a constant reminder of the importance of the different contexts, backgrounds and histories of people on the move and of how they shape their lives and emplacement strategies.

Through these experiences, professional and personal, I have learnt that to understand the reasons for and patterns of movement, and the future orientation of people who were forced into decisions to leave their place of origin, one needs to focus simultaneously on aspects of agency, structures, social positioning and everyday practices. All these elements intersect in specific contexts resulting in complex, varied, and dynamic effects and outcomes. In other words, rather than emphasising boundaries and territories, focusing solely on the states and examining normative models of integration and acculturation of the 'immigrant' or the 'refugee', this book offers insights into ideas of individual people and their orientation to connecting and belonging in specific contexts and points in time.

Problems with Centring on the State

Scholarly literature as well as policy documents focusing on the process of economic, social, political, and cultural inclusion of refugees or immigrants overwhelmingly emphasise the agency of the structural and institutional domains of the receiving societies. Terms such as integration, incorporation or settlement have been used by different authors as well as by different (state) actors involved in researching, conceptualising, regulating or supporting the process of social inclusion and adjustment of refugees and other newcomers.[5] Theories of citizenship have often been used to outline frameworks of meaning of the process of integration. Because citizenship guarantees legal, political, and socioeconomic as well as cultural and religious rights, it is centrally linked to social inclusion.[6] When social inclusion is viewed from the perspective of citizenship, conceptualised as a set of rights associated with its different aspects (e.g., Penninx, 2004a), then increasing social inclusion becomes an issue of developing instruments to facilitate access to these rights. These instruments of access and related policy approaches to integration depend on how the membership of the political community is conceptualised. Cross-country comparisons distinguishing between different national 'models' demonstrate that integration can be understood as assimilation or multiculturalism, or increasingly as a mixture of assimilationist tendencies and elements of multiculturalism (e.g., Bauböck et al.1996; Brubaker 1992; Castles 1995; Favell 2000; Soysal 1994). Hence, these and other studies document that the meaning of integration is differently defined in different states. For states promoting assimilation, it means socioeconomic and cultural cohesion based upon a quest for homogeneity. States allowing for multiculturalism understand and promote integration in terms of overcoming barriers to socioeconomic inclusion of ethnic minority groups, including refugees/immigrants. Some authors are however becoming increasingly aware that this overemphasis on the national unit results in overly abstract national-level models of integration (e.g., Soysal 1994). In recent years proposals and attempts have been made to focus more on the local/city level at which integration actually occurs (e.g., Favell 2001; Penninx et al. 2004). Regardless of these differences in meaning, approaches, and levels of analysis these conceptualisations of integration have one thing in common – the agency and instrumentality of the receiving state and its structures are at the centre of attention and inquiry.

Studies examining immigrant adaptation within the framework of acculturation represent the only exception to this emphasis on the receiving state, placing the migrant/refugee at the centre of analytic interest. The concept of acculturation has been widely used in cross-cultural psychology (e.g., Sam and Berry 2006). It refers to the cultural and psychological processes and outcomes of 'intercultural contact', and focuses on how refugees and other immigrants resolve dilemmas and difficulties involved in such contact (Berry 1997: 8). The negotiation of the relationship between retention of cultural identity and motivation to reach out and seek positive relations within the larger or dominant society will determine whether the actual outcome of the process of acculturation is assimilation, integration, separation/segregation, or marginalisation (Berry 1997).

Regardless of the scope and comprehensiveness of Berry's analysis, the model he proposed has been criticised by many. His critics argue that his acculturation model provides a framework for static and structural analysis, rather than for analyses of concrete individual or group differences in goals, beliefs, and coping skills (Lazarus 1997). They also point out that Berry's model does not adequately address the complexity of modern societies, and does not recognise and capture the range of different spheres of acculturation to some of which refugees and other immigrants chose to adapt more than to others. Instead, the model implies the assumption of a single monolithic majority society consisting of fixed dimensions along which immigrants move during the process of cultural transition (Horenczyk 1997: 35–36). Berry's critics also argue that the model fails to take into account changes in the newcomers' construction of their social and cultural worlds. They emphasise that during the process of acculturation the culture of origin often becomes reinterpreted or reconstructed without any change in intensity and extent of alliance to it. However, by linking the weakening of prior cultural alliances to the adoption of norms, values and behaviours characterising receiving societies, Berry's model treats culture as a monolithic and fixed concept, and therefore it is not capable of capturing and incorporating these complexities (Horenczyk 1997: 37–38).

Very importantly, Berry's model of acculturation is limited to the consequences of intercultural contact and does not allow for a fuller analysis of elements associated with adjustment to life in a new society that are not necessarily acculturation phenomena (e.g., acquisition of new skills). Adaptation and adjustment to the receiving society is much more than 'shedding culture' (Lazarus 1997). Finally, the model does not reflect the fact that the social practices of migrants are increasingly multi-sited and not confined by nation-state borders. Their sociocultural identities are becoming increasingly embedded in transnational social spaces. Their transnational practices allow them to experience the reality of movement and attachment simultaneously (Levitt and Glick Schiller 2004). The realities of transnational processes do not correspond to the notion of acculturation understood as a choice between adopting a new 'national culture' or rejecting it.

Outside cultural psychology literature, however, institutional arrangements within the receiving society remain at the centre of attention. This is because they are seen as determining the opportunities and scope for action, although immigrants, as individuals and groups, with their 'efforts and adaptation' are recognised as one side of the integration process (Penninx 2003). This further leads to a proliferation of (empirical) research on how immigrants/refugees adapt functionally by 'measuring' their integration in terms of language proficiency, housing, education, and employment, as well as showing some interest in their sociocultural adjustment approached analytically in a variety of ways. These studies assess how or whether refugees 'fit in' in the state-defined modes of integration, and thus they approach integration as a top-down process of adjustment. Not surprisingly, these studies show that the outcomes of integration are not uniform. Indeed, there are differences among different immigrant groups within the same country/policy context, as well as in how immigrants from the same country of origin adjust and attempt to incorporate themselves in different countries/contexts.

There is no doubt that immigrants, and indeed refugees, and receiving societies are unequal partners. Conditions of entry, that is, to the reception process and to membership, are critical for how immigrants become incorporated into receiving societies. In the case of refugees and their incorporation in new societies, these conditions are alarmingly and continuously deteriorating, leaving these people with fewer right-based and provision-based options concerning where and how they can make 'home' for themselves.[7] However, the primary focus of academic inquiry on the agency of the receiving state and its institutional mechanisms leaves us without much insight into how the people who are 'managed' and 'guided' by the receiving states actually 'nest' themselves in their new sociocultural environments; how they strategise and negotiate between continuity and change, existential needs and longer-term life plans, old loyalties and new identities. This leads to the processes of bureaucratic, legal, and public labelling of newcomers in general, and refugees in particular. As a result, they are often sympathised with or pitied, increasingly also feared, but seldom understood.

Rethinking Refugeehood: Focusing on Processes, Intersections and Agency

Debates on 'the refugee' as a category, and how refugees are to be distinguished from other migrants, are longstanding and ongoing.[8] One of the elements used in defining refugees is the involuntary character of their movement, prompted by political violence either perpetrated by the state or segments of the population, resulting in the breakdown of a society, armed violence, and dislocation of populations. Targets of this violence can be either individuals or groups considered opponents of the political elites, or other target groups, such as ethnic or religious groups. Conflicts of the 1990s also produced many unselected victims of the generalised violence characterising these 'new wars' (Kaldor 1999). Because of the international, national, transnational, and global character of the sociopolitical causes of refugee movements (Zolberg et al. 1989) and the resulting processes of (mass) victimization of local populations, including those on the move, refugees are very often approached and represented as victims, traumatised, passive and helpless, rather than as people who actively struggle to overcome their victimisation. These notions, devoid of agency, go hand in glove with the emphasis on the involuntary character of movement, implying a lack of choice and decision. Its link with contexts of sociopolitical turmoil, most often accompanied by physical, armed violence, constructs the flight as a life-preserving endeavour that is in opposition to life-betterment efforts.

This type of representation of refugees is often also prompted by the need to speak for or on behalf of refugees to secure their protection. A longstanding, highly politicised, and often heated debate on asylum rights in many parts of the world revolving around the issue of 'bogus' versus 'genuine' refugees seems to generate further the need to essentialise refugees and represent them as 'ultimate victims', hence, deserving international (state) protection. Refugeehood and victimhood are consequently often seen as one and the same. This fits well in the discourse surrounding the debate on 'genuine' refugees. In the current political and public climate 'genuine' refugees are only those fleeing for their lives, hence, acting upon instincts rather than any other human, moral, social or political need. If they strive for better lives they are not 'genuine'.

These essentialist notions of refugeehood are also linked to the concepts and experiences of terminal loss, bereavement, and disempowerment. Refugeehood and the experience of life away from one's 'true home' (Said 1984) or native place and culture is often described as 'the saddest of fates' caused by an 'unhealable rift' between peoples and their native places (Said 2000 [1993]). The loss of place, or displacement, regarded as an abrupt loss of basic material sources of livelihood as well as a radical challenge to one's sense of identity and belonging, has become central to the notion of refugeehood. There is no doubt that dislocation caused by flight, and the struggle to regain control and reestablish one's life, cause, as Eastmond (1997: 11) has put it, 'a social disruption at structural levels which leaves no domain of social experience untouched, with profound and existential consequences'. Viewed through this lens, refugeehood is centrally linked to feelings of utmost uncertainty and a grave sense of loss.

Becoming and being a refugee, however, is a *transformative* experience and practice, a process, rather than a set of static (disempowering) structures. This process also entails empowering experiences. It opens up new social spaces and opportunities for refugees, it also offers 'a plurality of vision', because new life circumstances allow for the awareness of two 'homes' and cultures, which are 'occurring together *contrapuntally*' (Said 1984: 35; emphasis added). This is because displacement or a loss of place, in specific circumstances and contexts, can be experienced as freedom from the preestablished sociocultural norms of the native society and country that often constrain individual behaviour and actions. For many women, for example, exile opens up their gender space by providing new opportunities linked to the process of reshaping gender roles within and outside the household (Eastmond 1993; Friere 1995; Korac 2004; Matsuoka and Sorenson 1999; McSpadden 1999). That forced movement and refugeehood are not only about loss of place and disempowerment, but should also be considered as the processes of place making, of regaining control and establishing oneself in the new life circumstances, has been increasingly emphasised in studies about refugees, diasporas and transnational communities. Malkki (1995: 517) was one of the first among refugee scholars to point out that emplacement is the flipside of displacement.

This call to rethink refugeehood by acknowledging it as a process entailing both disempowering and empowering experiences and structures is not another of many attempts to introduce a binary logic or opposition to the refugee studies discourse.[9] Nor is it indeed intended to undermine the plea of refugee advocates for the right of forced migrants to protection. Rather, the emphasis on displacement and emplacement is to make an analytical distinction between experiences and practices that occur simultaneously and intersect as a function of the interaction of structure and refugee agency. By pointing to this distinction, we can move away from the hegemony of victimhood in the refugee studies discourse, while still acknowledging that victimisation, loss and disempowerment are some of the central characteristics of refugee experiences. Both displacement and emplacement are critical for our understanding of refugeehood, which implies simultaneously experiences of victimisation and practices of overcoming it; experiences of grave loss, severe disruption of life, and radical challenge to identity, as well as processes of regaining control of life and reconstructing place and identity. In other words, agency and victimisation intertwine, constituting experiences of individual refugees. Because of a dynamic and dialectic relationship of these varied experiences and different practices, the notion of refugeehood becomes inseparable from the agency of people experiencing forced dislocation.

The recognition and *creation* of opportunities, however limited they may be within the context of forced migration, and the capacity to make individual decisions in specific situations, locations, and points in time, are all related to refugee agency. The focus on agency in approaching refugees enables us to perceive them as people like us, who have agency, sound judgement and reason for actions embedded in their past, politics, experiences of flight, and life way away from home. The notion of refugeehood devoid of agency effectively dehumanises people who are forced into decisions to migrate (Malkki 1996). It prevents us from understanding and approaching refugees as 'ordinary people in extraordinary circumstances' (Harrell-Bond 1999: 158) who need and indeed deserve our support in their struggle to regain control over their lives. The emphasis on refugee agency, hence, is a call to dissociate refugeehood from vitctimhood by exposing and subverting practices, both of the dominant state powers as well as representational practices within scholarly and other writings, through which refugees are constructed as powerless and incapable of making any decisions about their lives.

Refugees make decisions about their flight, however coerced they might be, and they create opportunities within the limitations of their predicament. This process is influenced by the intersection of micro and macro factors. Individual and group social positioning and local dynamics intersect with structural and global dynamics in different ways in specific contexts. This process is critically shaped by refugees themselves through their needs and aspirations. These are negotiated at different levels and scale of organization through networks of relations with various actors, including governmental and other institutions. Agency is hence 'embodied in social relations' (Long 2001: 15).

Researchers are increasingly emphasising the importance of agency for studying the experiences of people fleeing their places of origin and their forced dislocation (e.g., Essed et al. 2004; Korac 2005, 2003a; Turton 2003). The notion of refugees and other migrants as social actors who have the 'capacity to process social experience and devise ways of coping with life, even under the most extreme forms of coercion' (Long 1992: 22) has been introduced into the field of (forced) migration with the application of Giddens' concept of structuration to migration (e.g., Richmond 1993). Giddens (1984: 173) pointed out that social structures not only constrain behaviour and peoples' social lives, but also enable their actions. While he argued that the constitution of social structures cannot be understood without allowing for human agency, he viewed agency as embedded within institutional structures and processes (Giddens 1984: 11). This should not imply however that an actor 'follows a pre-given ideological script' (Dissanayake 1996: 8, cited in Long 2001: 15). Social actors and their agency are guided by both reflexivity and motivation. Turner (1988), among others, argued that a theoretical interpretation of social action must go beyond cognition and consciousness to include perceptions of security, trust, group inclusion, intersubjective understanding, and symbolic as well as material gratification, as important factors shaping agency.

Liminality and Refugee Agency

As social actors, refugees are continuously creating 'room for manoeuvre' (Long 2001) in the context of severely limited options and choices associated with forcible dislocation. They are actively engaged in confronting liminality. Turner (1967: 93) defined liminality as the phase 'betwixt and between', a state between separation from one social situation or group and reincorporation. As such, it is characterised by uncertainty and improvised existence based upon ad hoc short-term strategies at best, or day-to-day survival at worst. The liminal character of refugee existence is a consequence of the separation that is inherent in forced movements and therefore is part and parcel of the very nature of the experiences of forced migrants. It is also produced and reinforced by a variety of policy 'solutions' to the refugee 'problem', which keep people fleeing their countries of origin in situation of prolonged insecurity concerning their legal status and social rights. Bauman (2004) points out that in the current political climate refugees have become 'human waste', outcasts of modern societies. Reflecting upon the number and the situation of refugees in camps, as well as upon the consequences of restrictive admission policies in most countries of the world, which are forcing refugees to 'settle' in places that 'appear on no maps used by ordinary humans' (ibid.: 80), he argues that refugees are never to be free from the growing sense of transience and provisional nature of any settlement.

While liminal existence is indeed a severely disempowering experience, it is also a condition that refugees actively confront in a variety of ways in their search for and creation of solutions to their predicament. In this sense their actions should be considered as proactive and goal-oriented. This does not imply that refugees always have clear views of how their perceptions of reality are formed, and thus, that their strategies and actions are based on rational decisions and/or options.[10] As Long (2001) points out, choices, strategies, and behaviour of social actors, as individuals or groups, are shaped by 'larger frames of meaning and action' (ibid.: 14) formed through the links between the 'small' worlds of actors, and larger-scale 'global' phenomena and structures (ibid.). In uncovering the complexity of factors involved it is crucial, he argues, to contextualise actors' strategies through a systematic ethnographic understanding of the lived experiences of the variously located social actors (Long 2001:14–15). Without this type of contextualisation, the notion of refugee agency is as abstract as is the notion of victimhood.

Lived-in Worlds of Refugees: From Contexts to Processes

The centrality of context in approaching refugees as social actors enables us to uncover differences in their experiences and learn how they confront liminality in specific situations, define and redefine their goals and expectations. Contextualisation, hence, makes it possible for us to understand how structural elements intersect with the social positioning of individuals or groups and everyday practices. It allows a more complex and dynamic understanding of forced migrants as real people, thus deconstructing essentialist ways of thinking that refugees are essentially this or essentially that. The importance of an in-depth understanding of the lived-in worlds of refugees understood as social actors is twofold. It can contribute further to the conceptualisation and development of our understanding of refugees, who as actors are agents of social change. It can also advance our thinking on how to develop and implement effective policies and assistance to refugees.

Emphasis on the diversity of experiences involved in forced migratory movements sits uneasily with the bureaucratic need for standardised categories and with one-size-fits-all policies. Many authors have already criticised the way in which refugees are helped in camps and countries of (re)settlement. Because of the lack of appreciation of difference among refugees, the assistance provided is uniform and rigid. Much of the service provision, as research demonstrates, is based on approaching refugees as a universal category, denying them individuality, past life experiences and future aspirations. The recognition and link between these represents, however, the basis upon which refugees themselves may rebuild a meaningful place and life for themselves (Daniel and Knudsen 1995: 5). For many people who flee conflicts constructed as ethnic or religious strife, for example, the experience of displacement or of loss of place, and a range of social ties and meanings attached to it, often begins long before they actually dislocate. Their flight and subsequent experiences of displacement further challenges their identity. A significant part of the individual identity crisis experienced by people forced into decisions to leave their places of origin is linked to the process of becoming a refugee. It centrally involves confronting the stereotyping powers of bureaucratic notions rooted in institutional knowledge about who is 'the refugee' and how s/he is to be helped.

Policies and provision developed in response to the construction of 'the refugee' as a universal category are also not gender neutral. They most often reflect gender bias and unequal gender relations of power among aid workers and service providers, often resulting in non-recognition of the differentiated needs and problems of women and girls, and men and boys, or misguided interventions into gender relations of power within refugee families, households, and groups. This in turn leads to the escalation of gender-based tensions among refugees, cutting through all segments of their life and undermining their coping strategies and well-being (Hyndman 2000).

The hegemony of the notion of victimhood associated with refugees, which denies them agency and voice, leads to a paternalistic type of assistance for refugees, approaching them as passive recipients of aid who are prone to prolonging their dependency on organized forms of assistance (Harrell-Bond 1986; 1999). Although it is overwhelmingly assumed that refugee assistance is motivated by 'compassion' and 'altruism', suggesting the absence of any obligation and/or expectation, critics have demonstrated that the link between humanitarianism and paternalism is producing an overwhelming feeling of indebtedness and obligation on the part of the beneficiary (refugee) (de Voe 1986). Not surprisingly, these types of refugee assistance and aid often result in a range of psychosocial problems as well as in how refugees become incorporated in receiving societies or how they cope with their 'temporary' stay in refugee camps. Studies show that post-flight situations are equally, and often even more, stressful and traumatic than those associated with the pre-flight and flight experiences of forced migrants (e.g., Gorst-Unsworth and Goldenberg 1998; Lavik et al. 1996). Contextualising experiences of displacement and their meanings for specific people in specific circumstances can help bring about much needed awareness among policy makers and aid workers that refugees are not an undifferentiated category.

A call to contextualise the lived experiences of the variously located social actors through systematic ethnographic research of refugee situations is also a call to emphasise the importance of understanding how specific contexts shape the social positioning of forced migrants as well as their everyday practices. They also shape migratory processes, from global migration patterns to the social organization of migration and issues of incorporation. The emphasis on contextualisation is to highlight the importance of a shift from the state-centred to the refugee-centred approach to examining and understanding the processes as well as the consequences of forced movements of people. In this book, the call for a refugee-centred approach is to focus on how they organize their experience, form connections, reconstruct their social world, and create meaning through differently situated everyday practices and actions. The examination of the intersections of these emplacement experiences in specific circumstances and locations allows for a more complex and dynamic understanding of the processes of incorporation than a focus on the state and its interventions alone. In this sense, contextualisation serves as a microfoundation of mezzo and macro-processes.

The experiences of becoming and being a refugee in Amsterdam and Rome for the people in this research have been somewhat different, engendering different types of responses to their displacement and strategies for emplacement. In both contexts, however, the people whose accounts are presented in this book, although victimised in some substantial ways, were also agents or aimed to be agents of their own past, present and future lives.

Policy 'Solutions' and Types of Agency They Engender

Government programmes pertaining to refugee assistance and local support structures in receiving places play an important role in how the lives of refugees unfold, as many authors have already pointed out (e.g., McSpadden 1999). Refugee incorporation has become a much debated issue in the past decades. The reception and integration policies of European states vary widely, from highly centralised state-sponsored programmes to the provision of minimal and decentralised assistance. Regardless of these differences, however, a prevailing concern within the EU has been how to facilitate the decision-making process on asylum claims and how to deal with the 'mechanics' of settlement in order to meet the immediate and pressing needs of refugees.

European governments are increasingly opting for the establishment of specialised reception centres for the new arrivals (European Commission 2001). These centres are seen as an effective response to the growing number of people seeking asylum in the EU. They are regarded as an adequate 'solution' to the matters of security and provision of accommodation and other basic needs of forced migrants during the determination process, as well as for the management and deportation of those who are not granted permission to stay. Other measures relating to the functional aspects of settlement in receiving societies include policies and programmes offering access to retraining and education to enhance employment opportunities, access to health and other social services, and in some cases, the ability to participate in local decision-making processes. The level and character of these forms of assistance depend on the character of the welfare systems of the receiving societies, which tend to influence policies of integration. The effects of these policy approaches for the incorporation of those who are granted asylum are seldom examined, despite a growing realisation among researchers and practitioners working with refugees that such policies may effectively facilitate their long-term dependency, social isolation and stigmatisation.

The Netherlands and Italy represent contrasting types of policy approaches to admission, reception and integration of refugees. The Dutch system is state-controlled and embedded in a so-called welfare model of assisting refugees, while the Italian model is lacking an overarching strategy and is embedded in an ad hoc approach to refugee assistance.

The Dutch Rules

The Dutch model of refugee integration is based on a number of measures and interventions by the state intended to meet the immediate needs of refugees and to facilitate their gradual structural and institutional incorporation in Dutch society. The main goal of the Dutch integration policy is to 'activate citizenship' by enhancing the opportunity of individual migrants to exercise the responsibility involved in membership/citizenship in Dutch society (Lechner 2000). The emphasis on responsibility has led to a contractual relationship between the refugee/immigrant and the government/municipality as a basis for policy. The rights and obligations of both parties are guaranteed. The government/municipality is obliged to provide an integration programme, including language and retraining courses; the newcomer is obliged to complete the programme successfully within a specified period. If the newcomer fails to meet requirements stipulated in the contract/policy, the government might reduce his/her social security benefits or penalise those who receive income from other sources.

This policy is embedded in the country's well-developed welfare system and provides a considerable level of social benefits and services for refugees. The system is therefore favourable for those fleeing with children and the elderly. However, to protect the welfare system from abuse, the government introduced restrictive admission and reception policies. At the time of my research (2000–2001), those seeking asylum in the country usually experienced a two-stage admission and reception procedure involving a stay of up to forty-eight hours in an investigation centre (OC), and a stay of several months at a reception centre (AZC). The length of their stay at one of the reception centres depended on the duration of the determination process. If the outcome of their asylum application was positive, refugees were offered housing in one of the municipalities.

The Dutch reception system offers a well-developed system of housing refugees, dating back from before the introduction of reception centres and the new Integration of Newcomers Act. These were the times when, as Muus (1998) remarks, there was an overly strong emphasis on housing, to the point that it could be argued that all integration efforts were about accommodating refugees. Under the system in operation during my research, refugees could benefit from subsidised housing arrangements with municipalities after status acknowledgement. Only those who came before the stay in reception centres was obligatory had to make their own housing arrangements. Those whose status was acknowledged were also required to undergo compulsory language training, and had a possibility of retraining to enhance their prospects of finding employment.

For some people, however, in cases when a provisional permit to stay ('F' status) was granted, the reception procedure involved a third stage. This stage usually lasted up to three years and involved provision of housing and a modest allowance, but no provision directed at integration into Dutch society, such as compulsory language training, or the right to retrain and work. This phased, state-led settlement process may therefore last for years. A relatively relaxed naturalisation policy at the time of my research meant, however, that most of those who were allowed to stay in the country could obtain Dutch citizenship relatively soon after this period. Consequently, almost all of the people I met in Amsterdam were Dutch citizens.

Although the national government devises integration policy, the local municipalities and the NGO sector implement it on the ground. The Dutch NGO sector, whose work with refugees goes back to the 1970s, is well developed and funded. Traditionally, it relies heavily on volunteers, who are directly or indirectly associated with the Dutch Refugee Council (VVN). They offer specific forms of help to the newly arrived refugees during the initial phase of their stay, such as orientation in the new environment/society, including practical information and some language tutoring. Since the beginning of the 1990s, there has been a tendency to involve more professionals in work with refugees.[11]

The Italian Way

Italy lacks the legislative framework that could form a basis for social policy pertaining to the reception and integration of refugees. The reasons for this are twofold. On the one hand, Italy was until relatively recently a country of emigration and a transit country through which refugees and other migrants only passed on their way to other European and overseas destinations. By the end of 1998, however, there were over one million foreigners in Italy, making it the country with the fourth largest number of resident foreigners within the EU, after Germany, France and the UK (Pittau 1999). Although the situation has changed, the experience of previous decades still shapes the institutional memory of many governmental bodies. They still find it difficult to acknowledge that many of the refugees and other migrants actually come to stay. On the other hand, Italy's welfare system is relatively underdeveloped, which has led to a corresponding approach to assistance available to those seeking and/or granted protection. The assistance is minimal, because it is assumed that those needing support will resort to self-help within refugee and migrant networks. It is expected that this will encourage them to become self-sufficient in a short period.

Despite the fact that a new Immigration Law, enacted in 1998, stated that asylum seekers were to be accommodated at government-run centres, few such centres were established at the time of my research, in 1999–2000. Moreover, although the new law was enacted in 1998, corresponding legislation concerning asylum and temporary protection status had not been introduced at the time of this research. Italy also does not judicially recognise humanitarian refugees, but refers solely to the Geneva Convention. Consequently, populations fleeing the general violence and armed conflicts of the 1990s, for example Albania and the Yugoslav successor states, were granted temporary resident permits to stay, based on specific government decrees.

The people I met in Rome were granted temporary permits to stay, based on such a decree introduced in 1992. These ad hoc measures were effective between 1992 and 1997, resulting in 77,000 temporary residence permits granted to people fleeing the regions affected by the conflict.[12] This temporary status was usually granted without any lengthy determination procedure and included the immediate right to work and study. Because their stay was classified as temporary they did not qualify for permanent resident status which would eventually give them the opportunity to apply for Italian citizenship. Only those married to Italians had it, and some also had time-limited work-permits, renewable every four years.

While the humanitarian permit to stay in Italy allowed refugees to work or study, it also meant that the vast majority received no assistance to settle in the country. Thus, the system was not favourable for the settlement of those with (small) children and the elderly. Humanitarian (temporary) status also does not allow family reunification, resulting in fewer families settling in Italy. The government established fifteen reception centres for those fleeing the region. Their gradual closure began at the end of 1995; at the time of this research, these centres were closed. The centres could accommodate up to two thousand persons at a time. The exact number of those accommodated at such centres was not available, but there is a well founded indication that the number was not much greater than a couple of thousand (Losi1994).

Additionally, the NGO sector also initiated forms of assistance to refugees fleeing Yugoslav conflicts. The organization Consorzio Italiano di Solidaritá, founded in 1993, was particularly active. From 1993 to 1996, the organization helped approximately two thousand people fleeing the post-Yugoslav states. It helped in providing accommodation to these refugees through its own network of local organizations or volunteers primarily in smaller industrial towns in northern Italy. Initially, refugees were accommodated with Italian families, were helped to enrol in language courses and in some cases to find jobs. The regional governments financially assisted these programmes. In 1996, the organization started providing assistance for people fleeing other troubled regions of the world.[13]

The Italian NGO sector with a mandate to assist asylum seekers and refugees is, however, a relatively recent phenomenon. Most of the organizations were founded at the beginning of the 1990s. Some of these organizations have often innovative programs aimed at employment and/or educational needs of refugees, but due to their lack of organizational and financial capacity, they remain only small projects, inadequate to meet the needs of a growing refugee population in the country. Moreover, NGOs are unevenly spread across the country and less numerous than church organizations, which offer assistance to the destitute in general, including refugees. Church organizations and NGOs provide various types of assistance, ranging from emergency accommodation and free meals to language courses. However, the assistance they offer is scarce, particularly accommodation, and cannot meet the needs of a growing number of asylum seekers and refugees.

A Note on Method: Focus on Refugee Voices

As this book is committed to refugee-centred approaches to examining the processes and consequences of forced movements of people, its focus is on refugee voices. Because of its endeavour to reconstruct the actors' point of view in the variety of situations that they encounter in their everyday life this research is based on the methods of ethnographic research and case study. Research strategies to reveal the subjective world of the actor's experience are considered more appropriate for gaining knowledge about problems of displacement and the processes of emplacement than the social mapping of numerical data and statistical methods favoured by governments in examining different aspects of settlement and in evaluating outcomes of integration policies. Social surveys tend to generate structural models, as Wallman (1986) suggests, based upon 'categorical markers' or 'a once-for-all typology of people'. Such models, as she points out, present a 'tidier than life' account of social reality, in which the question of 'whether, when and how far the actor identifies with those who share the same categorical status' is never proposed (Wallman 1986: 223–24).

Throughout the book I refer to experiences of displacement and emplacement of refugees from the Yugoslav successor states who were granted asylum in Italy and the Netherlands. Data for this qualitative study was collected during eighteen months of ethnographic fieldwork in Rome (1999–2000) and Amsterdam (2000–2001), where there was a considerable concentration of people who were forced to flee the war-torn country. The study is based on different kinds of data obtained from refugees, NGOs, governmental and community organizations, and matched by participant observation in various contexts of social interaction.[14]

Emplacement is a process that can take a lifetime, so it is important to specify the time span to be examined, as well as the main unit of analysis. This study examined the situation of refugees from the successor states of Yugoslavia who arrived in Italy and the Netherlands between 1991 and 1995. It was considered that after six to ten years in exile these people were able to come to terms with some of their losses, to refine the perception of their situation in Italian/Dutch society, and to formulate their goals. My research focused on individual refugees, understood as agents who were actively involved in confronting liminality and in creating a meaningful place for themselves. It was envisaged that the analysis of individual cases and experience of displacement and emplacement would point to the factors that facilitate or hinder interaction within and outside the group of compatriots and the role of such interaction(s) in the process of emplacement as defined by refugees themselves. Hence, this study is not an investigation of the situation of 'refugees from the former Yugoslavia' in Rome or 'Bosnian refugees' in Amsterdam understood as an 'ethnic' or 'refugee community'. Rather, it is an endeavour to grasp the 'everyday praxis of group formation in its variability and context dependency' (Wimmer 2004: 4). Although the focus of the enquiry is refugee as individual, every effort was made to collect individual accounts of all family and household members, as it is acknowledged that families and households are often the basic units of survival shaping the individual choices, strategies and goals of their members.

Qualitative methods were used in this study for several reasons. Their use is linked to a critical view of a 'top-down' or normative approach to integration adopted in this study and its aim to give refugees a voice. Qualitative interviewing is considered as an important way of learning from refugees, and crucial in addressing the problem of 'asymmetry of power and voice' between the state and the refugees (Indra 1993). Robinson (1998: 122) has argued that 'since integration is individualised, contested and contextual it requires qualitative methodologies which allow the voices of respondents to be heard in an unadulterated form.' Further, qualitative methods help to avoid treating refugee subjects as 'data-gathering' objects, because they better address the exploitative tendency of unequal power relations embedded in the research process. Their use secures active involvement of refugees in the construction of data and knowledge about their lives. In this sense, qualitative methods are suitable for studies acknowledging research subjects as 'everyday theorists' (Cresswell 2004: 79) and legitimate 'agents of knowledge' (Harding 1987: 3).

This book does not aim to produce ambitious generalisations. Rather, it seeks to offer insights into the complexity of the process of emplacement based on an in-depth knowledge of a small 'slice' of reality. The empirical relevance of this research is enhanced by its comparative nature and its focus on the situation and accounts of refugees from a single country of origin in two different cultural and policy contexts. It was considered that people coming from the successor states of Yugoslavia bring to the receiving societies similar 'cultural capital' (Bourdieu 1984). They are of a similar background in terms of a social upbringing rooted in the shared socioeconomic system of their country of origin, the educational system and the system of values, together with some elements of shared traditions and culture. The ways in which this accumulated set of conditions of life position the refugee in a particular relation to others importantly depends on the policy and country context of receiving societies. Thus, the narratives of people in Rome and Amsterdam collected for this study do not claim to be representative of the situation of all refugees in the two cities and countries. They are, however, demonstrative of the issues and problems involved in the processes of emplacement confronted by similarly positioned individual refugees in different country contexts. Further, the accounts of people in this book clearly point to the fact that refugees are not a homogeneous category of people whose needs can fit a single so-called integration model.

During the fieldwork in Rome and Amsterdam, I established around 180 informal contacts with people who fled one of the successor states of Yugoslavia (around 120 and 60 contacts respectively). These contacts were useful for collecting general information about people's situation in Italy and the Netherlands. As these interactions were usually not on a one-to-one basis and, therefore, not suitable for collecting more personal data, I chose forty refugees in Rome and twenty in Amsterdam for formal, in-depth interviewing. In addition, I tried, as much as possible, to share day-to-day lives with refugees in both study sites and made every effort to participate in their social life. When the circumstances permitted, I visited them at work, at home, and took part at many social gatherings involving my respondents and their friends, who were either also refugees or people they met in exile. This enabled me to gain a more in-depth understanding of their social situation.

My principal concern in selecting interviewees for this study was to ensure they came from different networks in order to cover a variety of refugee situations, and avoid a danger of interviewing people with similar experiences (Bloch 1999). Contacts with the NGO sector, statutory agencies and community organizations in Italy and the Netherlands, as well as my own contacts with people living in the two cities/counties, assisted in making initial contacts with a number of refugees. These initial contacts facilitated the development of a web of informal contacts with people who were refugees in Rome and Amsterdam. These informal contacts were important in establishing a relationship of trust, which facilitated the process of identifying interviewees. This was important in addressing the problem of refugees often being intensely suspicious of institutions, government(s), and individuals representing these bodies, including researchers, the distrust being rooted in their experiences of exile (Moussa 1993: 36). Acknowledging the complexities, sensitivity and often insecurity of their situation in the receiving societies, interviewees were guaranteed anonymity and confidentiality, and assured that the names of places and institutions that could identify them in either their place of origin or Rome/Amsterdam, would be omitted. Therefore, the names that appear in the book are pseudonyms and the names of the places they come from or currently live and work are omitted.

The fact that I as the researcher come from the same country as the people involved in my study, meant that we shared the language and to some extent sociocultural background as well as the experience of life 'outside homeland'. These shared experiences and features of our identities were important in developing a mutual understanding and trust with the people in my study. However, our life circumstances were in most cases substantially different and these differences were aggravated in those cases in which our socioeconomic background and education were radically different. Edwards (1993: 18) argues that factors such as race, class and other social characteristics place both the researcher and the subject within the social structure and therefore are relevant to all social research. In order to reduce the problems in understanding which were embodied in these different locations, I often repeated to the refugees, in my own words, what they had said during the interviews, to see if they agreed with the interpretation. In this way, an effort was made to overcome barriers in understanding the words of the interviewees because of a 'lack of shared cultural norms for telling a story, making a point, [and] giving an explanation' (Kohler Riessman 1989: 173).

My methodological approach to doing this research was importantly informed and enhanced by writings of feminist standpoint theorists who argue that knowledge is situated (e.g., Harding 1987) and can be gained through a dialogical process, which is the way to approximate truth (e.g., Stoetzler and Yuval-Davis 2002). My own location and experience regarding the problems with ethnicity in the context of a conflict constructed as ethnic strife were radically different from the experiences of interviewees who were a minority population in their places of origin. However, the research process revealed that because we shared to a certain extent the system of values rooted in our social upbringing, it was possible to negotiate any differences in how we viewed the causes of the conflict and experienced its consequences. In a few cases in which the initial contact indicated a possibility of misunderstandings, distrust or even tension, subsequent communication focusing more on elements of the past life and experiences we shared proved to be invaluable for the development of mutual understanding and trust during the interview process. Through this type of interaction we were able to situate ourselves within our respective contexts, to reflect upon our individual (and group) positioning and experiences, and establish a dialogue.

I sought to interview people of different age, gender, ethnicity, marital status, parental status, education, region and place of residence before flight. The profile of the group of people in my research reflects the characteristics of the refugee population from the Yugoslav successor states in the two cities.[15] People in Amsterdam were older and of moderately lower educational level than those in Rome. Most importantly, however, practically all refugees in Rome were employed, except for a few young adults still living with their parents. Furthermore, people in Rome were overwhelmingly single or cohabiting, without children, and without family networks in Italy. In Amsterdam, parents or siblings of the overwhelming majority of those who were single were also refugees in the Netherlands. While intermarriage or cohabitation with the native population was present in the group in Rome, it did not exist among my interviewees in Amsterdam. Finally, the overwhelming majority of interviewees in Amsterdam had Dutch citizenship, while the majority of those interviewed in Rome still had temporary, humanitarian refugee status. In terms of the ethnic background of the people in this study and the region/state they originate from, for example, Bosnia-Herzegovina, Croatia or Serbia, the interviewees in both Amsterdam and Rome were overwhelmingly Bosniaks or of an ethnically mixed background from Bosnia-Herzegivina.[16] While the numbers of people belonging to these two backgrounds were identical among the interviewed in Amsterdam, the number of those from an ethnically mixed background was somewhat higher in Rome.[17]

An Outline of the Book

Chapter 1 provides a discussion of theoretical and conceptual concerns relating to the concepts of 'place', 'home' and 'transnationalism'. It challenges the centrality of 'origin' for understanding refugees as well as the notion of sited identities. Approaching refugees as people who have agency and who establish and develop social relations and ties according to their individual and group histories, cultural and political codes, as well as priorities and plans for their future can also help deconstruct the related 'naturalised' notion of 'community'. By emphasising the importance of examining emerging forms of interaction and networks of relations that refugees establish in exile for their emplacement this chapter also offers a framework for analysis of the 'voices' and experiences of refugees in this study.

The displacement of peoples from war-torn Yugoslavia is placed within its historical and sociopolitical context in Chapter 2. The social and political turmoil of the late 1980s, characterised by the exclusionary politics of ethnic nationalism that led to the creation of ethnicised forms of statehood in the region, is the context in which local populations were brutally victimised. Territories and regions which were most ethnically mixed, such as Bosnia-Herzegovina, were the most affected by radical nationalist claims for 'ethnically pure' territories. Many of those labelled as the Other in various regions of the once common country, either because of their ethnic background or politics, were forced to flee their places of origin. Chapter 2 examines the interplay between force and choice shaping the individual decisions of refugees in this study on when, how and where to flee. Experiences of war and accounts by refugees of the 'decision making' processes will point to some general features of the exile experiences of so-called spontaneous refugees, as well as the variations. I argue that in conceptualising forcible migratory movements it is critical to emphasise the centrality of people's agency in making decisions to move from their places of origin. This can bring into focus the exploration of how forcible migratory processes actually work in specific historic, political and other individual circumstances of the people on the move. By exploring the actual reality of the decision-making processes of forced migrants we can begin to address the problems of what has been termed 'management of (forced) migration' and a range of policy issues associated with it.

Chapter 3 outlines the transition experienced by people who fled from their places of origin in war-torn Yugoslavia to Italy and the Netherlands. This chapter presents individual experiences of arrival and of the first years in Rome and Amsterdam, by focusing on the transition from being 'ordinary people', who actively shape their lives, to refugees, a dependent, undifferentiated group without clearly defined social and legal status in the receiving society. The discussion reveals that refugees, although victimised, are far from being passive victims prone to dependency. They are survivors, actively seeking solutions to their liminal existence caused by displacement. Central to their place-making strategies developed upon arrival is their search for opportunities of support which allow for active participation and access to greater control over decisions about their lives. In searching for opportunities they focus on negotiating aspects of their past and possible options for their future, and actively develop strategies to confront their present, liminal condition. The chapter provides a commentary on the role and effects of different types of institutional support structure in facilitating the functional aspects of refugee settlement through which they start to regain control over their lives. It analyses two contexts of exile, one centralised, providing uniform and phased forms of support, and the other lacking almost any formal support system. Discussion points to the specific structural constraints of these two systems of support, which cause difficulties for refugees in their effort to tackle the state of liminality caused by their displacement. The analysis also reveals the connection between assistance strategies, the structural constraints they embody and the type of human agency they engender.

While Chapter 3 examines the processes of regaining control over life in exile through functional adjustment to the receiving societies, Chapter 4 explores other important components of the processes of emplacement. By pointing to the importance and complexity of the interplay between continuity and change for the process of reconstructing life in exile, the discussion examines the role of minority, or 'ethnic', and majority social networks in fulfilling these two important needs of people who are negotiating and developing their strategies of emplacement. The chapter explores the 'bonding' links between 'ethnic' networks and the need for continuity, as well as the importance of the type and quality of 'bridging' connections refugees have with majority groups for the need for change. The discussion also reveals how the different type and quality of social networks established, both bonding and bridging, is centrally linked to the type and character of the policy context in the receiving society. It points to the importance of formation and consolidation of both 'ethnic' and minority–majority social networks for the process of emplacement. The discussion reveals the centrality of bridging social networks, those between refugee and the majority groups, for refugee notions of belonging to their new sociocultural settings, as well as their general satisfaction with the quality of their emplacement in receiving societies.

The book concludes by exploring transnational dimensions of emplacement. By examining the emerging patterns of transnational lives of refugees and their effect on notions of belonging and the meaning of return, Chapter 5 offers a discussion of the changing meaning of citizenship and role(s) it has in the process of emplacement of refugees whose life trajectories are presented in this book. The analysis demonstrates that the sense of belonging to a community and notions of 'home' are reconstructed in new societies in a variety of ways, many of which correspond to neither local or national borders, nor policies which reflect notions of territorial and sited identities. Transnational place-making strategies therefore challenge the dominant conception of membership, integration and belonging linked to a single unitary realm of nation-state. In this sense, and in spite of the continuous importance of the nation-state, transnationalism, transnational links and strategies, have deconstructed it in some important ways, making citizenship no longer the main locus of identity for many refugees/immigrants. While the acquisition of formal citizenship rights is essential for the establishment of transnational place-making strategies, it appears to be less central to the notions and meanings of belonging of refugees in this study. The discussion in this book also reveals that social relations and connections that refugees make, become part of or strive for, occur both as localising processes, thus within a nation-state, as well as transnational processes spanning state borders. While bridging social networks help refugees to 'nest' into specific localities and become 'of place', 'ethnic' networks tend to span across local/national borders and 'nest' them in transnational social spaces. The dialectic relationship of these processes is continually negotiated through the place-making strategies of refugees developed in particular contexts and in specific points in time. Their emplacement, based on these strategies, will always lead to some level of pluralisation of identities, solidarities and membership forms.

Notes

1. Most of the funding for this research came from the Lisa Gilad Initiative. Additional funding was provided by the European Commission through the European Council for Refugees and Exiles, as well as The British Council, The Heyter Travel Fund, and The Oppenheimer Fund.
2. For more on labelling refugees see Zetter (1991; 2007).
3. This research formed the bases for my PhD thesis, entitled 'The Power of Gender in the Transition from State Socialism to Ethnic Nationalism, Militarization, and War: The Case of Post-Yugoslav States', Faculty of Graduate Studies, York University, Toronto, 1998. The thesis yield several publications, two of which are particularly relevant for some points of discussion in this book (see Korac, 2004; 2006).
4. For more on these types of settlement problems and their meanings see Žmegač (2005).
5. For a more detailed discussion of different terms used in both theory and policy see Castles et al. (2003a).
6. The majority of scholars in the field do not include gender rights as an important aspect of citizenship. However, there are authors who recognise it as central to the differentiated positioning of individuals vis-à-vis citizenship (e.g., Castles and Davidson 2000; Kofman et al. 2000).
7. Arendt (1966, cited in Xenos 1996: 243) has long pointed out that the problem of refugees in the modern age is not the loss of a particular place, but the possibility of finding a new one.
8. One of the recent debates on this issue includes exchanges between Adelman and McGrath (2007); Cohen, (2007); DeWind (2007); Hathaway (2007a; 2007b)
9. Refugee scholars are increasingly calling for analyses to overcome binary logic in conceptualising refugees, some extending this call to distinctions between displacement and emplacement (e.g., Doná 2007).

10. There have been different attempts to theorise migratory movements based on rational choice models, for example, those based on a 'place utility' (Wolpert 1965) or on a 'value expectancy' (De Jong and Gardner 1981).
11. The information on volunteers and professionals working under the umbrella of the VVN was provided by their representatives during my exploratory visits to the Netherlands in September 1999 and September 2000.
12. Data provided by the Ministry of Interior during an exploratory visit to Rome in November 1999.
13. Information and data obtained from the NGO representatives during an exploratory research visit to Rome in September 1999.
14. The information about refugees interviewed and community organizations contacted is given in Appendices 1 and 2, respectively. The list of governmental and non-governmental organizations contacted is given in Appendix 3.
15. Tables 1 and 2 in Appendix 4 show the social characteristics and legal status of the refugees interviewed.
16. *Bosniak* refers to a Bosnian-Muslim; this is the official term used by the government of Bosnia-Herzegovina.
17. Tables 3 and 4 in Appendix 5 show the ethnic background of the refugees I interviewed.

1

The Question of 'Home': Place-making and Emplacement

Negotiating entry into a new society as well as the adjustment to unfamiliar sociocultural settings and their structures is an integral part of refugee experiences. It involves a struggle to overcome or bypass the lack of rights and access, as well as a process of functional, cognitive, and value-based fine-tuning. It also leads to shifts in skills, knowledge, attitudes, world views as well as identities.

The process of negotiating entry is about the right to establish a 'home' in the receiving society, while negotiation of the series of changes and adjustments mentioned is about the process of creating a 'home' and becoming 'of place'. The 'home' here refers to a complex set of relationships that make acting possible and meaningful through shared understandings and shared interpretations of action, as Xenos put it (1996: 243). Consequently, negotiating entry, as well as the process of becoming 'of place', are shaped by different forms of contact and social interaction established by refugees. Through various forms of social interaction they struggle to fulfil their needs and aim to create a meaningful life and place for themselves in the receiving societies. This process is often ambivalent and highly contingent upon the conditions of different social arenas.

Home is a concept closely linked to the notion of place understood as a meaningful location that provides a sense of attachment to it. Many authors have argued that places are produced and made into meaningful locations through social activity and daily practice or through place-making projects characterised by the intersection of structure and agency (e.g., Appadurai1988; Cresswell 2004; Turton 2005). Place-making projects of refugees are affected and often contested by small-scale frameworks of interaction and institutional domains, as well as by more large-scale frameworks and distant social realms.

These cross-cutting domains, discourses and institutional constraints shape refugee place-making strategies, the meanings they attach to them, as well as their outcomes. They are also influenced by different types of refugee (human) agency and their modes of social action. The dynamics of this relationship are apparent at the local (micro) level, for example, through the ways in which local settings shape refugee opportunities, as well as by how their actions and practices influence important changes in the social fabric of these settings, ranging from economic to cultural. There is also a dynamic relationship between refugees and more distant social settings and domains. Refugees usually keep economic, social, political or cultural connections to their places of origin through transnational practices and links. They also establish links to places/countries in which their compatriots live and with whom they keep contacts through diasporic networks. Through a complex interrelationship of these different and dynamic social interactions and exchanges, which shape the material, moral and representational daily practices of refugees, they become 'emplaced' or create home that is meaningful to them. This dynamic 'process of "becoming"'(Pilkington and Flynn 1999), embedded in the practices described here, links their past, present, and future; through this process refugees develop 'a sense of place'(Migdal 1988).

Place, Home and Homeland

When place (and home) is understood as a process marked by openness and change, rather than 'a secure ontological thing rooted in notions of the authentic' (Cresswell 2004: 39), it is possible to envisage a variety of meanings of home and sense of place created and developed by refugees. This is because refugees are a diverse group of people, differentiated by age, gender, class, ethnicity, political beliefs, etc., and also, very importantly, because emplacement is a process and therefore a sense of place changes over time. Naila Habib's (1996) account on her search for home in exile, among others, highlights the centrality of 'the evolving meaning of home' for adaptation in exile, which is 'a dynamic and constantly changing process' (ibid.: 96).

The notion of home implies, as discussed so far, the literal (physical) sense of place, as well as other different but complementary dimensions associated with it, such as security, intimacy and its symbolic aspects. The category of home is however problematic and goes beyond its notion of meaning and care. Alongside intimacy and security, emphasised here, notions of home also entail the oppression, subversion, and exclusion of specific groups and/or categories of people, such as the young, the old, women, etc. In relation to these latter meanings of home, Douglas (1991) emphasises the 'tyranny of the home', and Martin and Mohanty (1986) point out how home excludes as well as includes and in this sense it is 'an illusion of coherence and safety based on the exclusion of specific histories of oppression and resistance, the repression of differences even within oneself.' (ibid.: 191).

Narratives and experiences of displacement or of loss of place are often coloured by this former type of rosy view of home, which then becomes a mythical place to which refugees long to return. Such narratives, and also often scholarly debates on refugees and displacement, conceive of home as a place of rootedness and authenticity, marked by permanence and boundedness. This also implies that home is a site of exclusion, central to the construction of 'us', people who belong in a place to which they have relatively immobile connections and whose identities are rooted in it. This kind of place is at the centre of much of the debate about refugees reinforcing the naturalisation of links between home and homeland, and implying that identities are fixed.

The acts of place-making are indeed political and contested, as Cresswell points out (2004: 122). This 'politics of place' (ibid.) is particularly transparent in the creation of the modern nation-state. Nation-state formation was, as Xenos (1996) argues, all about territorial identities marked off against other nations-states and against the Other, it inscribed borders both on maps and in the souls of citizens (ibid.: 238–39). This process, Xenos goes on to explain, led to the exchange of the home for the homeland, 'which exists as an imagined necessity rather than as a lived or historical contingency.' (1996: 240). Decoupling home and homeland, understood in the territorial, nation-state sense, is therefore critical for deconstructing refugees as people 'out of place'. A move beyond approaches to refugees as 'constituted by their displacement' (Cresswell 2004: 122), allows research and understanding of how they create place in a mobile (modern) world.

Territorially Bounded Places and Identities: Importance and Meanings

The notion that home can be made and remade (Xenos 1996) or the idea of place as process (Massey1997) is not a denial of the importance of territorially based identities, or homelands, for refugees or indeed for any other group of migrants. As Turton (2005) points out, debates about place and identity are at the centre of any conceptualisation of migration. For refugees, however, these links and connections gain specific meanings depending on the character and particular reasons for their movement. They then influence how people who are forced to flee their places of origin are conceptualised.

Forcible displacement of people, as numerous studies show, is often centrally related to the development of strong feelings of attachment to certain places. Indeed, the development of strong spatialised identities is linked to the nature of forcible movements that threaten or deny connections between peoples and places or homelands. As Eastmond (2006) reminds us, home moves us most powerfully as absence or negation.

Home as absence invokes powerful nostalgic narratives of home or place caused by prolonged absence from one's home and homeland. Home as absence often results in narratives and practices of symbolic recreation of place in which memory is always mediated by nostalgia. As nostalgia is never about the past as it was, but rather an active creation of the past in the attempt to remember it (Graham and Khosravi 1997: 128), home often becomes a mythical place or homeland. The production of homeland as a mythical place happens in real physical space but also and increasingly in cyberspace. There are numerous examples of 'cyberspace nostalgia' (Graham and Khosravi 2002) for places or political territories or entities that no longer exist, such as sites associated with Yugoslavia, which ceased to exist as a country and political entity in 1991,[1] or the city of Abaden, which was located at the Iran–Iraq border and entirely destroyed during the war of 1980–1988. Although the city no longer exists in real space, it has gained a virtual life in cyberspace (Graham and Khosravi 2002: 239). Such narratives, constructed in real physical space or in cyberspace, often have a tendency to gloss over any experiences of the 'tyranny of the home' or oppressive, exclusionary practices associated with it, as mentioned earlier. In specific circumstances, the processes and practices of symbolic recreation of place may lead to a mythologising of tradition and result in place-making strategies leading to actual ghettoisation and enclavisation of refugees (Shukla 1997), as well as to various transnational practices, an issue that will be discussed later in this chapter.

Threatened connections with homelands, or home as negation, also often result in powerful political movements in exile when forcibly displaced peoples struggle to re-create their lost states/homelands or continue their quest for sociopolitical change, aiming for a collective return. Studies of the Palestinians (Schulz and Hammer 2003), or the Chileans (Eastmond 1997), among others, demonstrate such place-making projects. Experience of these and other refugees in exile has led some authors to argue that: 'In the case of refugees, *political* allegiances and relations in the society of origin have a special significance', pointing to political activism oriented towards the 'homeland' (Wahlbeck 2002: 228), as the ultimate characteristic of the refugee.

Orientation to Place and the Politics of Belonging

There is no doubt that for some refugees political activism and allegiances with their country of origin will determine the character of their orientation to place and consequently their place-making strategies. The positioning of refugees within the context of conflict in their country of origin is often considered as determining differences between refugee groups. Joly (2002), for example, proposes the distinction between 'Odyssean' and 'Rubicon' refugees.

The first group includes people who belonged to a collective project before flight and took it with them into exile. For these people forcible movement and refugehood are primarily about displacement and loss of identity. Such is the case of Iraqi Arab refugees in London, who, despite their class, educational and political differences, belong to the mainstream population of the country and identify 'wholeheartedly with their home country' (Al-Rasheed 1994: 209). Their stay in London is thus seen as temporary, while flight is conceived as a 'communal strategy to save political ideas and practical programmes for the salvation of the whole nation.' (Al-Rasheed 1994: 210). This attitude towards the nation shapes the way in which they define their homeland, which is centrally marked by the symbolism of nationalism, rather than defined by geography, landscape or any other reference to a physical location of the places they came from (Al-Rasheed 1994: 211). Their place-making strategies or orientation to place become shaped by this type of identification with the nation and with the people they left behind, making return their ultimate goal. This, in turn, makes them unmotivated and unwilling to devise strategies to overcome marginalisation induced by exclusionary integration policies, as well as the racialised and xenophobic public discourse towards refugees in receiving societies (Al-Rasheed 1994: 212–13). Rather than devising strategies for reaching out, they opt for 'encapsulisation, whereby the community erects boundaries around itself through socialisation' with its members (ibid.: 213).

This type of orientation to place, and the politics of belonging it produces, has also been found to characterise refugees fleeing other countries and political contexts, resulting in their lack of interest in forging any links with the majority groups in receiving societies and, thus, mainstream society (e.g., Bousquet 1991; Fuglerud 1999; Wahlback 2002).[2] These and similar findings have often been taken as 'proof' that refugees and their identities are past-oriented. Based upon such findings and experiences of specific groups of refugees in specific contexts there is a tendency in the refugee literature to argue that for refugees 'the most significant relation is not within the host society' (Wahlback 2002: 225). Rather 'what matters [to them] is the social relation with the society of origin' (Wahlback 2002: 225).[3] Although this and other similar findings and arguments have led to an important emphasis on the transnational character of social relations of refugees (Wahlback 2002: 225), it has had the tendency of locking the notion of the refugee within ethnically centred social relations demarcated by their own ethnic boundaries.

For many refugees, however, for example for those whose political allegiances and relations in their societies of origin are underdeveloped, less significant or problematic, flight may be perceived not so much as a challenge to their identity, but as a new beginning and search for emplacement. These people may be considered 'Rubicon' refugees (Joly 2002), because their orientation to place is not informed by a collective homeland-oriented project. Such is the case of Iraqi Assyrians in London (Al-Rasheed 1994), for example, or of many Iranian refugees in Sweden who 'found themselves in exile at home', because alienation from their country of origin had begun before flight (Graham and Khosravi 1997: 126). Pointing to the contexts in which some groups of refugees may consider exile primarily as a type of 'homecoming' experience is not to deny that forcible movement of people is a severely disruptive experience, as Kibreab (1999), among others, has pointed out. Indeed, flight and exile entail an intensive and often trying search for identity and a meaningful place. The very existence of a variety of patterns of place-making strategies of refugees attest to the difficulty and complexity of these processes.

While Joly's typology is certainly useful, it is critical to remember that there are many (subtle) differences in the type and character of political allegiances refugees create in their places of origin. These differences will be shaped by the character of the political turmoil people experience as well as by their location within specific segments and strata of the native society. The acknowledgement of this is additionally and increasingly important, because more and more people are fleeing their places of origin en masse, forced by generalised violence, rather than by experiences of individual persecution. Politics and political allegiances have a very different role to play in the lives of those who are forced to flee their homes by this type of political turmoil. How refugees experience and conceptualise exile and emplacement will therefore depend on the circumstances in their country of origin, the positionality of people forced into making decisions to flee, and the different stages of their life cycle. All these elements and their interplay imply different world views and life projects of refugees. Some will be more politicised and oriented towards the collective (group), while others may be less preoccupied with macro-political levels and concerned primarily with their own family group or individually set goals. This type of contextualisation can explain, for example, why the responses of Bosnian refugees to painful memories and losses associated with causes of flight and exile were less collective and politicised than were those of Chileans (Eastmond 2000: 77–80). The lack of political allegiances or ambivalence towards identifying with any collective projects oriented towards the country of origin does not make people fleeing political turmoil and violence any the less refugees. Differences in political orientation or activism of people fleeing their homes will however affect their place-making strategies and how they attempt to emplace themselves.

Finally, and very importantly, world views and life projects of individuals who fled their places of origin cannot be approached and explained by focusing solely on their country of origin or their ethnicity and culture, as they are not the only factors shaping their value systems, identities, and notions of belonging. Gender, class, stage of life cycle, as well as the situation in and the experience of the receiving society, to mention just a few of intervening factors, always intersect in a variety of ways with attributes of group belonging, and shape actual individual strategies of 'nesting'.

Emplacement, hence, always occurs in specific locations and is characterised by shifting identities and the changing character of belonging. Rather than being fixed, claims and attributes of group belonging are situated and produced in complex and shifting locales, that is, in a 'translocational' sphere characterised by the interplay of a range of locations and dislocations in relation to ethnicity, national belonging, gender, class and race (Anthias 2001: 634).[4] The focus on place-making and emplacement, thus, enables us to analyse 'identity as situated process' (Stepputat 1999) and to move away from searching for the most important determinant characteristic of 'the refugee' or from developing typologies of refugee groups.

Links between Peoples, Places and Cultures: The Question of Community

The notion of the 'natural roots' of refugees being in specific territories and cultures is problematic because it nurtures the expectation that those coming from the same society will have a type of 'natural' bond to each other. Based on such ties, they will aim to form themselves into a 'community'. These links and bonds will provide them with much needed emotional support, and help them overcome social isolation. This belief or expectation leads to the lack of recognition of the often oppressive, divisive and exploitative tendencies characterising groups of refugees coming from the same country (Van Hear 1998). How these negative aspects of community affect individual refugees will always be contextually specific. It will depend on their gender, age, class, and education, their ethnic, religious and political belonging and affiliation. These axes of differentiation will intersect in a variety of ways depending on how individuals and groups are positioned within the different political and sociocultural contexts of the country of origin.

While divisive and other negative tendencies characterise all migrant communities, causing factionalism and segmentation, there is evidence that they are particularly characteristic of refugee communities (Al-Rasheed 1994; Gold 1992; Griffiths et al. 2005; Salinas et al. 1987). Given that reasons and causes of flight are often sociopolitical upheavals that have been increasingly marked by ethnic, class, or religious divisions, refugees usually bring with them internal hostilities and histories of oppression and exploitation. This often results in internal divisions and social pressures within refugee groups. Such tensions cause exclusion or alienation of those who are perceived as the Other or who see themselves as different from the majority group and their goals and aims.[5] For these reasons, creating 'a community in the singular' (Anthias 2002), understood as having shared values and goals, as well as a high level of social cohesion, may be difficult for many refugees. It is important to acknowledge this both in research and the development of policy. Naturalised links between places, peoples, and cultures within refugee discourse have to be constantly challenged. If left unquestioned this type of 'bonds of nationalist thought' leads to 'methodological nationalism' (Wimmer and Glick-Schiller 2003) implying that the movement of people and the character of the links and bonds established by those on the move can be understood only if the nation-state is at the centre of analysis.

Group and Cultural Identity as an Organising Principle for Incorporation

The problem with naturalisation of the notion of community is not only conceptual, preventing us from acknowledging and understanding differences and tensions within groups of compatriots. The problem is also practical and political when such an understanding of community is linked to policy initiatives in receiving societies aimed at encouraging social inclusion and the participation of refugees and other newcomers in receiving societies. Multiculturalism is one such policy framework characterising an increasing number of receiving societies. In most of these societies it means, as Anthias (2002: 279–80) points out, that the dominant group or culture creates the frame of reference and the agenda for participation by minority groups. In this sense, this type of multiculturalism remains within the minority culture framework, which is based on the notion of hierarchy of cultures, rather than equality.[6]

When refugees (and other newcomers) are seen as naturally rooted in their cultures and identities, their cultures become idealised, understood as fixed, static and given. This boxing of cultures in distinct and unchangeable cultural containers leads to ignoring important differences within, as well as to the establishment of hierarchies between cultural groups. The former tendency often results in cultural bias and labelling of some groups (of refugees) as 'traditional'. The latter is often associated with perceptions of the culture of the receiving society as superior and, hence, the one to which refugees have to adjust, implying a one-way process of change. The tendency to label refugees and other newcomers as belonging to inferior cultures is particularly dangerous. Because of its emphasis on *inferiority*, rather than on *difference*, there is the implication that cultures of those labelled as 'outsiders' cannot be negotiated (Tabboni 1995: 19).

One of the implications of this framework is that the organising principles for dealing with newcomers (and refugees) in receiving societies are conceptualised and based upon their identity and incorporation as ethnic groups or communities. This emphasis on the groups understood as 'communities' and on their (group) cultural rights is often seen as a way of mobilising their resources from within for integration purposes (Penninx 2004b). The problem with this approach is, however, that identities only exist in context and in relation to particular aspects of societal participation, as pointed out earlier. This sits uneasily with the homogenising tendencies associated with sociocultural identity as the organising principle for incorporation. Further, it poses the problem of the relationship between group and individual rights. The issue of group rights as citizenship rights have been long debated. Affirmative or positive action programmes relating to special provisions for disadvantaged groups have been both strongly supported (e.g., Goldberg 1993), as well as critiqued for reproducing categories of disadvantage (e.g., Anthias and Yuval-Davis 1992) and for being incompatible with equal human rights. Are group rights to be associated with ethnic groups/minorities and individual with the rest of the society? Also, what if cultural/group rights challenge or override the rights of the individual? Kymlicka (1995), for example, in his attempt to address this question, points to the differences between minority rights which safeguard their interests, and those that impose restrictions on their own members. He, however, fails to address satisfactorily the latter problem and the way it should be dealt with in a multicultural society. Finally, and very importantly, this raises the issue of who represents the group; whose voices are to be acknowledged as the 'authentic' voices of culture and ethnic origin?

The Question of Community Organisations

Regardless of all these unsettled issues concerning sociocultural identity as the organising principle for incorporation and becoming 'of place', many refugee and other migration scholars argue that refugees and other migrants are best helped by encouraging the establishment of their own associations. Refugee and immigrant organizations are considered not only important for keeping the sense of continuity with past lives and identities through maintaining ties with the society and culture of origin, but also for establishing links with the mainstream society and for overcoming social isolation and marginalisation. Penninx (2004b), for example, argues that immigrant organizations are 'the expression of mobilised resources and ambitions', and may become an accepted part of civil society (and a potential partner for immigration policies) (ibid.: 13). These organizations are therefore seen as important in forging a sense of belonging to the receiving society through the recognition of the group (cultural) rights of minority populations.

There is indeed an indication that such organizations can be helpful for orientating and incorporating some specific refugee groups in specific contexts (receiving societies), as demonstrated in studies of Kurdish refugees in Britain and Finland (Wahlbeck 1999) and Somali and Kurdish refugees in London (Griffiths 2000), for example. However, research also reveals that if encouragement of this type of group organising through policy is uncritically applied to all refugees irrespective of their individual and group histories as well as circumstances of displacement and emplacement, it can lead to the formation of 'contingent communities' resulting in their further marginalisation and disempowerment (Kelly 2003, 2004). Kelly's research on Bosnian refugees in Britain shows that this happens in receiving societies which centre their institutional systems primarily on group access and group provision of essential services for refugees. When refugees fail to form a functional and meaningful community association, measured by the standards of the receiving society, they become further marginalised and disempowered (Kelly 2004). This assumed role of refugee community organizations in policy and academic literature has also been challenged by Griffiths et al. (2005, 2006) and Hopkins (2006).

The problems related to a naturalised notion of community, discussed here, stem from the concept of sited identities, an assumption that has been radically challenged by the transnational and mobile reality of the modern world. Transnational links that cross the borders of states are emerging from the process of globalisation and increased migration.[7] As the result of these processes, refugee (migrant) communities are becoming importantly transnational in character. They are embedded in ties and networks criss-crossing national borders, which affect their daily lives in exile and increasingly shape the meanings of belonging and orientation to place.

Transnational Practices of Place-Making

The importance of transnationalism and transnational links for studies of forced migration goes beyond their relevance for the decision-making processes shaping migration movements of people forced into flight (e.g., Borjas and Crisp 2005; Crisp 1999; Koser 1997). They are also central to the processes of emplacement of refugees and to their place-making strategies. Transnationalism and transnational practices have expanded the boundaries of meaning of specific locations and conceptions of home. They allow for a dynamic and complex shaping of meanings and links between peoples, places, cultures, belonging and identity. Some forms of transnationalism and transnational practices may be 'enforced', while many others are voluntary.

The 'enforced' links often emerge out of pressing feelings of responsibility to help financially family and friends. They may also be related to involvement in administrative affairs linked to property claims, as well as pressures often posed by community organizations to display loyalty to the country of origin by contributing financially to its development (Al-Ali et al. 2001: 591). In a way, therefore, they are imposed by a range of social pressures relating to the circumstances of flight and the situation in the sending country (Al-Ali et al. 2001).

Many refugees, however, visit their places and countries of origin regularly and willingly. Through these visits they reconnect with family, relatives and friends, as well as with aspects of their culture and social life that are missing from their 'other' home. Experiences of transnationalism affect the ways in which refugees conceptualise place; it often becomes conceptualised through different but complementary dimensions of home, associated with the different material, sociocultural and symbolic resources of each place. In this process of emplacement, it is the receiving society that is usually perceived as the 'practical' home (Graham and Khosravi 1997) associated with the material and legal 'security dimension' of place (Eastmond 2006). Conversely, the country of origin is perceived as the 'cultural-spiritual home' (Graham and Khosravi 1997) linked to the 'emotional dimension' and fulfilment it offers (Eastmond 2006).

Piecing together different dimensions of home through transnational practices or transnational place-making may be grounded in the physical reality of geographical territories, but it can also take place in the virtual reality of cyberspace. Graham and Khosravi's (1997) study, for example, points to the development of the former type of transnational place-making strategies among Iranian refugees in Sweden. In their search for missing dimensions of home, refugees often engage in temporary recreations of home through regular family reunions. These events often take place in alternative and not necessarily familiar geographical spaces that are easily accessible to most of the family members and relatives, some of whom live in their places of origin, while others are scattered around the world.

When missing dimensions of home, such as a specific form of sociability extending beyond family and kinship ties, cannot be re-created in physical reality, through regular reunions for example, refugees often create them in the virtual reality of cyberspace. Moving across borders in cyberspace allows refugees to piece in virtual spaces into the 'place' in which they feel at home. Eastmond's (2006) study of Bosnians in Sweden and Graham and Khosravi's (2002) study of Iranians attest to such types of emplacement into cyberspace territories. Graham and Khosravi emphasize that because of its quality of 'annihilating distance' the Internet bypasses spatial divisions and links people and places that are normally separate (Graham and Khosravi 2002: 219). In this sense, 'cyberspace can be an alternative "territory," where a transnational community or a virtual neighbourhood can be constructed' (2012: 228).

Transnational cyberspace practices generate richness and diversity of ideas and social relations. Therefore, cyberspace territories, like real territories, provide a site where the meaning of ethnic or national identity is reshaped. Cyberspace connections and networks of compatriots across borders encompass national and transnational processes (Graham and Khosravi 2002). Consequently, depending on specific circumstances and contexts, as in real space, cyberspace activities may either deterritorialise identities or intensify them as well as produce 'a passion for locality' in the form of 'cyberspace nostalgia', as discussed earlier in this chapter.

Through various types of transnational practices refugees link and engage with their new and old homes. Through these processes they negotiate a way of being and a way of belonging, to borrow from Levitt and Glick Schiller (2004), and combine them into one experience and social field. It is important to acknowledge though that not all refugees can engage in this type of negotiation through transnational practices. Many have restricted rights to movement or return; others may not have skills or material resources for such activities either because they are unemployed, financially insecure or not well educated. Nonetheless these practices, and the information and other material or symbolic outcomes they engender, are not entirely isolated from the rest of the population. Graham and Khosravi (2002) observe, discussing the limitations in accessing cyberspace, for example, that although the Internet may be '*directly* accessible for a small, privileged and educated elite', online information and practices can be communicated to people in a variety of forms (ibid.: 228–29 emphasis added). In other words, limited skills, unemployment and financial insecurity are not a barrier to getting involved in transnational practices, but they do shape their forms.

Transnationalism and 'Homelessness'

Returning, even if it does not involve a more permanent residency, may very often be also problematic; it may result in feelings of 'otherness' caused by the transformative experiences of exile, as well as the often radical changes in the places of origin.[8] The interplay of these two processes may transform the country of origin into a 'foreign' place. Transnational practices may therefore further challenge one's notion of belonging, identity, and meanings of home. They may provoke even more acute feelings of homelessness linked to the realisation that home is *nowhere*.

This situation of having 'no place' may lead to the condition of hybridity. Central to the possibility of a person (migrant) being linked to two places at once, but belonging to neither, or the condition of hybridity, is the idea of the 'in between space', introduced by Bhabha (1990, 1994). This 'in between space' implies the lack of a central cultural narrative and produces a counter-narrative of a 'Third Space' avoiding 'the politics of polarity' (Bhabha 1994: 38). In this sense, people occupying the 'Third Space' are seen as cultural brokers. The role of cultural brokers is often associated with (intellectual) elites whose hybrid artistic products have been the primary focus of scholarly attention. Bauman (2005), among others, has argued that hybridity is more a prerogative of elites than other strata of the population. Accounts of many refugees coming from all walks of life demonstrate, however, that many of them find themselves too 'to be "between" cultures and into none' (Habib 1996: 100).

Feelings of homelessness brought about by transnational practices described above may stimulate more intense transnational links and practices among compatriots scattered around the world in their search for missing dimensions of home, as already discussed in the previous section. Conversely, such feelings may also result in the realisation of the strength of ties and affinities to the new home as empirical studies demonstrate (e.g., Muggeridge and Doná 2006: 423).

Ties with the New Home

The importance and role of developing ties and affinities to the new home for refugee emplacement is often neglected in literature about refugees (and other migrants). The emphasis on the centrality of 'origin', as discussed so far, has often led to arguments that refugees are not *interested* in or willing to have much to do with local populations. But is that really so? As argued earlier in this chapter, refugees create a sense of place through various forms of social interaction. It is through the social contacts they establish and the way these shape their practices that refugees struggle to fulfil their needs and aim to create a meaningful life and place for themselves in the receiving societies. The contacts they establish may be co-ethnic networks established within groups originating from the same country; cross-ethnic, created through inter-ethnic contacts among compatriots or between people originating from other countries; and minority–majority networks developed between members of minority groups and majority groups. The latter groups, the majority, refer to those often also constituting mainstream society, and more generally, to the groups not considered 'ethnic'. Many of these types of relations are initiated and tied through the institutional structures of particular local settings (e.g., church organizations, community groups, NGOs, municipalities). They can also be established through semi-invisible micro-links of sociability linked to informal contacts between diverse groups of people in urban areas through which they may, in some contexts and circumstances, develop a positive web of support. Jane Jacobs (1961) pointed to the importance of social networks developed through seemingly 'unpurposeful' and 'random' contacts of neighbours in cities through which they form social networks and relationships of trust.

Some of these informal networks of support are embedded in *bonding* social networks, established among co-ethnics and thus within the (ethnic) group boundaries. The importance of social networks among co-ethnics for the process of adaptation of those newly arrived has long been established (e.g., Gurak and Caces 1992; Williams 2006). A positive web of support that can and often is created through *bridging* social networks has been less often acknowledged as a critical resource for reestablishing the lives of refugees and other migrants. Particularly lacking are explorations of the roles of connections developed between minority (ethnic) and majority groups. If considered, minority–majority bridging social networks are most often regarded as a by-product of so-called successful integration of individuals who, as Castles (2000: 199) argues, 'normally cluster together and develop their own infrastructure', but in time, if they are 'successful immigrants', make links with mainstream social frameworks.

Discussion in this book challenges the notion that it is somehow natural for newcomers to cluster together. This notion implies that ethnic and cultural boundaries are fixed, embedded in shared and unchanging norms, values, as well as a sense of belonging to community, defined in the singular. It also suggests that newcomers themselves, first and foremost, aim to 'nest' themselves within a co-ethnic milieu. This naturalisation of co-ethnic clustering in receiving societies makes it difficult to recognise that the process of nesting is a multi-dimensional practice characterised by a dialectic relationship between different types of social links and connections influencing the goals and attitudes of individual migrants. The way in which this relationship is played out is always contextual, shaped by historic, economic, sociopolitical and cultural situations and characteristics of both the places of origin and destination. Likewise, it will also always depend on the circumstances of individual or group dislocation that tend to shape their goals and attitudes.

The emphasis on social networks and trust as the entry point into the analysis of how refugees create home or a meaningful place for themselves in receiving societies, links social capital to the processes of emplacement. The value of social networks through which we bond with similar people and build bridges between diverse groups and individuals has been recognised through the introduction of the idea of social capital (Dekker and Uslaner 2001: 3). Social capital is understood here as a social-relational concept, encompassing norms of reciprocity and trust; it is created and shaped by social context(s) over time (Coleman 1990). Putnam (2000) introduced the concept of 'bridging social capital' to emphasise its potential to generate broader identities and reciprocity as opposed to 'bonding social capital' which 'bolsters our narrower selves' (2000: 22–23). He pointed out that 'bonding and bridging are not "either-or" categories' (ibid.: 23). Rather, 'many groups simultaneously bond along some social dimensions and bridge across others' (ibid.). Consequently, by putting emphasis on the formation of bridging social capital, people searching for ways to reconstruct their lives in exile do not necessarily have to abandon their ethnic identity or 'roots' and links with their native cultures. Werbner (1999: 18) points out that migrants (and refugees) must inevitably engage 'in social processes of "opening up to the world", even if that world is still relatively circumscribed culturally.' By reaching out and seeking meaningful contacts outside ethnic boundaries, it is possible to negotiate a meaningful relationship and balance between continuity and change, and reconstruct life in a way that reflects both one's past and present situation and identity. In this sense, in this book I explore how refugees make place for themselves by gaining control over their lives and negotiating continuity and change within it. These processes are embedded in a complex web of social relations and interactions that occur in receiving societies. Through these interactions refugees re-create their lives and create home for themselves.

Taking Control and Reconstructing Life

To understand how refugees go about their lives after experiencing dislocation, how they re-create them and create home, as the discussion in this chapter indicates, it is critical to examine the processes of negotiation between different types of loyalty and attachment to places emerging from the simultaneous processes of nesting in more bounded, local spaces and in transnational ones. While elements forming these attachments are locally situated, their meanings and how they shape one's sense of belonging, identity, as well as practices can be fully understood only in conjunction with their global underpinnings. This process of 'nesting' or of emplacement' is embedded in a variety of place-making strategies consisting of economic, social and cultural (multi-sited) practices. They are embedded in two analytically distinct processes: the process of taking control of one's life and of reconstructing it. These two paths intersect and neither can be understood as a prerequisite for the other. In this sense they are overlapping rather than stage-sequential processes. Distinguishing between them is important analytically however, because they help examine how refugees confront uncertain and improvised conditions brought about by their dislocation, and understand how their agency shapes their processes of 'nesting'.

The process of taking control of one's life is centrally linked to how refugees confront the abrupt loss of basic material sources of livelihood as well as of social status, both of which are associated with forcible displacement. This dimension of emplacement consists of a set of functional adjustments to the new society, such as learning its language, finding housing and employment or undertaking education and retraining to adapt to the circumstances of the labour market. Their inclusion in all these areas, which are vital for their becoming self-sufficient and independent, entails a process of negotiating entry and having rights and access. Therefore, the legal statuses of refugees, as well as a range of socioeconomic rights they may or may not have, importantly determine how this process unfolds.

The process of taking control of one's life is however much more than access to or control of (basic) material and economic resources. This dimension of emplacement encompasses a much broader meaning of livelihood that, as Wallman and Buchanan (1982: 5) point out, is 'never just a matter of finding or making shelter, [or] getting food to put on the family table'. They argue that: 'The tasks of meeting obligations, of security, identity and status, and organising time are as crucial to livelihood as bread and shelter' (ibid.). Regaining control over one's life is about interplay between existential and other needs, interests and values of particular individual refugees or groups in specific contexts. It is as much about its meaningfulness from the point of view of refugees themselves as it is about their successful adjustment to the rules and norms of receiving societies. Consequently, many who may be regarded as successful by receiving societies may not regard themselves as such, as they may find that how they regained control over their lives is lacking in meaning they themselves aim for. Conversely, those who may be 'objectively' judged as not well integrated may not perceive their situation in the same way, as they may find it a condition that gives them enough 'room for manoeuvre' in achieving their emplacement goals. These goals are not a static category; they change over time, reflecting the changes in life projects of refugees, which are dependent upon the stage of one's life cycle, time spent in exile, and other interrelated variables. Refugee agency is central to making the process of regaining control of one's life relevant to one's changing interests, value systems, and needs. How they regain this control is shaped by both the conditions and contexts of the receiving societies as well as those beyond national borders. These become interrelated through the transnational practices of refugees and intersect in transnational places, as already outlined in this chapter, and this will be further discussed later.

The process of reconstructing life is shaped by the interplay between the need for continuity and that for change. It entails a continuous process of negotiation and is a less readily visible and 'measurable' dimension of emplacement than the process of taking control over one's life. The need for continuity implies a search for links with social roles, meanings and identities embedded in one's life as it was before flight. The need for change requires a flexibility and openness to reshaping (some) of these old roles, meanings and identities. This process of change is centrally linked to one's ability to make sense of the rules underpinning social structures and societal relations in the new society. If the process of change is perceived as meaningful rather than imposed, it enhances the process of restoring continuity of one's life.

The need for continuity importantly draws on sources provided by social networks and ties with compatriots or ethnic networks. By seeking friendships and support through this type of social network refugees search for acceptance within a hierarchical system and personal reference based upon similarity of positions held before flight and the sociopolitical turmoil that caused it. Knudsen (1991: 27) observed that this type of acceptance gained through ethnic networks is central to negating the enforced equality and uniformity of the 'refugee' label, which renders personal histories invisible.

The need for change requires a flexibility and openness to reshaping (some) of these old roles, meanings and identities. This process of change is centrally linked to one's ability to make sense of the rules underpinning social structures and societal relations in the new society. The need for change is linked to the type and quality of connections with majority groups. As receiving societies do not consist of a single monolithic majority, refugees may develop different types of links with different subgroups of the receiving society with which they are interacting. Networks with majority groups facilitate the access to the types and quality of societal resources that are otherwise not readily available to refugees. As complex formations that 'channel, filter, and interpret information, articulate meanings, allocate resources, and control behaviour' (Fernández-Kelly 1995: 219), minority–majority networks are important for enabling the use of the considerable human capital that refugees bring to receiving societies, as studies demonstrate. A study about refugees in the labour market in Portland, Maine, USA (Mamgain and Collins 2003) demonstrated, for example, that refugee men and women belonging to an established ethnic group were supported by these networks in finding a better paid first job. However, only those who established social connections with the majority groups benefited from what may be regarded as a longer run success.

These networks are indeed loosely bound with asymmetric ties, varying in content and intensity, as well as in access to power and resources. Nonetheless, they give members 'indirect connections to other social circles' (Wellman 1981: 188). A web of interpersonal relationships occurring between 'ethnic' or minority and majority groups at the micro-level of society is also central to the process of localising, or becoming part of the local social fabric. This is because these relationships are constitutive elements of socially produced notions of belonging to specific localities and sociocultural contexts. They are an important element of change, creating new identities, loyalties and notions of belonging, all of which are central to emplacement.

The process of reconstructing life is, thus, centrally linked to the possibility of establishing, developing, and maintaining different types of social relations in the new society. An important feature of the experience of displacement is a loss of family, kinship, friendship and wider ties with community and society. Thus, displacement affects the 'social world of refugees', which Marx defines as the sum of all their relationships and of the forces impinging on them at any moment of their experience (Marx 1990: 189). One of the important elements of the process of emplacement therefore is the formation and consolidation of social networks, both 'ethnic' and minority–majority. This is because emplacement does not take place in a social vacuum; rather it occurs within the context of intra- and inter-group relations. In specific contexts and points in time some of these relationships and networks will be supportive, others will represent a challenge for emplacement.

The emphasis on the importance of the consolidation and development of both 'ethnic' and minority–majority social networks points to the fact that refugees, especially during earlier stages of their 'nesting', function in more than one social world – the one that is familiar and the other that has yet to become known. Refugees ascribe different meanings to each of these social realms and sets of social relations associated with them. These sets of relations interact and intersect in different ways, depending on the context of exile, and affect how refugees negotiate the relationship between continuity and change. Analysis of these two dimensions of emplacement, the process of gaining control and of reconstructing life, can bring to our attention bottom-up knowledge on how emplacement unfolds in different societal and policy contexts from the point of view of refugees themselves. This type of analysis can help support the very mechanisms of inclusion that refugees themselves as social actors value, produce, develop or shape, and hinder those they actively confront. This is important because not all forms of inclusion are empowering and because not every individual or group can or indeed want to be included in all societal spheres. An insight into these processes and their recognition in both conceptual and policy terms highlights the importance of approaching incorporation as a two-way process requiring *mutual* adjustments and change.

Notes

1. See Cyber Yugoslavia at www.juga.com
2. It is important to note that this type of finding cannot be considered applicable for the entire refugee population fleeing one country and/or settled in one place. Fuglerud's study of the Tamil diaspora in Norway found that the group studied was inward looking, oriented towards their place of origin and not keen on making contacts with the local population. There are however many Tamils living abroad who actively seek ways to connect with the locals in the places where they have settled, and at times experience contacts within their 'community' as oppressive and 'forced'. Some preliminary findings/interviews with Tamils living in Europe done by Michaela Told as a part of her ongoing PhD research, entitled 'A Gender Perspective on Transnationalism of the Sri Lankan Diaspora Communities in Germany', are a good example of such an attitude. Michaela Told

is a PhD student at the School of Social Sciences, Media and Cultural Studies at the University of East London.

3. Joly (1996) has also emphasised the centrality of the relation to the home country and by extension to the past for the identity of refugees.

4. Anthias (2001) introduced the concept of translocational positionality, and argued for focusing on location/dislocation and positionality to emphasise the importance of spatial and contextual dimensions of identity. Focus on location and positionality, she argues, 'acknowledges that identification is an enactment that does not imply fixity or permanence' (Anthias 2001: 633). Rather, narratives of belonging or location, as Anthias prefers to call them, 'are emergent, produced interactionally and contain elements of contradiction and struggle' (ibid.: 633).

5. Kunz (1973) referred to these different groups within groups of refugees coming from the same society as 'vintages'.

6. Altheas (2002) differentiates between liberal multiculturalism characterising most of the societies in the world, and reflexive multiculturalism which is aspirational and refers to a possibility of different ways of being that is compatible with transnational and transethnic identities, as well as notions of hybridity.

7. A more detailed discussion of transnationalism as a field of research is beyond the scope of this chapter. For more on this growing and rather fragmented theoretical field of research see Faist (2000); Glick-Schiller et al. (1992); Glick-Shiller (1997); Vertovec (1999).

8. Some of the best accounts of the problems of returning and feelings of 'otherness' can be found in exile literature, for example in Kundera's novel *Ignorance* (2003)

2

Experiences of Displacement: Force, Choice and the Creation of Solutions

I fled Bosnia partly because of the bombs, which I got to experience a great deal, partly for fear of being conscripted, and mainly because of the collective madness which left no room for dialogue. (Omer, 33-year-old refugee from Bosnia-Herzegovina, in Rome since 1992)

Decision to flee one's place of origin is always made in specific social, political and historical contexts in which individuals or groups feel their lives and well-being are threatened. The negotiation of elements of force and choice informing these decisions or those linked to deciding about secondary migration should be regarded as fundamental to our very understanding of the refugee and refugeehood. Understood as agents or 'purposive actors' (Turton 2003), refugees come to be seen as actively creating solutions to their problematic situation, negotiating elements of force and choice embedded in their predicament. And very importantly, in creating solutions individual people, as the discussion in this chapter will reveal, have different alternatives available to them, all of which are not only a consequence of external constraining forces and factors, but are critically shaped by their age, gender, socioeconomic status, connections and networks. Moreover, these are only some of the factors shaping their individual situation as well as their perception of their safety, well-being and prospects for their future.

My primary concern in this chapter, discussing narratives of displacement of people I met in Rome and Amsterdam, is not to examine how much choice they had in deciding to move, or how reactive their decision-making processes to flee were. Hence, I am not concerned here to determine whether they can be classified as 'voluntary'/'proactive', thus, as having choice/agency, or 'involuntary'/'reactive' migrants, hence those who lack choice/agency.[1] Nor do I want to explore how one type of migration can transmute into another, 'sometimes as a matter of strategy, sometimes by choice or circumstances' (Van Hear 1998: 50–51). Instead of attempting to classify people involved in my study along some type of continuum or discussing when they can no longer be considered forced migrants, and how they become economic migrants, I want to point to their agency that is central to forcible displacement, as pointed out in the Introduction. I want to explore how and why they made specific decisions and how they have been creating solutions to their predicament by searching actively for options and therefore choices. Many of these choices or options they created could not be captured by the idea of a continuum. Yet they might have been critical for individual refugees, their families or groups of people in how and why they fled, as well as how they have been negotiating and shaping their place-making strategies.

The Mass Exodus of People from War-torn Yugoslavia: The Quest for Ethnic Purity and Territorial Cleansing

In August 1995, the then Serbian independent newspaper *Nasa Borba* published an article stating that four and a half to five million people in the war-torn region of Yugoslavia were forcibly displaced.[2] The data included refugees granted asylum in one of the Yugoslav successor states, internally displaced persons, and approximately seven hundred thousand people who fled the country after the beginning of the wars, seeking protection elsewhere in Europe and beyond. When contrasted with the figure of twenty-two million, which was the total population of the country before the war, these data mean that every fourth or fifth citizen in what was once Yugoslavia has been forced into a decision to flee her/his home.[3]

Conflicts emerging since the 1990s, often called 'new wars' (Kaldor 1999), have been overwhelmingly internal and marked by the divisive politics and ideologies that have transformed ethnicity into an effective weapon of war. In contemporary conflicts, the process of boundary formation between 'us' and 'them' as well as of identifying 'the enemy within' occurrs at the communal level, spreading fear and hatred of the Other. Goodhand and Hulme (1999: 17–18) point out that in this type of war 'the community' 'represents the nexus of conflict action'. It is at the community, micro level, they emphasise, where most of the physical violence and suffering occurs (ibid.). Indeed that is why current wars generate massive refugee movements, because forcible migration of particular groups or 'ethnic cleansing' of local communities has become a tool in establishing new ethnicised forms of statehood based on the politics of exclusion. The explosion of conflict, causing unprecedented forcible displacement of people, can be attributed to the processes of globalisation, structural changes in the world economy, and politics, that is, the establishment of the 'new world order'. Countries hit by these structural changes were often also characterised as 'weak states', such as in Somalia and many other parts of Africa (Nafziger et al. 2000), and/or experiencing the rise of nationalist and separatist movements, such as in Yugoslavia.

The first signs of socioeconomic crisis in Yugoslavia, caused by the structural changes in the world economy and politics, emerged in the 1980s. The economic crisis began in the 1970s following the world oil crisis and the reprogramming of Yugoslavia's foreign debt. Changed terms and conditions of servicing the debt caused a drastic fall of all economic indicators and after 1982 resulted in an increase in the percentage of the population living below the poverty line, from seventeen to twenty-five per cent (Woodward 1995: 52). As the standard of living in socialist Yugoslavia has been steadily rising, especially after 1965, the impact of this economic decline on people's lives was visible and demoralising.[4] In such circumstances, ethnic nationalism became a compelling antidote for the difficulties society would have to confront during the process of economic, political and social restructuring dictated by the IMF and the World Bank. The nationalistic discourse of the late 1980s in Yugoslavia was constructed in opposition to socialist ideology. Its exponents successfully manipulated the millions of citizens who felt socially insecure and rootless as a result of the restructuring that had accompanied the dismantling of state socialism.

After the end of the Second World War, socialist Yugoslavia experienced one of the most rapid processes of urbanisation in history (Jancar 1985: 204). Before the war, eighty per cent of the population in the country was rural; as of 1978, however, more than seventy per cent of the population lived in urban settings. The millions of people who had moved from rural to urban areas within the time span of a single generation never fully integrated into the urban milieu. In the 1970s, approximately four out of every five workers in the cities were peasants within their own memory, bringing with them rural values and norms into the cities (Denitch 1972: 34). They belonged to neither a rural nor an urban life, but somewhere in between. For many Yugoslavs, rapid industrialisation and urbanisation increased the importance of wider social connections and social identifiers, which were linked to the ideology of a 'workers' society'. Consequently, the significance of extended family ties, traditionally forming strong bonds at the communal level, as well as the set of values linked to religion and other forms of more traditional social identifiers, weakened. These changes were not accompanied by an equally rapid process of social and political development. The lack of social mechanisms to incorporate rural–urban migrants into communities meant that these newcomers remained linked to one another through networks of friends and kin from home areas, effectively remaining socially excluded.

They were often subjected to ridicule as anything associated with rural roots and peasantry was considered a subject fit for humour. Culturally they were subjected to the pressure of the mass media that portrayed the urban and modern existence as the only desirable one (Denitch 1972: 32). Thus, a new set of meaningful and strong social identifiers strengthening the individual sense of stability and identity as well as wider group cohesion were never developed, causing a considerable proportion of the population to feel rootless and with poorly defined social status and identity.

Such rootlessness bred a sense of insecurity – a condition that was effectively exploited by the socialist state in its efforts to forge a collective identity and provide millions of people with a sense of belonging. During the years following the fall of the Berlin Wall (post-1989), this rootlessness, as I argued elsewhere (Korac 2003a), was also fertile ground for the revival of ethnic nationalism. The dismantling of state socialism triggered the onset of a personal and collective identity crisis for the population in the region; it also heightened people's sense of economic and social insecurity, because they were no longer protected by the shield of the socialist state. Ethnic nationalism, which promised millions of people a sense of belonging and sense of security at a time of radical changes, had a powerful appeal.

The first order of the day for the post-socialist nationalists was to create a base for an ethnic national identity that would support their projects of ethnically exclusive states. To get this support they first had to secure political power over sub-federal territories, as this was their power base. Denitch (1972) explains how the Yugoslav system of decentralisation was based on the identification of leadership not with ethnic but with geo-political (Republic) interests. Given that none of the Republics were ethnically homogeneous, the local leadership was formed within the Republics. Such formed leadership, in time, became the leadership on the federal level, but its power base remained in the Republics. Denitch rightly argued, back in the 1970s, that this system had 'a build-in tendency to develop localism and to encourage nationalistic demagoguery' (1972: 34). Regardless of these built-in weaknesses of the system, in 1990 the voters were still ambivalent about supporting the radically nationalist projects of their leaders. This ambivalence was not surprising in a country which, in ethno-national terms, as Woodward (1995: 32) noted, was a land of minorities, in which most communities and large parts of the country were ethnically mixed, and no group had more than a regional majority.

Multi-ethnic communities were sites not just of peaceful multicultural coexistence but of genuine cohesion (Kaldor 1999; Korac 2004). Ethnically mixed marriages were one of the significant demographic and cultural characteristics of Yugoslav society (Morokvasic-Müller 2004). Although ethnically mixed marriages, as an expression of good multi-ethnic relations in the region, were more typically found in urban settings, they were also common in rural settings in the areas with the most ethnically mixed population. At the time of the 1981 census, the number of people in ethnically mixed marriages and from ethnically mixed backgrounds was greater than the number of ethnic Albanians living in Kosova, or the number of Montenegrins, Macedonians, Bosniaks and Slovenes in wider Yugoslavia (Petrovic 1985).[5] This group, of approximately two million people, was in fact outnumbered only by Croats and Serbs (ibid.). In such a context, the nationalists' aim for 'ethnically pure' states required a radical shift in discourse. History and language were to be purged of any notion of peaceful coexistence, as cultural 'cleansing' was a precursor to war.

Commenting on the results of the first multi-party elections in the country, in 1990, Woodward (1995: 118) points out that: 'The voters did not make a clear choice for nationalists and independence. They did push the nationalist momentum further, not because of the voting results themselves, but because of the use politicians made of them.' It can be argued that the revival of ethnic nationalism in the region was in essence a 'state nationalism' rather than 'nationalism from below' (Milic 1993). The primary social divisions and inequalities in the country during the years leading to war 'were not defined by ethnicity but by job status and growing unemployment' (Woodward 1995: 44). Politicians engineered war propaganda, targeting the ambivalent voters. In their rhetoric, they claimed that the 'unnatural' socialist regime had replaced religion, tradition, shared blood and kin for the emancipation of the working class, women, and proletarian internationalism. The nationalistic discourse, for its part, offered a set of values constructed as traditional, which could easily be perceived as 'natural'. According to these 'new' values, men were assigned the role of the 'real warrior', while women were expected to take on the responsibilities for the reproduction of the group, as well as custody of cultural values and identity.[6] Rural–urban migrants were the initial group from whom the 'real warriors' were recruited, and they eagerly mobilised behind their leaders.[7]

Divisive politics and policies became the precursor to armed violence, and the role of the media and media representations were a particularly important means in creating boundaries between 'us' and 'them', as well as of identifying the 'enemy within'. As in other conflicts constructed as ethnic strife, for example in Rwanda, the role of the media was central to spreading fear and hatred among populations at the communal level.[8] As Parin (1994: 41) pointed out, television and radio were tightly controlled and were 'serving the populace a diet of lies, invention, and propaganda, sometimes horrifying, sometimes sentimental.' Hence, the 'television war' started long before the outbreak of the armed conflict.[9] In his analysis of the importance of this kind of 'war' for the outbreak of actual violence, Parin (ibid.) refers to a statement of Marco Altherr, the then Head of the International Red Cross delegation in the Yugoslav successor states, in which he asserted that television was in large measure responsible for atrocities on both sides of the conflict in Croatia, 'by having aroused instincts of revenge and unleashed reciprocal acts of retribution.'

Divisive politics, through cultural 'cleansing' and war propaganda, led to the outbreak of violence and ethnic and territorial cleansing in many parts of the country. The heaviest fighting took place in areas with the most mixed populations in Bosnia-Herzegovina and Croatia. The quest for ethnic purity and associated exclusionary politics in areas unaffected by the war followed territorial cleansing of ethnic minorities in the war zones. The overwhelming majority of people whose experiences and accounts are presented in this book come from the war zones, in which their lives were directly endangered, but there are also those who felt threatened or victimised in places and territories in which no armed conflict occurred. They too felt that by choosing flight, they were opting for life with dignity and without fear.

Given the centrality of ethnicity for the identity politics of war, the identity of many people involved in this study had been radically challenged even before they decided to flee in search of safety. The violence targeted and victimised different ethnic communities or individuals labelled as 'the enemy' or 'the Other' in particular localities, specific political contexts, and at different points in time. This meant that people fleeing this worn-torn country could not see themselves as 'a nation in exile', which shares a common past and political project for their future. They overwhelmingly perceived themselves as victimised by political and historic circumstances, rather than as protagonists in this conflict. There were some, very few, for whom the importance of their ethnicity, as well as the creation of independent (ethnicised) states of *their* people, has become an important focus of identification, due to their war-time experiences. Nonetheless, this cannot be defined as the emergence of a shared political project and ideological conviction creating a sense of a strong social bond among compatriots living abroad. They are not linked by a shared political struggle for sociopolitical change aiming for a collective return, as with the political conviction and activism characterising some other groups of refugees.[10] Hence, they fled in search of safety, creating on their way opportunities to take control over their lives and to create better prospects for their future, rather than with the aim of reconstructing their lost homeland in exile.

How One Makes a Decision to Leave and Where to Go?

Narratives of journeys of the people I met in Rome and Amsterdam attest to the complexities involved in the interplay between force and choice which is central to the experiences of refugee displacement. Although the overwhelming majority fled the war zones and many after experiencing a direct threat to their lives, it is still difficult to distinguish between those who came to Italy or the Netherlands fleeing from individual persecution or generalised violence and those wanting to escape poverty and social injustice in their quest to gain control over their lives and to better their situation.[11]

Reasons for 'Staying Put' and/or Fleeing

Nermin and Kemo are two Bosniaks from different parts of Bosnia-Herzegovina, who fled in 1995; Nermin first to Croatia and then to Italy/Rome, Kemo to Serbia and then to the Netherlands/Amsterdam. Among the people I met, they belong to those few who 'stayed put' the longest. Their reasons for staying in war-torn Bosnia for almost the entire duration of the war were as different as are their life and displacement trajectories. Nermin, who was thirty-one years old when I met him in Rome, was a Bosnian army conscript, who fought in Bosnia and was wounded more than once. In late 1994, he found himself in ill health and with low morale for any further fighting. He decided to escape to Croatia, where his father moved before the war after divorcing his mother. At the time, Nermnin thought that he would stay there, but did not. He explains why he decided to move on and where to go:

> When I got there I realised that the situation in Croatia wasn't much better than in Bosnia, there was no fighting, but the misery was the same. I had to find another solution. The only thing I could afford was a trip to Italy. I came to Ancona in March 1995. I'd paid to be smuggled on a ship, I felt like a criminal. The only contact I'd had was a young woman from Bosnia-Herzegovina who was here in Rome. I didn't even call her – I just came.

Kemo, who was twenty-three years old at the time I met him in Amsterdam, was underage for being conscripted during the first years of the war in Bosnia. His father died before the war and soon after, his sister and her husband went to Germany as guest-workers. He and his mother remained in their hometown, which, during the war, happened to be in a Serb-controlled part of Bosnia. Both of them resisted his sister's pleas to leave the town. They were refusing to succumb to 'fear and madness around them', as Kemo put it, and I would add, to the reality of their experiences of mistreatment and intolerance. Although his narrative points to many instances of ill-treatment and discrimination primarily at the hands of local authorities, it also reveals problems with many local residents. Consequently, they were forced into a life of isolation for almost four years. His account of war-time friendships and support from some of their neighbours and people with whom they forged close relationships during this period also provides an explanation of how they managed to survive. It reveals how their lives were made liveable and their resistance to leaving their home meaningful. Although Kemo and his mother were adamant that they did not want to flee, they also knew that if the war was not over by the time he was eighteen years old and thereby eligible for the army, then they would have to leave Bosnia. And so they did, in the summer of 1995, their journey planned and coordinated by his sister from Germany. Kemo explained:

> On our route we passed through Serbia, went to Hungary using passports of our Serbian friends who kind of looked like us. My sister, who lived in Germany, organized for us to transfer to Germany on forged passports she bought through a Slovak connection. That is how we reached Germany and my sister, but we didn't stay there because my sister's in-laws, at the time refugees in the Netherlands, advised my sister to 'send' us there immediately because of a good prospect to get permanent residence in the Netherlands.

In creating solutions for their predicament, Nermin and Kemo were also among those very few who were forced to use illegal ways of reaching their destinations. By doing so, they not only risked being caught and eventually deported, but they also put their lives at risk, in the hands of unknown smugglers and criminals. It is well documented that smuggling and trafficking in migrants has become a multi-million dollar business, stimulated by restrictive reception measures and border controls imposed by the receiving countries of the North (Castles 2003; Cornelius and Tsuda 2004; Van Hear 1998). As most of the other people reached Rome or Amsterdam between 1991 and 1993, at the time when control of the EU borders was not so strict and when the admission policies for people fleeing war-torn Yugoslavia were more relaxed, they reached their destinations without adding another layer of fear and danger to their already precarious situation.

Intermediate Places and 'Solutions'

The journeys of many people I met in both Rome and Amsterdam also took them first to one of the Yugoslav successor states, to Croatia or Serbia and Montenegro. A significant minority fled first to other EU countries, such as Denmark, Germany or the Netherlands, before reaching their final destination. Those who first fled to Croatia or Serbia and Montenegro obtained or could obtain the right to stay, but decided to move on because of the political and/or economic situation there. Misa, who was forty-two years old when I met him and his family in Rome, left Croatia and fled to Serbia in the summer of 1991. As a Serb, married to a Croatian woman, he, his wife and children found their lives intolerable in their hometown, as his children were threatened at school, his wife at work, and he lost his job. When Serbian houses started being blown up, night after night in their neighbourhood, they decided to go.

The timing of their arrival in Serbia, at the beginning of the conflict in Croatia, as well as their good qualifications, needed on the labour market, and Misa's contacts in Serbia, meant that soon after arrival they were 'up on their feet again'. Both of them landed jobs in their professions and children were back at school. This type of smooth transition is by no means typical of the situation of hundreds of thousands of refugees and internally displaced persons in Serbia.[12] Those who arrived later confronted not only problems of meeting their very basic needs, but also felt unwelcome, as the duration of war, the growing number of refugees, as well as internal socioeconomic and political problems made many Serbian citizens either outright hostile or indifferent towards refugees. Misa and his family, although relatively well-settled in Serbia, decided to flee yet again, in the winter of 1993, after he was called to fight in Bosnia. Misa explains how they made their decision to flee again and why to Italy:

> Within twenty-four hours of receiving the call-up papers, we decided to go to Italy. Italy was the only solution because we didn't want to go far. I have a mother and both of my wife's parents live in Croatia; we didn't want to be far from them. So Italy was the only solution. A friend of mine from Croatia was already in Rome, so that was helpful.

Others who shared Misa's pattern of flight had more typical experiences of displacement in the Yugoslav successor states. They had to endure the hostility, poverty and misery of refugee camps, or other types of living arrangements they were offered or able to afford. One of them was Mirsad, a Bosniak who was twenty-five years old at the time I met him in Rome. He fled Bosnia-Herzegovina with his parents and a younger brother in early 1993, and went to Croatia. They settled in a small town near the Croatian coast where he continued his high school education. By the summer of the same year, they realised that they could not cope any longer. Mirsad recalls the situation at the place where they lived as refugees:

> They didn't like us much. That was the time of the wars [between Bosniaks and Croats in Bosnia-Herzegovina]. There were very many refugees and lots of hatred. That is why my father decided to move the family to Rome. We joined my sister who fled here in 1992 [she fled to Italy before they came to Croatia].

Those who arrived in Italy or the Netherlands after spending some time in other EU countries, decided to move on primarily because they were unable to obtain legal status. In some cases, however, they decided to move on because they hoped for more security and opportunities to consolidate their lives elsewhere. In most cases, their decision-making process cannot be described as an entirely rational system of weighing the pros and cons of moving on or 'staying put'. Sinisa was forty years old when I met him in

Amsterdam; he and his wife fled Bosnia-Herzegovina in the spring of 1993, just after the beginning of the war. As he and his wife are Serbs, who found themselves living in a Bosniak-controlled territory when the war began, they not only feared for their lives because of the constant shelling of their town, but also felt discriminated against, were at times abused, and hence they experienced heightened fear for their safety as well as their future. They managed to get out and reach Croatia, hoping to move on swiftly to Britain, where he has a distant relative, but with whom he had long ago lost touch. He had visited London a couple of times in the past and thought that 'that might not be a bad place to live.' As Sinisa was not able to get in touch with his relative and obtain an invitation letter, their request for visas was rejected. Instead, they went to Germany, because their friends, who were well-established there, sent a letter of guarantee. Sinisa's account details how they ended up in Amsterdam and how the decision was made not to stay in Germany:

> Although our friends were willing and able to help us to get up on our feet again [find work, accommodation, etc.], we didn't want to stay in Germany because we didn't feel good there. At that time, all other so-called rational reasons were in support of a stay, but we'd decided to follow our instincts. From there, we went to the Netherlands to be closer to England and to wait for the opportunity to get there. We heard from an acquaintance from Croatia, who lived in Amsterdam, that Bosnians are well received in the Netherlands. We had his phone number, so we phoned him up from Germany, and he invited us to come and stay with him until we figured out what to do next.

These accounts and other narratives of people I met in Rome and Amsterdam show how social networks and transnational connections were in many instances essential for providing financial and other resources as well as the organizational infrastructure for the journey. Nonetheless, their decision to leave their place of origin or to undertake secondary migration were for the most part based on their own perceptions of security issues and/or the prospects of regaining control over their lives at the places where they lived. Only in exceptional cases, involving a very few young adults, was the decision to flee and leave parents behind made by their parents and prompted by (distant) family members living abroad.

However, even in such cases, these young adults, as other refugees in my study, made further migration choices based on their own perceptions of their situation, their prospects of gaining legal status, continuing education, finding meaningful jobs and having better prospects for their future. Such is the case of Goca, who was thirty-one years old at the time I met her and her partner in Rome. She was a student in Bosnia-Herzegovina before the war. During the months leading to the outbreak of violence, her parents and her aunt, who was a guest-worker in Germany, put pressure on her to go there and 'stay with her for a while'. Although reluctantly, Goca left in March 1992, just weeks before the armed conflict started in her hometown. Meanwhile, similar pressure was put on her boyfriend who, at around the same time, went to Montenegro to 'visit his relatives' there. Fearing that he may be conscripted if he registered as a resident there, he crossed the Adriatic and went to Italy. The only contact he had was the telephone number of a friend of a family friend who had settled in a small town in the north-east of Italy. Although separated, Goca and her boyfriend kept in touch. She recalls the way it was in Germany and how she came to Italy after less than six months:

> I started working [in Germany] but I didn't have any papers, even a tourist visa was impossible to get because the war in Bosnia had just started. My stay was illegal. In June 92, my boyfriend managed to come to Italy where he'd got a tourist visa and then he invited me to join him.

In shaping perceptions of opportunities open to them, information on the situation in other EU countries gained through social networks and transnational connections was very important in negotiating, and at times guessing, the possible gains and losses involved in different migration choices available.

Reasons for 'Choosing' Rome/Italy

The accounts of migration choices of people I met in Rome reveal that the overwhelming majority came to Italy because that was the only country they could reach, as it was nearby and because Italy was one of the last EU states to introduce a visa regime for nationals from the Yugoslav successor states. An additional factor that played a role in the decisions of refugees to flee to Italy was their perception of this Mediterranean country as in some way being similar to their countries of origin. Senad, a Bosniak from a town in the south-eastern part of Bosnia-Herzegovina close to the Adriatic, was one among quite a few of the people I met in Rome who emphasised this quality of Italy as their country of choice. Senad was forty-two years old when I met him. He fled to Rome in 1992, because he had Italian friends, a family friendship dating from way back before the war. Although this friendship connection was an important 'pull' factor for him to come to Italy, Senad had nonetheless considered other options he had had before flight. He explains why he decided to come to Italy:

> If I went somewhere north [Northern Europe] where you have cloudy skies for months, where there's no sun, even with all the good things you get there, I don't think it's all there is to being happy. We were born on the Mediterranean, and this is a Mediterranean country, the closest to us [people from the Yugoslav

successor states]. We're used to eating a fig here and there, to cheating someone a little here and there, and then to being kind and helpful to total strangers – that's the Mediterranean atmosphere.

The most important reason for deciding to flee to Italy, however, was having some sort of contact there. Most of them knew at least one person in Rome. In most cases the people they knew were also refugees from one of the Yugoslav successor states. Usually they were acquaintances or friends with whom they had long since lost touch. Some also came to join their siblings who were already refugees in Rome. A few had Italian friends in Rome from before the war, such as Senad, or war-time friendships with Italians who were on aid missions in their hometowns before their flight. These contacts were not only an important source of information, but also an important source of psychosocial support that is paramount for people forced into decisions to leave their places of origin.

Ending Up in Amsterdam/The Netherlands

For the most part, decisions to settle in the Netherlands were circumstantial, rather than resulting from a planned, rational, informed decision. A significant minority, however, had chosen the Netherlands as their destination, because they wanted to join family members who were already refugees there. Most did so either through a family reunification scheme applicable to those with a family member who had already been granted a full (Convention) refugee status in the Netherlands, but a few applied independently. Although both Italy and the Netherlands introduced ad hoc regulations allowing for the admission and reception of people fleeing war-torn Yugoslavia, the Dutch, unlike the Italians, introduced a legal basis for temporary status in 1994. This Act allowed temporary protection only for those fleeing Bosnia-Herzegovina who arrived after April 1993; those fleeing other regions had to enter the regular asylum procedures. Introduction of these measures also meant that all those who entered and applied for asylum in the Netherlands during 1992 and before April 1993 were granted refugee status. Consequently, the number of people from Bosnia-Hercegovina, and Bosniaks in particular, granted refugee status was relatively high.[13]

In very few cases people were advised by relatives or friends living abroad to go to the Netherlands, because at the time of their flight the Dutch had relatively relaxed determination procedures towards refugees from Bosnia-Herzegovina. Such was the case of Nermin and his mother, for example, whose flight was supported and coordinated by his sister living in Germany, as described earlier in this chapter. Nermin initially thought that he would be joining his sister in Germany. He explained how and why he and his mother ended up in the Netherlands:

When we finally arrived in Frankfurt, I felt free and safe, although I was carrying a fake passport and didn't have permission to stay in Germany. But my sister was instructed by her in-laws, who live in the Netherlands, to send us promptly there. They told her that we stood a much better chance of sorting out papers to stay in the Netherlands than in Germany. My sister's friend drove us to the Dutch border almost immediately upon our arrival in Frankfurt. At the time, I didn't think there was much difference between these two countries, so I did not mind going to the Netherlands. What was important to me was that I'd be relatively close to my sister and able to visit regularly, once my papers were sorted.

In even fewer cases, people I met in Amsterdam had chosen the Netherlands because they had information on their relatively generous welfare model of assistance to refugees. Because of the current trend in the EU to lower their welfare standards for refugees and make their societies 'less attractive' destinations, it is important to examine the circumstances under which the generous welfare system of another state becomes a decisive 'pull' factor in choosing where to flee. Slavenka was one of those very few people who came to the Netherlands attracted by the type of provision for refugees, or that is how one may 'categorise' her. On closer inspection, however, her account of the interplay of force and choice paints a different picture. Slavenka fled her hometown in Bosnia-Herzegovina in mid 1994, and went to Croatia with her mother and brother, leaving her father behind. As her mother is a Croat from Bosnia with relatives in Croatia, they benefited from these contacts and initially considered their situation there tolerable. However, with the number of refugees in Croatia growing and the war in Bosnia-Herzegovina dying out, many Bosnians lost their status and their benefits with it. This shift made the lives of many hardly liveable. Slavenka, who was twenty-five years old when I met her in Amsterdam, explained their circumstances in Croatia after they lost all support and why she and her mother came to the Netherlands in April 1995:

> We'd lost our accommodation in the place where we settled [in Croatia], there wasn't any financial assistance, it was difficult to think about continuing education because it was hard to find any work and even harder to work and study. My mother couldn't find any work, and the situation in Bosnia was the same, no money, no work. When we came here [to visit relatives] we saw that our relatives had managed to have some kind of normal life here. They had social benefit, which is pretty good here in the Netherlands. That was more than we could dream of, and we decided to apply for asylum.

When these and other experiences of the people making the decision to move are juxtaposed to the current political debates about 'bogus refugees' and the attempts of governments of the receiving societies to distinguish between elements constituting economic reasons for movement and those which can be considered political or involving abuse of basic human rights of peoples from many troubled regions of the world, it is not hard to see that these heated discussions are misleading. They do not reflect the fact that conflicts, causing massive exodus of people fleeing war and generalised violence in the past decades, go hand in hand with the destruction of vital economic means of support of the populations caught in these wars. The states involved in these conflicts also rarely observe and protect the rights of refugees or those internally displaced. Hence, it is misleading to treat the decisions of people to escape poverty and social injustice caused by violent political upheavals, or those made after fleeing the immediate danger for their lives, as somehow making them 'lesser refugees' or 'forced migrants', and therefore, less deserving of our support in rebuilding their lives.

Flight and Creation of Solutions: Agency and the Role of Social Networks

The discussion in this chapter has demonstrated that even when the initial choices of whether, when and where to flee are extremely limited, when elements of force prevail, it is the agency of the people that makes them move in the first place. It also makes them continuously open to the new and originally unforeseen alternatives or areas of opportunity often affecting the choice of their ultimate destination during their initial journey or provoking secondary migration. Reasons for making specific migratory decisions about where to go may appear far removed from the initial 'pushing' force to migrate, as is the case with some of the experiences presented in this chapter. On closer examination, however, it becomes clear that they are inseparable from the original motivation to flee, which is not simply to preserve life, but to regain control over its continuity in a meaningful way. In this sense, it can be argued that forced migration always entails at least some degree of choice and should be regarded as proactive. It is always embedded in active search for and creation of solutions, however unsatisfactory these solutions may be initially.

The process of creating solutions underpinning the decision-making processes of people fleeing their places of origin, and thus their agency, is enabled and sustained by a range of types of social networks and transnational connections, as revealed in this chapter, and as pointed out by others (e.g., Borjas and Crisp 2005; Crisp 1999; Koser 1997; Van Hear 1998). The forcible character of these processes, hence, the prevailing lack of proper, long-term planning, and often the need to make decisions ad hoc, are central to this type of migration. Consequently, the forcible character of migration usually requires fast mobilisation of resources, and therefore this type of movement critically depends on networks and transnational connections characterised by 'weak ties' (Granovetter 1973, 1985). Such ties are based on loose connections with acquaintances, friends of friends and contacts emanating from circumstances, rather than any closer relationship. The centrality of weak ties in facilitating flight points to the very agency of the people making decisions and actually making the move. It reveals the process through which they create powerful resources in the situations and circumstances of severe disempowerment characterising forcible displacement.

The emphasis on the agency of refugees brings into focus the exploration of how forcible migratory processes actually work. Through this type of inquiry refugees are no longer seen as the objects of our knowledge, assistance and management, but as having a central role in the creation of our understanding of 'the refugee' and in the formulation of our responses to their predicament. By exploring the actual reality of the decision-making processes of forced migrants and emphasising the centrality of people's agency we can begin to address the problems with a range of policy issues. Contemporary public and policy discourses on refugees are inflexible, rigid, and uniform, representing refugees as a category of people who pose threat to our security or as passive victims who impose a burden on our welfare systems and societies. Such representations, as well as policies reflecting them, leave little or no room for acknowledging and making a constructive use of the powerful human resources and human capital of the people who are forcibly displaced. The discussion in the next chapter continues to examine the issues of agency of the people forced into decisions to flee their places of origin by exploring the narratives and experiences of the people in my study after they reached Italy and the Netherlands.

Notes

1. Attempts to address the issue of the blurred boundaries between forced and unforced migration in the form of the continuum of 'force' and 'choice' (Van Hear 1998) and of 'reactive' and 'proactive' migration (Richmond 1994) are well known efforts to fit different types of migrants into a single conceptual framework. The former, proposed by Van Hear, distinguishes between voluntary and involuntary migration as the two opposite ends of the continuum, pointing to more choice or options and less or no choice or options, associated with the respective ends of the continuum. The latter, proposed by Richmond, distinguishes between proactive and reactive migration, at the two opposite ends of the continuum, pointing to those with agency and those with no or very little agency. In Van Hear's framework, forced migrants are at the 'involuntary' end of the continuum, while according to Richmond's conceptualisation they cluster around the 'reactive' end of the continuum.

2. The data come from an unnamed UNHCR report and refer to the then latest instances of 'ethnic cleansing' in Srebrenica and Zepa (Bosnia-Herzegovina) and in the region of Krajina (Croatia). Cited in Klarin (1995: 5).

3. These data aim to emphasise the overall consequence of the divisive politics and ideologies that have transformed ethnicity into an effective tool of war in the region, rather than to gloss over important differences in the extent to which some ethnic nations, Bosniaks in particular, were victimised by these politics. Also, the emphasis on the more general characteristics of nationalist politics in the region does not indicate my lack of awareness and recognition of unequal relations of power among ethno-national groups in these wars, and consequently, their differentiated responsibility for the crimes and atrocities committed in this conflict.

4. By the end of the 1970s, the standard of living, measured by GDP per capita, in the most developed parts of the country, such as Slovenia, reached the level of the poorer countries of the developed world. For more on the type and character of Yugoslav socialism and its economy see Zukin (1975).

5. Kosova is the Albanian name for the territory in which the Albanians are a majority population. The more frequently used name Kosovo is a Serbian word for the same territory in which the Serbs are a minority population.

6. Many authors have emphasised that women are central to producing and maintaining cultural and group identity (e.g., Yuval-Davis and Anthias 1989; Yuval-Davis 1997; Walby 1992). During the growing process of militarisation associated with the escalation of armed conflict, women often become specifically targeted because of these roles. This is because the identity politics of wars constructed as ethnic strife assign women with 'honourable' roles as 'Mothers of the Nation' and 'Symbols of the Nation'. They became increasingly seen as precious property to be controlled and 'protected'. The intersection of discourses of gender and nation, thus, tend to essentialise the relations between women and men, preparing them to take on their 'traditional' and/or 'natural' roles: men to sacrifice their lives and women to sacrifice their husbands and sons.

7. A mini-survey, undertaken by an independent journalist in Belgrade in 1991, that profiled fifty volunteers in the Serbian paramilitary forces who were members of the Serbian Radical Party (SRP), showed that most of the volunteers were of rural background but with a permanent residence in one of the regional urban centres in Serbia. The leader of the SRP, Vojislav Seselj, is accused of committing war crimes in Croatia and Bosnia-Herzegovina and is currently standing trial in The Hague.

8. For more information on the role of the media in the conflict in Rwanda see Malvern (2002) and Des Forges (2002).

9. For more information on the role of the media in the Yugoslav conflict see Žarkov (2007).

10. In some instances, as mentioned in Chapter 1, people fleeing political upheavals and conflict share such social bonds embedded in a shared political struggle to re-create their lost states/homelands, as is the case of the Palestinians (Schulz and Hammer 2003) or the Chileans (Eastmond 1997) or the Iraqi Arabs (Al-Rasheed 1994).

11. As the conflict between Yugoslav successor states caused the largest mass displacement of people in Europe since the Second World War, the UNHCR

prompted governments of the receiving countries to introduce temporary protection measures for these refugees. Temporary protection meant that a person can be granted temporary asylum if fleeing situations of generalised violence in contrast to refugee status which guarantees the permanent protection of persons fleeing conditions of individual persecution as stipulated in the Geneva Convention of 1951.

12. In 2000, Serbia & Montenegro (formerly known as the Federal Republic of Yugoslavia, and, as of 21 May 2006, split into two independent states), was ranked the third country among the top ten refugee receiving countries in the world, when ranked by refugee population per 1,000 inhabitants (Castles et al. 2003b: 6).

13. Information provided by the Ministry of Interior during an exploratory visit to The Hague and Amsterdam in November 1999.

3

Regaining Control Over Life:
Dependency, Self-sufficiency
and Agency

After being forced into decisions to leave their homes, the people I met were eager to regain some sense of normality in their lives. This was the recurring theme and the common thread running through their narratives and the goal which was driving and shaping their actions. During the early stages of their journeys the desire to have a normal life again meant first and foremost a search for safety and a place in which they could start regaining control over their lives. Their narratives reveal how they actively sought ways to legalise their status as well as to overcome destitution caused by their displacement. The former was the primary reason that brought them to either Italy or the Netherlands; the latter shaped their initial survival and 'nesting' strategies as well as future plans. Most of the people I met in Rome and Amsterdam, especially those younger and single, but also those with children, had fairly clear ideas about their immediate plans and, therefore, their priorities. In this sense, my research supports arguments that the process of refugee settlement is goal-oriented, regardless of a range of insecurities and uncertainties it also entails (e.g., Valtonen 1998). Even if they did not have a clear preference about whether they might decide to stay or return, their accounts of their initial hopes about their lives after they fled home reveal their desire to create a meaningful 'place' for themselves in both receiving cities/countries. This was regardless of whether their stay was to be only temporary or permanent.

Almost all emphasised a need to be actively engaged in regaining control over their lives. This, in turn, would create much needed space and opportunity for making further plans and decisions about their future, allowing preparation for either meaningful return or staying where they were.

For some, this meant getting a job and earning enough to get by, as well as being able to help those who had stayed behind. For others, it meant finding ways of recognising their degrees and skills, or of finding opportunities for retraining or gaining work experience in lines of work in which their previous professional experience could be useful. For those whose education was interrupted by war and the subsequent flight, this meant exploring the opportunities of continuing or restarting education. For those with children of primary education age, this also meant continuation of their children's education.

In this sense, although the period upon arrival was marked by disorientation and in some cases profound feelings of despair, loss and bereavement, they also came with a hope to consolidate their lives shattered by war, and make meaningful plans for and decisions about their future. Italy and the Netherlands, where they sought refuge, and Rome and Amsterdam, where they were actively seeking ways to overcome their liminal existence, were critical junctions in this process. Their encounter with the situation in Rome/Italy and Amsterdam/the Netherlands, ranging from socioeconomic and policy structures and contexts to cultural and those which can be termed 'the way of life', shaped in different ways these initial hopes, energies and convictions.

Following the Rules in the Netherlands

Problems with a 'Phased' Approach

Restrictive admission policies as well as the phased approach to reception and integration, outlined in the Introduction, shape the process of incorporation of refugees in Dutch society. The accounts of people in this study speak of how their initial encounters with the Netherlands, its policy systems and people, shaped their perception, attitudes and strategies of 'nesting' there. Smilja, a 48-year-old woman who fled Bosnia-Herzegovina with her son, recalled the process she was subjected to immediately upon arrival:

> I felt terrible there [at the investigation centre], because for the first time in my life I was surrounded by the police. I was photographed as if I was a criminal, my fingerprints were taken, I was strip-searched, people in uniforms were escorting me back and forth, I was questioned in a foreign language I could not understand, and I was separated from my son who was eighteen years old then. At the other centre [the reception centre] I was constantly crying at the beginning, and I wanted to go back regardless of what could've happened to me there. No one told us when all the interrogation and questioning would stop, and when we'd be allowed to live normally. All we were told was wait.

Photographing, fingerprinting, and strip-searching was a shock to all the people who were subjected to it. For some, it was an experience of exceptional humiliation for which they could not see any justification. After all, they were fleeing persecution, human rights abuse or outright attacks on their lives. They could not fathom why they were treated like criminals when they finally reached safety.

This type of mistreatment of people fleeing their countries of origin is provoked by an increasing number of people entering Europe from around the world and seeking protection. The mistrust and indignity with which the admission and reception procedures are marked are conveniently justified as 'security measures', necessary to guard 'our safety' and keep 'our humanitarian efforts' protected from abuse. The discourse surrounding refugees has radically changed in the past couple of decades. During the Cold War era, refugees were predominantly coming from the Eastern, 'communist', part of Europe seeking refuge in the 'free world'. For political and ideological reasons they were treated as heroes. This type of treatment was very much helped by the fact that their numbers were relatively small and that most of them belonged to elites in their countries: they were typically scientists, academics, artists and sporting heroes. Additionally, and very importantly, they were white and European, although East European. This is not to argue that refugees have been historically treated with respect. There were always those who were treated with suspicion and viewed as villains.[1]

People fleeing their countries of origin in the past two decades are perceived as a different 'kind' of people, not like those who were reaching Western borders from behind the Iron Curtain and the grip of communist ideology and persecution. Many are seen as reaching Europe and other countries of the developed world for economic reasons, putting pressure on the welfare systems of these countries at best, or posing a security threat at worst. Thus, in the name of security and in an effort to protect the well-being of 'genuine' refugees, many of the people I met in Amsterdam, certainly all those who were obliged to enter regular determination procedures upon arriving in the Netherlands, had to endure this procedure and learn to live with the experience. In finding ways to come to terms with the humiliation involved in the reception procedures some of them, including Smilja, sought to normalise it by explaining (in retrospect) that the process was 'well and professionally organized' and 'part of a normal procedure', but the problem was that no one took the trouble to explain to them the reasons for putting in place such procedures for the newly arrived.

The people I met in Amsterdam were offered a vide range of different services developed and organized to provide for their needs. Through these services and provision they were in contact with both professionals as well as volunteers working with refugees. This well-developed and organized infrastructure and provision for refugees and other newcomers was due to the organizational and financial capacity of municipalities and the NGO sector, which are responsible for implementing integration policies. It is also because of the responsibilities that individual immigrants have towards the Dutch state to 'integrate', as outlined in the Introduction. Hence, either professionals or volunteers specialising in work with refugees and other migrants were the people leading them through the process termed integration. For some, this was a positive experience. Ivana, a 47-year-old single mother from Bosnia-Herzegovina, for example, said that she was 'very satisfied with the patience and readiness of the Dutch to help and make the lives of refugees less onerous.' This and other positive views were linked to good experiences of communication with volunteers who were either so-called refugee workers or language tutors. When they went beyond the formal 'script' of what was required in their contacts with refugees, their gestures of kindness, openness, and spontaneity were perceived as bridging initiatives of people who were reaching out in solidarity to a stranger in need. Ivana, for example, remembered a refugee worker at the reception centre with profound gratitude. She brought a sewing machine from home one day for Ivana because she could not find one available at the centre. She also remembered how important it was for her to be invited to a birthday party of her language tutor. This gave her the opportunity not only to learn first-hand about 'Dutch customs and ways', but more importantly to feel like a normal human being again, a person who is accepted and valued for who she is.

Most of the refugees I met, however, experienced this phased, state-led orientation programme and functional adjustment to the new society as a pressure to 'adjust in the way the Dutch see fit', as Kajo, a 37-year-old Bosniak put it. He arrived in mid 1992, and was still in the process of getting his professional skills recognised when I met him, in 2001. Kajo, as well as other people in Amsterdam, perceived his experience in the Netherlands as a form of social control which hardly left any space for the process of mutual adjustment and individual agency. Boris, a 35-year-old man from Bosnia-Herzegovina, summarised the views of the people I met:

> I do what I am told to do, and everything is going according to 'integration' rules that we 'refugees' have to follow. We didn't have to integrate really, you see, we just had to do what we were told.

The dissatisfaction and at times the bitterness of the people I met in Amsterdam concerning their situation were caused by their acute feeling of loss of agency. To realise their goals they had to reclaim the right to agency and find 'room for manoeuvre' within the system of rigid integration rules. Those who did not have to stay in so-called reception centres, because they had close family members in the Netherlands and were therefore required only to report there once a week, were more likely to organize their lives around their own priorities and goals, rather than those defined by the receiving state and their policies. This was mostly reflected in finding ways and opportunities to learn the language faster as well as to be 'free and independent' in searching for organizations and agencies that may be able to help them to get on with their lives, as Miro, a 27-year-old man, explained.

The state-led process, implemented by local authorities and NGOs and carried out by professionals, started while the people I met were still in reception centres; on average, they stayed in these centres from several months to over a year. Most of the people I met appreciated the fact that they were 'not left to their own devices' when they first arrived, as Emir, a 51-year-old Bosniak put it. Nonetheless, the actual support offered and the character of the contacts with professionals and volunteers working in these centres were overwhelmingly perceived as not suited to their individual situations, plans and needs. While some, such as Cica, a 34-year-old nurse from Bosnia-Herzegovina, appreciated the opportunity to learn about 'the life and customs in the Netherlands', the country they 'did not know anything about', through contacts with refugee workers or language tutors at the centres, the people I met overwhelmingly regarded the system and support developed for them as lacking in knowledge and information about their culture(s) and backgrounds, as well as depriving them of agency. My research indicates that this is not a problem specific to the Netherlands, but applicable to other countries with similar reception systems and integration policies. Tanja's account of her life in Denmark, where she and her mother originally fled from Bosnia-Herzegovina in 1993, reveals shared views among the people who experienced similar systems. When I met Tanja she was twenty-two years old and living in Rome. She arrived there in 1998 on a student exchange programme, after obtaining refugee status in Denmark. At the time of my research, she thought of her stay there as long or longer term. When recalling her experience in Denmark she said:

> I wasn't happy there, I felt kind of 'programmed'. I can't say that everything was difficult, but I felt kind of labelled as a refugee. They're [the Danes] always somehow distant and they always look at you kind of differently. The Danes couldn't cross that barrier and look at us as people who have had some bad experiences but are trying to get over them. I always felt kind of labelled.

Refugees I met in Amsterdam complained about 'being taught how to turn on the light and use the lavatory … instead of being given a good language course appropriate to our skills and needs', as Boris, a medical doctor from Bosnia, recalled. He was one of those who came with a strong conviction and plan to do whatever was required to continue work in his profession. He was well aware that this may take time and certainly a lot of effort and hard work on his part, but he was full of energy and enthusiasm for a new beginning.

Boris also envisaged the possibility of medical doctors not being in demand on the Dutch labour market. In such a case, as he was 'functional' in English, he thought of searching for possibilities of finding work with one of the international organizations providing medical assistance in conflict regions around the world. As some of these organizations have their branches in the Netherlands, Boris hoped that they would be interested in benefiting from his two-year long experience of work as a medical doctor in his hometown in a war-ridden part of Bosnia, before he and his wife had decided to flee. It comes as no surprise that he was critical about the situation he found himself in upon arrival. It took years before he was actually able to find and start a language course tailored to his needs and even more to undertake compulsory (additional) medical training in order to have his diploma recognised. Boris came to the Netherlands in early1994; he got a job as a medical doctor in a hospital in Amsterdam in early 2001.

Others, who came to the Netherlands with less articulated plans and needs, primarily those older and less educated, from small towns or semi-urban areas/settlements, were satisfied at first, because they were 'alive, not hungry or cold', as Nadan, a 59-year-old Bosniak, put it. However, as time went by dissatisfaction with the lack of privacy and 'normality' in their lives crept in. Some, like Nadan and his wife, spent almost two years 'living' in one corner of a big room, with three other families, in a reception centre accommodating some 1,200 refugees.

When the stay in reception centres did not exceed four months accounts of the experiences of life in them tended to be less negative. For the most part, the time spent there was viewed as being 'in transit' as Smilja put it, as 'a short break', a time to recuperate, before moving on with their lives. In a few cases, the accounts of the time spent in the centres had a positive tone. Kemo was one of those who viewed his stay at the reception centre in a relatively positive light. He was eighteen years old when he arrived from Bosnia with his mother, as mentioned in Chapter 2. They were sent to a reception centre in which they did not have to share a room with other people, giving them a sense of privacy. Almost immediately upon arrival he started attending the Dutch language course daily. The classes were held in the nearby town, rather than the centre. This gave him a sense of purpose and a reason to go out to town rather than to stay in and feel confined to the perimeter of the centre. A very important element of Kemo's positive memories of the reception centre was the experience of the cultural and racial diversity among the people there. He said:

> There were people from different countries there, particularly from Africa and Asia. I was happy to have the opportunity to get to know people from other parts of the world. We communicated in English, which I knew a little at the time, but during the three months that we were there, my spoken English improved; that was an unexpected gain from these contacts too.

Appreciation of the cultural and racial diversity of the reception centres was not however shared by all. In most cases associations with people at the reception centres were seen as forced and therefore as something they had to endure rather than engage with. In some cases cultural and particularly racial diversity provoked racist feelings of superiority because they were European and therefore thought of themselves as more 'modern' in their outlook and value systems. In most cases my discussions with them revealed that these feelings of superiority were embedded in ignorance and a lack of any prior first-hand experiences and contacts with Africans or Asians.

Leaving the reception centres and moving into their own accommodation meant a new stage in the process of regaining some kind of 'normality' in their lives, at least in terms of having privacy and improved standard of accommodation. Those whom I got to know while in Amsterdam all had good accommodation (measured by Amsterdam standards of public housing) and well-equipped flats. However, the problems of the lack of agency in dealing with their individual situations, plans, and aims, remained for many. As did the discrepancy between how they were perceived by the Dutch, professionals and volunteers with whom they were in touch, and who they really were in terms of their individual and group histories and backgrounds, skills, knowledge, world views. Smilja, a nurse from Bosnia-Herzegovina, for example, remembered being shown 'how to use the fridge and how to switch on the television', when she and her son moved out of the reception centre into their own accommodation in Amsterdam. These and numerous other similar experiences were perceived as humiliating and not really helpful. The official 'to do' and 'check lists' of professionals or volunteers who were helping them to start their lives in Amsterdam often did not reflect their situation, aspirations, plans, and needs.

Although research indicates that one of the main reasons for the Dutch people to volunteer as refugee workers or language tutors is their openness towards immigrants in general, and their concern for the situation of refugees in particular (Hollands 2001), the structural conditions under which these contacts take place do not seem to reduce cultural distance or prejudice. Direct, interpersonal contacts with refugees challenge perceptions that they are not people like 'us', make volunteers aware that they are most often self-reliant and independent, and leads to a more differentiated understanding of 'other' cultures, Hollands' study demonstrates (2001: 304–6). Through these contacts volunteers learn, frequently with surprise, that refugees are often very well educated and come from middle or higher class backgrounds (ibid.: 306). While this realisation led some refugee workers to become aware of the potential contribution of these people to Dutch society, it led others to disappointment because of their expectation that refugees are 'poor people in need' (ibid.: 306–7). Hollands concludes that one of the factors contributing to this specific prejudice is the lack of understanding and knowledge about migration or refugee movements, and lack of awareness of the political context in which support and help for refugees is provided (ibid.: 307).

Humanitarian commitment to helping people in need is clearly embedded in the structural framework of a minority situation in which the culture of the receiving society is ranked as superior (Knudsen 1991: 30–34). The experience of such a notion of cultural difference caused 'a certain level of resistance', as Boris put it, to the country which has become their 'homeland now'. Hence, many of the people I met in Amsterdam formed a somewhat negative attitude towards Dutch society, regardless of the fact that they all also emphasised their gratitude for being allowed to stay in the country and for being granted material and other support.

Problems with 'One Size Fits All' Programmes

Frustrations and bitterness caused by the character of assistance also reflect the prevailing tendency to provide assistance through 'one size fits all' programmes, as pointed out in the Introduction. One of the many problems with this approach to assisting refugees became apparent in discussions about experiences of learning Dutch, which reportedly was one of the main obstacles to a more rapid process of regaining control over the lives of the people I met in Amsterdam. Only those who came as young children or in their teens, as their parents reported, did not have difficulties learning the language. The problem in learning Dutch, as they pointed out, was to a large extent caused by the fact that the language training system is linked to the phased system of rights and obligations associated with various legal statuses.

While awaiting the decision on their asylum claim, language courses are not compulsory. They are organized at the reception centres and taught by voluntary language tutors. These courses are not geared towards the specific age or literacy/educational level of refugees; hence, they are not effective, particularly for younger and better-educated students. Cica, a 34-year-old nurse from Bosnia-Herzegovina, explained why she gave up attending language classes at the reception centre in which she and her husband Boris, stayed: 'We would spend days repeating one word, on and on, because many people could not follow.' Only after convention, 'A', or humanitarian, 'C', status is granted, does language training become obligatory, when it is taught by professionals, and offers a variety of modes depending on the intensity, age and educational level of students. Given that the determination procedure was usually very long, many refugees started learning the language after twelve and often more months in the Netherlands.

Further, the social isolation of refugees from the society and local communities created by their often long stay in reception centres contributed to the lack of opportunity to practice and improve the language. Additionally, for many younger, well-educated refugees, English was the language they tended to use in day-to-day communication with the Dutch for many months after leaving reception centres, because it was easier and also because the Dutch speak it well. For older and less educated people I met, who did not know any foreign languages prior to their flight, learning Dutch was even more difficult, because they were not used to learning other languages.

Problems of the inflexibility of types of assistance provided in reception centres during the determination process also emerged in discussions with the people who came with determination to reestablish themselves in their professions, once granted permission to stay. Some of them, like Kajo, for example, took the initiative to find out early on what he would have to do in order to get his university degree recognised, if granted asylum. He was eager to find out as much as he could, so that he could start preparing himself for examinations while awaiting the decision, rather than sitting idle, 'measuring time by the occurrences of breakfast, lunch and dinner', as he put it. However, all his efforts were in vain, there was no one who could answer his questions or willing to point him into the right direction. Hence, Kajo and the others with similar plans had not only to postpone the acquisition of adequate language skills required for work in their profession, but also the process of obtaining information about what the skill recognition process entails.

The dissatisfaction and frustration caused by the system of support offered in the reception centres point to yet another problematic dimension in the assistance offered to refugees soon upon their arrival. It is focused upon immediate day-to-day problems, rather than simultaneously on the future and the past of the refugees (Knudsen 1991). The problem with this type of approach to assistance is evident when contrasted with the accounts of the people who were subjected to it: they themselves focused on rethinking aspects of their past and possible options for their future. In doing so they were actively developing strategies to confront their present, liminal condition.

Getting Food on the Family Table and Beyond

Employment is one of the core components of incorporating newcomers into the receiving society, acknowledged as such by both the refugees themselves and the receiving society. It is also one of the most difficult problems to tackle, because of a complex set of intervening parameters. These range from the situation in the labour market of the receiving society and policies that progressively exclude newcomers from formal labour markets or their specific niches, to the character of the language and professional skills of newcomers.

These problems are compounded by the fact that in most European countries, including the Netherlands, people who come seeking asylum and protection do not have the right to work until after they are granted legal status. This process tends to last for years, rather than months. These prolonged periods of liminal existence and insecurity severely undermine the agency, determination and hopes of people to take control over their lives. By losing precious time needed to adjust functionally to their new environment, through learning the language and finding meaningful ways to earn their keep, they also often lose a 'feel' for their professions, they worry about their skills becoming 'rusty', all of which undermines their self-esteem.

Around half of the people I met in Amsterdam were employed, and another quarter was studying or in the process of getting their formal skills recognised.[2] The level of labour-market participation of the group was similar to the general level of employment of refugees in the Netherlands. In 2000, the unemployment rate among the Dutch population of working age was three per cent, whilst the unemployment rate among refugees was thirty-five per cent.[3] Most of the refugees found work through channels other than the employment office, which should be a first step towards the labour market. Both Brink's (1997) and my research indicate that refugees tend to find jobs either through commercial employment agencies or their own networks. Those employed or studying felt particularly exposed to the 'all-embracing pressure to adjust, both at professional and personal level', as Kajo put it. As many of the people I met in Amsterdam were well-educated, with approximately one third having a university degree, and an equally high number with a technical or other vocational qualification on a secondary level, many were in fact underemployed because of the many structural and social barriers in the Dutch labour market and society.[4]

In an attempt to tackle some of the barriers that exclude refugees and other newcomers from labour-market participation, some of the local NGOs, such as Emplooi, developed a type of one-to-one supportive programme for assisting refugees in finding employment. This initiative involves 'matching' individual refugees with Dutch volunteers who have experience and contacts in specific niches of the Dutch labour-market. A person seeking work and a volunteer develop an employment strategy based on a carefully made assessment of the individual needs and circumstances of the job seeker. They together define tasks and identify ways of accomplishing them. After the initial, preparatory phase is over, the volunteer contacts employers who may be interested and able to offer a suitable position. This 'tailor-made' approach to refugee employment has proved to be effective, but due to a very limited number of organizations involved in this type of programmes, their structural and organizational capacity prevent them from reaching out to refugees and from meeting their needs in any systematic way.[5] None of the people I met in Amsterdam, for example, had heard about this organization and the type of programme they offer.

Underemployment was particularly high among well-educated people. Those few who had jobs adequate to their education and skills were resourceful, patient and lucky enough to find ways to undergo the process of skills recognition in order to be back in their professions. They were also almost exclusively men. It took them on average up to seven years to do so. Boris, the Bosnian doctor, was one of them. For him, as well as for a very few other people who succeeded in their efforts, the assistance provided by a Dutch privately funded organization, the University Assistance Fund (UAF), was instrumental in securing the financial assistance necessary for continuation of professional careers.[6] All of them learned about the organization through their own, informal channels, rather than from one of the numerous organizations or individuals working with refugees. Boris recalled the way he was approached by the organization's staff, after he contacted them:

> I had two interviews there, one of which was about my reasons for coming here and about my legal status and the difficulties I had in obtaining a permanent residence permit. That interview was more detailed and serious than those I had during the determination procedure. After these interviews, I was accepted as their client and they agreed to pay my additional professional training. I was paid the university fees, most of the course books, and some of the travel expenses.

This study indicates that the opportunities and possibilities for affording both the time and financial resources necessary for the process of diploma recognition are gendered. In the cases of married couples, especially if with children, but also of those cohabiting, it was almost exclusively men who undertook the process, while women took on a supportive role and found jobs they could get without any or much retraining. This was the case regardless of women's education and employment history. In very few cases in which women also decided to recognise their professional skills and diplomas they often experienced marriage/relationship breakdowns, as was the case with Spomenka who settled in Rome. Her experience will be discussed later in the chapter. The highly educated women in this study and all other people I met who did not want or who could not find ways to recognise their degrees and skills, but instead had decided to retrain and find jobs in new professions and lines of work, spent on average up to five years establishing themselves functionally in the new environment.

To Work or Not to Work: Is This a Gendered Question?

Many of the older or less educated people responded to the perceived control and pressures to comply with the prescribed settlement programme by reducing their life aspirations and by effectively excluding themselves from wider society. Nadan was one of them. As he said:

I have decided to live peacefully what is left of my life here. I don't feel any urge to earn much and own this or that. I can't get a real job [because he was in his late 50s], I can only work as a volunteer, and I don't want to do that. It's hard for me to live on social benefit, but I am not ashamed because of it. I am not here because I wanted to come. It was someone's politics that brought me here, and it's someone's politics to accept me and keep me here.

This choice of 'early retirement', as Smilja, the nurse from Bosnia, described her decision not to seek employment, was overwhelmingly, although not exclusively, gender specific. Women in their late forties or older, who could not find employment in their professions, were more likely than men to take jobs that paid the same or slightly better than social benefits or to volunteer for Dutch organizations. In most cases, their spouses would spend most of their days in their local community organizations, either working as volunteers or socialising.[7]

The difference in attitude between men and women concerning underemployment revealed in my Amsterdam study is linked to the issue of how men and women develop survival strategies in exile (Eastmond 1993; Friere 1995; Matsuoka and Sorenson 1999; McSpadden 1999). Friere's (1995) psychodynamic assessment of exile experiences of Latin Americans in Canada demonstrates that, given comparable time in a new country and similar settlement experiences, gender identity associated with women's traditional roles and responsibilities seems to be linked with the development of successful survival strategies in women. She points out that in most societies and cultures, 'work only adds an additional, secondary role to their [women's] core identity as mothers and wives' (1995: 21). Men's core identity is by contrast, work-related and supported by a number of traditional socioculturally established roles of 'authoritative figure', 'provider' and 'protector' within the family and community (Friere 1995; McSpadden 1999). In exile, as Friere further emphasises, men become painfully aware that their occupational status, sources of power, and political agendas are non-existent or meaningless in the receiving society. She argues that although both women and men in their new places of settlement experience psycho-emotional disorganization and individual identity crisis, women tend to reconstruct their core sense of identity more successfully than men; they are more likely to achieve a sense of a continuity of meaningful vital roles in new societies than men (Friere 1995). Consequently, I would add, women tend to be more open to whatever opportunities arise in the receiving society.

The Lucky Few: A Counter Account

A significant minority of refugees involved in my Amsterdam study did not have to endure the experience of reception centres, either because they came before the stay was obligatory or strictly controlled, or because they had close family members already in the country. They all considered themselves 'lucky', because they 'heard terrible stories about the situation in these centres' as one of them put it. Avoiding the reception centres not only spared them the hardship of having no privacy, and of forced associations with people with whom they did not have much in common, as well as the idle existence these places engender – it also gave them greater space and opportunity to initiate a focused search for solutions, as mentioned earlier in this chapter.

Sinisa and his wife arrived in Amsterdam in May 1993, without a clear idea whether they wanted to stay, or move on to Britain.[8] As, at the time, stay in reception centres was not yet obligatory for those fleeing Bosnia-Herzegovina, they stayed with 'an acquaintance from Croatia'. Their host put them immediately in touch with a local NGO called We for Peace, which helped them obtain humanitarian (C) status by June of the same year. This organization was founded in Amsterdam, as a local, civic initiative by a couple of enthusiasts, soon after the first large influx of people from the Balkans had arrived. It aimed to help the people fleeing the war-torn region legalise their stay and obtain some type of assistance to settle.[9] Both Sinisa and his wife are well-educated people who were in their early forties at the time I met them. His account outlines the 'settlement programme' they devised for themselves and its outcome:

> We arrived just in time to submit our applications to the local police through that organization [We for Peace]. At the beginning we were not given any social assistance and I did all kinds of manual jobs. I also immediately started to learn Dutch, because I wanted and needed to achieve some kind of security here and that is impossible without learning the language. It was a pretty good summer course. In the autumn, we started getting social assistance and we continued with language courses throughout that year, because we had more time given that we didn't have to work. Meanwhile, we heard from friends about a very good, intense, language course at the university. We enrolled, and attended classes every day, for six months. By the end of 1994, we successfully passed the exam of language competence at the highest level. Since we had day-to-day communication with native speaking people, our neighbours and at local shops, banks, etc., and not only during the language classes, we'd started to avoid using English and started practising Dutch, in the summer of 1994. That was helpful for learning the spoken language. In early 1995, I read an ad in the newspaper about a training course in business consulting and planning, I applied and was accepted. After very intense training of seven months, I got my diploma in late 1995. It took four months to find a job, and I have been in this firm since May 1996.

All those who, like Sinisa and his wife, did not have family members already in the country also spent their first days or months with friends or acquaintances from war-torn Yugoslavia. Others stayed with Dutch people whom they happened to meet while they were holidaying in the Adriatic before the war. Some met their Dutch hosts while they were on aid missions in their places of origin or the first asylum. Such was Mira's case, for example. This 30-year-old woman from Bosnia-Herzegovina met a Dutchman while she was in Croatia, where she first fled. When she finally reached the Netherlands, in April 1993, he put her in touch with a Dutch family; the people who provided her not only with her first accommodation, but who also paid for one of the best and most intensive language courses in the country, which she successfully completed. Within a year, she was ready to continue her interrupted university education. Meanwhile, her stay had become legal and she secured financial assistance for her studies through UAF. In September 1994, Mira started a four-year programme of studies, which she completed in two years. Mira explained why she did it so fast:

> It wasn't because I was very smart or over ambitious, but because I had no more time to waste. I was already much older than my fellow colleagues, I was 24 years old when I started.

At the time I met her in Amsterdam, she was a successful, self-employed professional.

There were also those who did not have any such contacts when they arrived and they found their first shelter in one of the many squats of Amsterdam. On arrival, all of them worked illegally to earn their keep. These were low-paying jobs, such as babysitting, housecleaning, and waiting tables, done mostly by women, or a variety of manual jobs, done mostly by men. As with Sinisa and his wife, they were all granted social benefit soon after arrival, which freed their time for more intensive language training, retraining and job searching. It took on average up to three years to learn the language and find employment in their professions or in line with their skills. This was considerably less then time spent by those who could not follow their own 'settlement programme'. People I talked to emphasised how important was for them to learn the language quickly and adjust functionally to their new socioeconomic environment. This gave them a sense of security and control over their lives.

As the discussion so far has demonstrated, Dutch policies pertaining to the functional aspects of settlement render refugees 'passive recipients of aid' (Harrell-Bond 1986). Refugees are seen as policy objects, rather than agents actively involved in the process of their adjustment, and as people who devise their own strategies of 'nesting'. The liminal condition of peoples' existence in receiving societies becomes even more complex and difficult to tackle when aggravated by long and heavily bureaucratised determination procedures, as well as by uniform assistance provision which does not correspond to peoples' goals and life projects. Consequently, many refugees in the Netherlands remain unemployed and dependent on social funds. Many are not able to practice their professions, not because their skills are not needed in the Dutch labour market, but because of the many structural and social barriers that prevent them from doing so.

Struggling to Survive in Italy

The Self-reception 'System' in Rome

The overwhelming majority of people from war-torn Yugoslavia arriving in Italy encountered profound problems in achieving a minimal financial security, because very few received even minimal assistance, as pointed out in the Introduction. The first years of the people I met in Rome were characterised by a struggle for physical survival, as they were not provided with any type of assistance to settle in the city. Although many considered this 'a major blow', as Jusuf, a 42-year-old Bosniak, explained, in retrospect, almost all of them emphasised the importance of not having to feel that they 'owe anything to anyone here', as Milena, a 33-year-old woman, also from Bosnia-Herzegovina, put it.

The lack of an organized attempt to meet the group needs of refugees in Italy forced them to rely on their skills and resources in settling in Rome. Jusuf's account of how he managed to survive after he fled Bosnia, where he was detained in one of the concentration camps, mirror's the experiences of most of the people I met:

> We were without any kind of assistance here and we were forced to do all kinds of things [jobs] just to survive … They [the government and the NGO sector] gave us absolutely nothing. Accidentally, a lot of people I knew also found themselves in Rome, those who came to Italy a year or several months before I did, so they helped me with accommodation and finding some small jobs. I got by during the first months thanks to their help and the help of other people [refugees] I met during that period; until I managed to find a steadier job and became more independent.

During their first years in Rome, they spontaneously formed networks, which served as an alternative self-help reception 'system' dealing with their most pressing needs, such as finding accommodation and work. Mirza, a 36-year-old Bosniak, explained how and why these networks and friendships developed:

> For us who found ourselves here [refugees from war-torn Yugoslavia in Rome] it's normal that networks and friendships have developed. The situations we

were faced with when we arrived here were extreme: no papers in the beginning [for those who arrived before the 1992 Decree was enacted], no job, no help, war in our country; so those strong ties were made. Even today, we live a much more stressful life than Italians do.

Although some had acquaintances, friends and relatives already in the city, many more arrived without having any contacts. They learned about places 'where the folks from our country meet', such as cafés or other public places and spaces. Most often they obtained the information from Italians they met during their first days in Rome or other people, often foreigners living in the city with whom they could communicate in English or French, the languages that many of the people I met spoke.

The absence of both a national integration strategy and a corresponding welfare structure, as pointed out in the Introduction, have contributed to a situation in which both government organizations and the NGO sector in Italy continually deal with emergencies. This lack of a national integration strategy as well as the underdeveloped NGO sector, have undermined the ability of organizations dealing with refugees to plan their activities and programmes properly. They are often unable to meet even the most pressing existential needs of refugees, such as accommodation, for example. As a result, those who arrive in search of safety are often forced to sleep on the streets of the towns in which they wish to settle, and experience the hardship and humiliation of being homeless in a literal sense of the word.

Most of the people I met in Rome had relatively good rented accommodation in the city (measured by Roman standards of rental accommodation). Single people, but sometimes also couples, often lived in shared accommodation. Some could afford to live on their own, which was not the case until years after their arrival. When they arrived, most found their first shelter in apartments of known and unknown refugees from the region. Dragan, a 38-year-old man from Serbia, explained how this self-help system worked:

> During the first five years [1993–1997] I'd been staying in a flat in central Rome, which became some kind of a 'cult place'. It was a huge flat where there was always a lot of us [refugees from war-torn Yugoslavia], known and unknown people. Five of us were sharing the place for financial reasons, to share the costs. There were five bedrooms, plus a living room. A whole bunch of people would hear about 'the place to stay' and would come by; some of them would stay for a couple of nights, some much longer; we were from all ethnic origins.

Dragan's narrative of this past experience was unequivocally positive, at times even nostalgic for the type of solidarity this and similar arrangements entailed. During my research I heard many accounts of and references to this and other 'cult flats' in Rome. I learnt how known and unknown people would come and go, contributing financially when and as much as they could. Most often their stay was short, but if it was longer, the 'lodgers' contributed financially for day-to-day expenses, such as food, electricity, etc. However, almost all the accounts revealed at least some difficulties caused by a 'huge telephone bill' left unpaid after a 'friend' had left or tensions because s/he did not want to leave. Regardless of these troublesome incidents, these past experiences were not narrated as memories of hardship but most often as accounts of victory over disempowering conditions of their lives when they first arrived in Rome, and they were told with pride.

Shared accommodation with other people from the region, immigrants from other countries, or at a later stage with Italians they happened to meet early in their stay, became a housing model for many. There were some, of course, who spent their first nights at Termini train station,[10] and others who could not think of any other solution but to spend their first nights and their last money in inexpensive hotels. Only two refugees found their first shelter in the dormitories of one of the church organizations or NGOs in Rome. These organizations usually also ran soup kitchens on their premises for the destitute and homeless, including refugees. Those few who were helped with accommodation obtained the information by a stroke of luck, rather than any organized effort on the part of the providers. Therefore, the small number of people provided with temporary shelter was not only due to the general lack of such provision in the city. It was also the consequence of the general lack of information about services available to refugees, as well as the lack of a well-established NGO sector at the time when most of the refugees interviewed for this study arrived, in 1991, 1992 and 1993.

Moreover, even those very few people who were lucky enough to obtain temporary accommodation through one of the NGOs found that these organizations had very little or no time, financial and human resources to meet their other needs. Nermin, one of the two people I met who were helped in some way by the local NGOs, explained the problems he encountered:

> They [NGOs] tell you about all kinds of services they offer, but I haven't heard that anyone got a job, or that anyone got any other help but accommodation and food [a bed in a dormitory and a soup kitchen]. They have it all on paper. I know, for example, there's a possibility that the *comune* [municipality] pays half of your rent, but that's not what's happening in reality. They keep saying that they're in some kind of *emergenza* [emergency] and that's why they can't do it.

The absence of a systematic strategy for reaching out to refugees only intensifies problems with assistance. Hence, the lack of information about (scarce) assistance available is a continuing problem. Similarly, a very few government-run programmes for assisting refugees, such as financial assistance for those who would like to start small family businesses, are very hard to obtain. This is either because of the lack of information about this type of assistance or because of the highly bureaucratic procedure for applying and decision making. Therefore, it is common for resources allocated by the government for such programmes to remain unspent at the end of a fiscal year.[11]

Earning One's Keep: The Gendered Shape of Luck

The men I met in Rome experienced more difficulties in securing shelter and jobs than women did. On arrival, a general pattern of finding jobs emerged. Most of the younger women would find work within a matter of days as live-in housekeepers or nannies. This was due to the situation in the labour market in Rome that offers opportunities in domestic services,[12] but it was also related to the kinds of social networks the women from the region had in the city. During the 1970s and 1980s, a number of young women, predominantly from Dalmatia, Croatia, and Herzegovina, the south-eastern part of Bosnia-Herzegovina, would come to Rome for six months or a year to work as live-in housekeepers. They would earn a little, learn the language, and return home. Before their flight, many of the women I met in Rome had direct or indirect contacts with women from the region who did this kind of work. These contacts were instrumental in gaining vital information about how to search for work in domestic services. After the first refugee women found work, these served as a source of information and contact for those who arrived later. Vesna, a 33-year-old woman from Croatia, explained one of the many ways in which these initial contacts and networks were established. Her account also details the pattern of work and life of most of the women during their first year in Rome:

> During the war [in Croatia], my parents used to go to a nearby shelter regularly, at the time when our neighbourhood was heavily shelled. In the shelter, they met a middle-aged woman who happened to know a woman, Helena, who was a live-in housekeeper in Rome in the late 1980s. That is how I got in contact with her, and she helped me find my first job in Rome. I was among the first to arrive here, I helped many other women who came later … The way for us women was first to get a job as a live-in housekeeper. You stay in a family until you've saved enough money which enables you to look for a new job. It took me ten months and when I'd set enough money aside I left the family. When you leave the family you worked for as a live-in housekeeper you find a flat and your jobs are either in a café or cleaning people's houses.

Nuns of the Croatian Catholic Church in Rome were also helpful in assisting women, irrespective of their ethnicity or religion, who arrived with the first influx of refugees. Italian families in need of domestic help and/or childcare would usually contact the nuns in search of reliable help.[13]

A live-in housekeeper's job would not only secure a modest salary for women, but also accommodation, food and an environment to learn Italian. In some cases, women were actively encouraged by their employers to take Italian language courses. All the women interviewed described their period of work as live-in housekeepers as a 'difficult period'. Emira, who was twenty-eight years old when I met her, explained the nature of these difficulties:

> These were difficult times for me, not because they behaved badly [the family she worked for], but because I was there to do a job I never did before, I was always protected in my family … I stayed there for six months.

Additionally and very importantly, this period was described by all as a 'prison-like' experience. As they lived with their employers, they were usually 'on duty' all day, except for one day a week. Vera, who was thirty-four years old when I met her in Rome and studying, remembered her first job as a live-in-housekeeper:

> I'd spent a year in that family and then I found another job. It was a really exhausting job, I'd be working all day long and I'd be so tired in the evening that I couldn't even watch television, which I had in my room. I wasn't even reading newspapers, or a single book, during that period. I knew very little concerning money matters – what they were paying me at the time, I'd soon realised was actually very little.

The problem they faced was a lack of control over their time and a feeling of isolation from the outside world, as the time for phone communications with friends or relatives was also limited; besides most of them knew none or very few people in the city and could not afford time to search for contacts. Emira explained her feelings of isolation at the time:

> The first three months were especially difficult because I didn't know anyone, but then with the help of a nun of the Croatian Catholic Church with whom I had initial contact through a family friend in my hometown, I found out about the places where the folks from our country [Yugoslavia] gathered and so I went there and met a lot of them … That was the church of Santo Geronimo [St Hieronymus] in front of which people of all ethnic origins [from the Yugoslav successor states] would get together. There, I met many people I'd known before but wasn't even aware that they had got here as well.

The change of employment was an important step forward for these women even when they stayed in the cleaning business, because it meant greater freedom.

The situation for men finding their first jobs was particularly difficult because of the characteristics of the labour market in Rome. In most cases, the first work men found, commonly through contacts women developed with Italian families they worked for, were manual and low-paying jobs such as building, painting, gardening, and so forth. The problem with this kind of work is not only that it is poorly paid, but that it also may be not paid at all, as many Italians employing immigrants informally, as my research indicates, tend to avoid paying them after the completion of the work. Hence, their first months, even years in some cases, depended on sheer luck in finding a trustworthy boss. Unlike many women whose jobs, although low paid, were paid regularly, men often had to work hard and long hours for little or no pay. This situation made the lives of many miserable, because the vast majority had no savings and thus no means to sustain themselves. The fact that men had not only to find jobs immediately, but also affordable accommodation, compounded the problem. Srdjan, a 32-year-old man from Serbia who came to Italy in 1993, explained the problems men had to confront during their first year(s) in Rome:

> I found my first job through people I knew [through the refugee networks] and I got to carry bags of cement to the third floor, and I didn't get paid in the end. In such a situation, you don't know how to react. Your language is poor; you have no one to protect you. So, that first period, in which you are supposed to earn some money to have something to start from, proved to be very disappointing. All we could afford to eat was *pasta bianca* [plain pasta] sprinkled with either sugar or salt. This went on for a long period of time, about one year, when all we could do with our tiny incomes was to pay the rent.

Sharing the Burden: Families with Children

The lack of any kind of assistance made the lives of those with small children and the elderly particularly difficult, and most of them left before my research took place. They either moved to other parts of Italy where it was easier to find work or resettled in a third country. In families that stayed on children who were in their early teens when they arrived often had to work and contribute to inadequate family budgets. Milan and his family was one of these very few that stayed on. At the time of their arrival his children were twelve and fourteen. Milan said:

> We somehow managed by ourselves at the beginning; the children were out of school for a year, they'd worked a bit here and there, the older one went to our friends' [Italian] shop; this was the man we were staying with, who had a photo-optic shop. He learned how to take photos and sell glasses and other things, and the younger one went to a watchmaker's shop and even learnt how to fix watches. During that year they learnt some Italian, not in school but through contacts with Italians.

Aca, his son, who was twenty-two years old when I met him, talked about how he felt during that year when he did not know the language, did not go to school and did not have any contacts with his peers, apart from his two-year-younger brother, and when he had to work. He said:

> At the beginning, not knowing the language made me feel like a mummy. I shut up all the time. In the shop [photo-optic where he worked] there were grown-ups only, which meant that I did not have anyone else around me [of his age]. That's how I learnt Italian, I had to learn it fast, I had to communicate ... I also learnt that being alone is very important, you get to learn a lot about yourself ... I think I grew up during that period, I learnt many things about myself that I did not know before.

Those few whom I met who were in their teens when they fled with their families all shared the feeling of growing up fast. Not all of them continued school, however, after the initial year or two during which they had to work to contribute to their family budgets. Faruk told me why he did not continue his education, interrupted by war at the age of fourteen. After he and his family arrived in Rome he and his older brother and sister had to work because their parents could not find any job. But after over a year of working to earn their keep, he 'felt like a little man' and could not bring himself to the idea of going back to school, although the family no longer had pressing financial difficulties. Instead, he continued working. He was a waiter in a restaurant in Rome at the time I met him.

Even when children did not work, either because they were too young or because their parents made every effort to spare them the experience, financial and other insecurities deeply affected family lives requiring children to step in and fill in roles they would not normally be expected to do. Here is Silva's account of her family's first year in Rome:

> The older daughter was old enough to help me in those difficult moments, so she did her very best, even more than could have been expected from a child that age; but we [she and her husband] could not afford any other help. It's difficult to describe it now, but everything was functioning quite well. My husband and I'd worked in all kinds of shift combinations, so she's been our only help; she was exceptionally resourceful and mature for her age, she was only nine years old then. My younger daughter was very little then and she had to be looked after and helped during her first days and months at school ... We practically did not have any family life. My husband and I worked in shifts, so we wouldn't practically see each other for days. I can't really explain now how the two of us and the children managed. I was spending so little time with my daughters and I felt so sorry for them, especially for the older one; she was helping us and we were not able to give her any support and help at school because we didn't speak the language ourselves.

It is worth pointing out here that the increased responsibility of Silva's daughter for the maintainance of their family life was not an exercise of her parents' (or her father's) desire to control their daughter, as is often the case in families experiencing dislocation (e.g. Bek-Pedersen and Montgomery 2006). My contacts and time spent with the family indicate that this was indeed due to the lack of resources and opportunity to organise family life in any other way during their first year in Rome, because of the lack of any assistance for those settling with children in Italy. At the time I met them, Silva and her husband Misa were happy and supportive of their daughter's contacts and friendships with her peers, her adjustment to life in Italy, as well as hopeful that the experience of hardship during their first year of family life in Rome is not going to affect their daughter in any negative way.

Studies show that refugee children assume greater responsibility within the family, because of their adaptability as well as because of an inversion of the hierarchy of responsibility within the family structure (e.g. Anderson 2001). In the Europen context of settlement, a children's role in helping their families to cope with a variety of challenges in receiving societies is primarily that of communicator with the wider society, as they very often assume the role of interpreter for their parents. In the Italian context, however, the right to work granted with the humanitarian permit to stay in the country, combined with the lack of an initial recepotion system, put an additional, heavy burden on refugee families, and children in particular: many of them had to work and help their families 'get by' during first months of their stay in Rome.

The Importance of Self-Respect

The experiences of hardship in finding shelter, learning the language, finding work and becoming independent without any assistance were interwoven with feelings of self-respect for being active in finding solutions and for being self-sufficient. The importance of maintaining self-respect was paramount among the people I met. So much so that even when some form of assistance was available, in the form of provision of free meals at Caritas,[14] for example, the refugees tended to avoid relying on it. A typical explanation for such an attitude comes from Stipe, a 24-year-old man from Bosnia-Herzegovina. He arrived in Rome in the summer of 1992; at the time I met him he was a barman in a very well-known café. Recalling his first year(s) in the city, he said: 'I was happier when I was hungry, I felt better with an empty stomach than to be among the crowd there [people frequenting the soup kitchen run by Caritas].'

Although the refugees confessed to being on poor diets for months and some even for years upon their arrival and hence in dire need of food, they emphasised the importance of dignity as the critical factor that kept them going. As they were allowed to work and, therefore, were permitted some level of choice as to whether or not to rely on aid, almost all of the interviewees opted for independence, often regardless of the hardships involved.

The fact that they did not rely on aid made them aware that this situation has potential benefits for their day-to-day interactions with Italians. Milka's account echoes the experiences and views of the many people I met. She was forty-five years old when I met her and her family in Rome, where she was employed as a housekeeper. The family had financial difficulties for years, as her husband Milan was not able to find any steady work for a very long time. Even so, Milka said:

> There was nothing here, no assistance or any kind of support for us, and I'm glad about that. Everywhere they look at foreigners as people on whom the taxpayers' money is being spent. I think that's one of the major issues in most EU countries today, and it's less so in Italy. We've earned [she and her husband] whatever we have here. If I'd gone to Caritas to ask for something, I'm sure my neighbours would be looking at me in a different way. This way, they respect me.

The perception of the problems they encountered in Rome was also shaped by information about the experiences of their friends and relatives in exile in other European countries.

These transnational networks and connections put their own experiences into perspective. Branka explained how she, for example, formed her attitude towards her situation in Italy. This university-educated woman, who was thirty-three years old at the time I met her, fled Bosnia-Herzegovina in 1991. She and her partner first went to the Netherlands to stay with a Dutch acquaintance, but as they were not able to find any work and legalise their stay, they decided to go to Italy in search of permission to stay and a seasonal job in the North. After a year of unsatisfactory working arrangements, a series of circumstances prompted them to move to Rome, where she has had a range of low-paying, service sector jobs. At the time I met her, she was a waitress at a bar-discotheque. Branka said:

> While I was in Germany [visiting], I met a guy from Bosnia who'd been a refugee there and he told me about their experience. Everything was perfectly organized for them – reception, accommodation, children's education, financial support, you name it. Our people who found work there were always paid for doing it, not like in Italy where it often happens that you don't get paid. Therefore, their situation in Germany was much better. But their papers didn't allow them to go where they wanted – for example, someone who lived near Stuttgart wasn't allowed to go to Munich. They lived like prisoners, well-off prisoners though. My papers here allow me to go wherever I please. So, the way I feel about my status and life here is perhaps best described by the title of Milan Kundera's book *The Unbearable Lightness of Being.*

Tanja, a 22-year-old student and a part-time sales person in a retail shop in Rome, gave yet another account of why she felt better off in Italy than if she had been in some other European country. She explained in the following way the situation of people from her hometown in Denmark, where her mother is also a refugee:

> Our people there have become overly humble and they have lost a lot of dignity. Many just go on living on welfare, they have lost self-respect and many have become drug addicts or alcoholics. You can see that they have grown old so fast. They have become ruined, old and apathetic.

There was a unanimous agreement among the refugees I interviewed that their compatriots in exile in Denmark, Germany, Sweden, the Netherlands and Norway, for example, enjoyed a better standard of living. Nonetheless, there was also a shared view that the policy systems in other countries have many negative effects, because they undermine agency and effectively enhance dependence. Cica compared the situation of her partner's family, who are refugees in Sweden, and their circumstances in Rome at the time I met her. Her partner had graduated from a university in Rome and found job in his profession shortly before I started my research. Cica was also in the final years of her studies and working part-time to contribute to their budget. She said:

> Compared to my partner's brother and his wife in Sweden, we're about the same level now, only it was much more difficult for us to reach it. Even that may turn out to be an advantage, because that difficult life is a valuable experience. My partner's family has been more or less in the hands of the Swedish government, which has been leading them through their lives step by step. Their only problem at the beginning was how to manage with the social benefit they were getting, so as not to make it last fifteen instead of thirty days. It's true that they are still much better off financially than we are, but altogether we're about the same.

Organized programmes of reception and integration, such as the Swedish system, were seen as disabling individual initiative, hence, undermining self-esteem, or as limiting basic rights, such as the right of free movement or the right to work. As a consequence, their compatriots in these countries were often described as inward-looking, preoccupied with the past and socially isolated.

Working from Day One: Pros and Cons

One of the main sources of their empowerment in the Italian context, as my research indicates, was the right to work. This is best revealed in the account of Mirsada, who, after fleeing with her elderly parents and her sister's family of five, had to work in the service sector for a number of years, regardless of her university education and considerable professional experience. At the time I met her, she was employed with an NGO, the job she found through contacts she established with Italians during the first years of her stay. Mirsada's account summarises the role of work in the lives of those I met in Rome:

> I think that working here made us feel better, regardless of what kinds of jobs we've had. I think that's what helped us keep our wits about us, and I think that's what kept me sane all these years. We've been working all the time, we were occupied with something, there was no assistance – here's a house, here's the money. I have contacts with many of my friends from Bosnia, for example in Norway; they say they can't work at all. In the last two years they've started some kind of additional training, but otherwise they're together all the time and preoccupied with stories of the past. I think it's good that we've started a new life here. You have to start at once; you can't live in the past.

Nerim's account is yet another example of this shared attitude. Soon after he arrived in 1995, he moved out from his 'emergency shelter' offered by a friend, into temporary accommodation provided by a local NGO.[15] While doing a series of menial jobs, he also completed training for so-called cultural mediators, which secured him a job in a local *Questura* (the local police headquarters).[16] Nermin got the information about this training opportunity through an Italian whom he happened to meet during his early days in Rome. This job allowed him not only to make some savings that facilitated the continuation of his university education, interrupted by the war, but also to establish gradually a web of contacts with Italians enabling him to continue earning as a self-employed IT consultant, after his contract as a cultural mediator was over. Nermin said:

> Practically everyone who wanted to work found a job, those who wished to study enrolled in university – they've been studying very slowly, okay, that's on the whole because of the lack of assistance here, so they had to work. Frankly, I don't know where I'd be today with my life here if someone gave me a flat and a half a million *lire* a month. Perhaps I would have started studying, probably I would, but I don't know if I'd be feeling better right now, how determined I'd be to do something with my life here … I'm not saying that the financial support isn't important – assistance in getting a place to sleep and something to eat, what I call 'economic zero' … All of us here started from more or less the same material basis; we all started from below that economic zero, as I call it.

Although the importance of work in developing successful coping strategies was emphasised by all the people I met, it was not perceived as a straightforward way to empowerment.

They all prized the right to work, which came with their humanitarian status in Italy. However, they contended that the lack of an initial reception system forced them to become self-sufficient at a high cost. They were forced to enter a niche of the labour market from which it is very hard to move up the economic and social ladder. Rada's words echo the accounts of many I met in Rome. She was thirty-two years old when I met her, working as a sales person in a retail shop. Rada articulated the situation of many I met in Rome:

> It was a struggle in the beginning [in 1993, when she arrived] and it is the same struggle now – to have a place to sleep, to have something to eat. There's no security here, I work an awful lot and it's a vicious circle from which there's no way out. I'm okay for them [the receiving society] and that holds while I am relatively young, while I'm free [single], while I am able to give. God forbid that I should fall ill or that I should have some serious problem. I can't even imagine what would happen then ... I don't see that any of us has settled down so that she/he can say that she/he's satisfied.

For those with an interrupted education, the cost of the immediate need to find any kind of work was delaying or abandoning the idea of its continuation. Cica, who came to Italy in 1992, to join her boyfriend, was a student in Rome when I met her, as mentioned earlier in this Chapter.[17] She recalled how she struggled to continue her education, interrupted by the war and the subsequent flight:

> I couldn't bear my life here anymore. It boiled down to 10–12 hours of hard and senseless work that could only secure basic living. We couldn't even dream of continuing our studies and planning for the future ... All they [the Italian government] did was to give us permission to stay and work, but we had to do everything else ourselves ... But when my partner and I could finally afford to continue our studies everything changed. I'd regained my hope for the future.

The opportunity to study, for those who were able to afford it, was perceived as a way forward, a further step towards a common goal: to bring normality and meaning into their lives. Although it marked the beginning of a new stage in their lives, combining university education and work to earn the living was a challenging experience. Alija, who was thirty-one years old and studying when I met him in Rome, recalled how he managed to earn enough to continue his education, interrupted by war, by playing guitar in the Metro.[18] Although that early period 'was not easy', he felt pretty much in charge of the situation, because he did everything in his power 'to make something positive happen'. The continuation of his studies, he felt, was 'compensation for all these efforts' and as if his life 'regained purpose after all'. Alija explained how he felt about his achievement at the time of my research and what type of difficulties he was still facing:

> It's been quite a while since we've started [he and his girlfriend studying] because we are working at the same time. I'd go to the university in the morning and play in the afternoon. It's hard when a colleague from the university comes along and asks what you are doing there and you're like 'playing music in the Metro'. It wasn't easy at all considering my previous 'software' [upbringing and attitude towards life]. We [he and his girlfriend] were constantly under enormous financial pressure because we had enough money to pay university fees and living expenses for one semester at the time. There were a few situations when we were literally left with zero money. But in such situations we were also lucky to find jobs … There's definitely a measure of bitterness in me for having had to put up with all this shit [*sic*] to be able to get where I am now … That means that the country I'm living in didn't give anything to me. But at the end of the day I can say that I am happy because there are many who haven't succeeded in making a decent living and getting on with their lives.

Indeed, a majority of the people I met were not lucky, able or resourceful enough to continue their education or to find jobs in their professions. They had low-paying, service-sector jobs, which usually meant work involving long and antisocial hours. Yet, they were well educated and often with considerable experience in their professions. Milena, a 33-year-old architect from Bosnia, explained why she works as a waitress in a bar in Rome:

> It is very difficult for architects here. I know a whole bunch of Italian architects who are out of work or work for peanuts, not being able to cover their basic costs; they can afford that because they live with their parents, or the parents support them, which isn't the case with me. So I am compelled to work in a bar, and I do my professional work when I can, part-time, when I find one. Here you have either to make compromises or you have to have good connections. It is very difficult to gat a job on the basis of your diploma and skills only; nobody is interested if you don't have all kinds of connections. I found some part-time jobs through friends [Italian] but often I wasn't even paid, it was pure exploitation. We'd agree on everything, that the job would be paid when it was done and then it wouldn't get paid for two years. Then I gave up, because I could see how it was.

Barriers to skill recognition or to employment of the highly educated were profound, but not exclusively due to the fact that the people I met were newcomers lacking the right type of connections and social capital. Some of the barriers were structural and due to the characteristics of the labour market in Italy; in some sectors of the economy jobs were scarce as Milena's account indicates. Additionally, the scope of the informal economy is considerable, allowing exploitative working conditions for both the local/ indigenous population and newcomers.

The Right to Work, Informal Economy and Barriers to Skill Recognition

People I met also often worked in the informal economy, regardless of their right to work. However, most of them did not perceive this as a sign of any specific discriminatory practices towards refugees, but as the situation in the Italian labour-market, placing many Italians in a similar position.[19] Vesna, for example explained the situation in an IT firm where she worked when I met her.[20] She was among those who were successful in moving out of her initial line of work, after completing training for IT specialists, which she undertook while working as a cleaner, and which secured her a job in her new profession. Vesna said: 'everyone in the firm works like that [informally], our boss decided not to have many legal [formally employed] workers.'

Those who tried their luck in finding work in their professions without undergoing skills recognition had, however, different perceptions of discriminatory practices towards refugees and other immigrants in the work place. Those who were in medical profession, such as nurses, dentists or medical doctors who found jobs in private clinics in Rome, spoke of severe exploitation. Silva, who was 41 years old when I met her and her family, worked as a nurse after she learnt Italian well enough to search for that kind of job.[21] She recalled her situation while working in a private clinic in Rome:

> When I had that illegal job in the hospital [when she was not formally employed as a nurse] I was paid ninety thousand *lire* a month and my Italian colleagues were paid over 2 million for the same job. However, I had to shut up because I needed that work so badly because we [she and her husband] had to support a family of four.

As Silva could afford neither time nor money to get her skills recognised, she searched for other solutions, and at the time when I met her she had a secretarial job with a Church organization.

Others, very few, who decided to take the laborious rout of skills recognition, were confronted with profound difficulties in obtaining information on what is needed for such undertaking. They complained about Italian bureaucracy which is a 'total mess', because it provides one with 'all kinds of contradictory information', making it 'practically impossible to find out what was needed without connections', as Spomenka, a medical doctor, put it. She was 38 years old when I met her, her estranged husband and their children in Rome. They fled Serbia in April 1993, fearing her husband's conscription. From the winter of 1993, when she and her husband successfully completed language courses, to March 1995, they were not able to find their way through the labyrinth of Italian bureaucracy and obtain the right information about what is needed for their diploma recognition.

During that period, Spomenka, as almost all other women I met in Rome, worked as a domestic. By a stroke of luck, nuns of the Croatian Catholic Church with whom she got in touch soon after their arrival, recommended her to work for 'a family of a former Italian ambassador'. The family had 'all the right contacts' in the Italian Foreign Ministry, hence, she and her husband were finally able to obtain information needed, and start the process of collecting and translating documents required, as well as preparing for additional examinations and writing a thesis. It took them two years to complete the process and additional year and a half to be granted membership in the medical association in order to be eligible to seek employment in their profession. This process was not only laborious, but it also required substantial financial resources and, thus, severe sacrifice and hardship on the part of those who decided to embark upon such a route. In the case of Spomenka and her family, the experience of hardship resulted in her broken marriage and her young children being often left alone, unattended, for prolonged periods of time while she was at work or preparing for examinations. Spomenka's life was made bearable because of the support she had from nuns of the Croatian Catholic Church, who helped with her children's education, for example.

Agency and Lack of Security

Because their status, for the most part, was temporary, and because most of the people I met in Rome were underemployed, with low-paying jobs, none felt that they had succeeded in making a secure place for themselves in Italy. They felt that they lacked a sense of stability that would allow them to plan their future. When defining the losses involved in their flight and exile, they characterised them as losses of economic welfare or uncertain prospects for their future, but not so much as loss of personal agency. The latter aspect of their situation in Rome and Italy was regarded very highly.[22]

The settlement 'rules' characterising the Italian reception process meant that the people I met in Rome were prompted to take initiative in creating their own local support systems and solutions to their precarious situation. These systems were importantly based on networks of support developed by compatriots, within and across ethnic lines. They were also centrally linked to numerous informal and spontaneous contacts with Italians they established in various social settings, as will be discussed in the next Chapter. Through such spontaneous and informal webs of support they actively participated in regaining control over their lives.

Clearly, the absence of experience of reception centres and contacts with professional or voluntary refugee workers associated with an organized assistance programme meant considerable hardship in settling in Rome. However, it also saved this group of people from a systematic bureaucratic labelling, ascribing them a common identity associated with the role of a victim or of sick/traumatised persons. The process of forming such a bureaucratic identity, as Zetter (1991) emphasises, is deeply non-participatory in nature and usually renders refugees powerless. As my discussion reveals, the lack of integration policies and of rigidly mapped settlement rules affects the way in which people employ their agency. At one level, the Italian system formalised their liminal condition by granting them temporary legal status; in doing so it denied them security. At another level, the same system allowed them a scope of initiative in their struggle to become functional and self-sufficient. Their active search for opportunities to improve their precarious situation and better their lives helped them to cope with the insecurities of their status in an active and constructive way. Although difficult, the process allowed them a sense of agency and dignity. Additionally and very importantly, the fact that deportations of illegal immigrants in Italy were rare and regularisation of illegal immigrants in the country was frequent made them more relaxed about a possibility of losing their right to stay.[23]

The discussion of the refugee situation in Rome has demonstrated that the right to work and/or study granted with the humanitarian permit to stay in Italy, combined with the lack of an initial reception system, meant that those more resourceful in terms of their skills and social networks, or those with 'the right' demographic characteristics were more likely to 'get by' and eventually to 'get on' with their lives by finding a way into Italian society and its structures. This resourcefulness, however, was not only a matter of having adequate and needed skills or of their age, gender, parental or marital status. In the case of some people fleeing the Yugoslav wars, ethnicity had also become a powerful 'resource' in settlement, for others it had been detrimental (Korac forthcoming). For Roma refugees fleeing these conflicts the need to develop an alternative self-reception system in Rome, because of the absence of a well-developed national one, meant that their only possibility of survival was to seek support from their relatives and friends already living in Italy. However, their relatives and friends led segregated lives, living in so-called nomad camps around major cities. The consequence of this segregation, as Sigona (2003) points out, was extreme marginalisation and exclusion of the Roma population in Italy. By turning for support to those labelled 'nomads', Roma refugees from war-torn Yugoslavia settling in Italy have been confined to a segregated existence and extreme marginalisation, experiencing racism and social isolation, regardless of the (temporary) rights granted on their arrival.

Problems with Refugee Assistance

As the discussion in this Chapter revealed, the people whose accounts and experiences are presented in this book, although victimised, are far from being passive victims prone to dependency. They are survivors, actively seeking solutions to an existence made liminal by displacement. Central to this process is their active search for opportunities of support which allow them dignity, by letting them make (informed) decisions about their own lives.

The two settlement contexts examined here characterised by a centralised, uniform and phased forms of support, on the one hand, and by a lack of almost any support, on the other, led to different ways in which people were regaining control over their lives. The way in which the two 'models' of settlement are juxtaposed here is not to imply that one is better than the other. Both contexts embody specific structural constraints causing difficulties for refugees. The Dutch context undermined their agency by implementing rigid settlement rules and effectively has limited individual initiative. This resulted in often substantial discrepancies between how refugees themselves defined goals and meaning of their functional adjustment, and the normative policy assumptions about what these should be. This mismatch causes stress and frustration, as well as prolonged dependency, which often transmutes into a long lasting one.

The Italian context opens up a space for individual initiative and active participation, hence, it does not undermine agency. It does so by virtue of not having any systematically implemented assistance strategies or integration policies, not because the system in Italy is intentionally developed to challenge non-participatory character of existing models of assistance/policy. The way refugee assistance is approached in Italy is congruent with the government's intention of minimising their assistance and making it fit the character of Italian welfare system. It also mirrors the still widespread belief that Italy is not a country of immigration and the society in which people come to settle. The absence of assistance creates a fracture within the existing exclusionary structural systems, such as their temporary status or barriers to employment in specific niches of the labour-market. This fracture created by the lack of policy within an otherwise exclusionary system gave some refugees, those more resourceful or of the right ethnic, gender or class background, more space to engage actively in the process of gaining control over their lives. Consequently, the Italian system does not address one of the fundamental questions concerning refugee assistance: How to enhance their agency, make the full use of their human capital, and support the establishment and further development of their social capital?

For all these reasons it is important to emphasise that the discussion so far is not an argument against provision of assistance to refugees. Nor it means that welfare programmes, such as Dutch, necessarily create lasting reliance on government support. Rather, it aimed to point to the connections between assistance strategies or policies, structural constraints they embody and the type of agency they encourage. This discussion also pointed out that it is difficult to talk about a 'good' or 'successful' model of settlement policy. Policy systems tend to be 'one fits all' programmes, while refugees are a heterogeneous group. Thus, the proper understanding of assistance strategies and policy interventions should be centrally linked to examination and understanding of this heterogeneity allowing for flexible policy measures that would provide support without denying people their agency, identity or human capital.

Notes

1. For more on this see Kushner and Knox (2001) and Marfleet (2006).
2. More specific information on employment and training/retraining is provided in Table 1, Appendix 4.
3. Data provided by *Emplooi*, an organization assisting refugees in finding employment in the Netherlands.
4. Vocational high schools (the total of 12 years of schooling, with last four years in vocational education) were widespread in the Yugoslav education system.
5. The information provided by representatives of *Emplooi*, during my exploratory visit to Amsterdam in September 2000.
6. The University Assistance Fund (UAF) is based in Utrecht; it provides assistance to asylum seekers and refugees to continue their university education or to continue their professional careers.
7. Al-Ali's (2002: 90) study of Bosnian refugees in the Netherlands indicates similar gender pattern.
8. Their decision to flee Bosnia-Herzegovina, pattern of flight and reasons for coming to Amsterdam are discussed in Chapter 2.
9. The information obtained by the founders of *We for Peace* during my fieldwork in Amsterdam in 2000–2001.
10. The main train station in Rome.
11. Information obtained from a UNHCR representative during my exploratory visit to Rome in November 1999.
12. For more information on the character of the labour-market in Italy, and the opportunities immigrants have in domestic services see Reyneri (1998).
13. The role of the Church in assisting immigrants to find this type of job is also discussed by Reyneri (1998).
14. Caritas is a prominent church organisation operating in Italy and worldwide. Caritas, as other church organisations in Italy, provides support for destitute, including refugees and other immigrants. Caritas, among other things, runs soup kitchens in Rome.

15. Nermin's decision to flee Bosnia-Herzegovina, his pattern of flight and her reasons to come to Italy/Rome are mentioned in Chapter 2.
16. Cultural mediators have been introduced in Italy aiming at orientating newcomers upon their arrival and at helping local authorities and service provides to understand and respond to their needs.
17. Cica's decision to flee Bosnia-Herzegovina, her pattern of flight and her reasons to come to Italy/Rome are mentioned in Chapter 2.
18. Underground train system in Rome.
19. Reyneri (1998) analyses the scope and the character of the informal economy in Italy and discusses whether it is created by the increasing number of illegal immigrants or it is sustained and shaped by it.
20. Her experience of finding her first work as live-in housekeeper and the pattern of work and life during her first years in Rome, are mentioned earlier in this Chapter.
21. Their decision to flee Croatia, their pattern of flight and their reasons to come to Italy/Rome are 'voiced' by her husband Misa in Chapter 2.
22. Valtonen's (1998) research of the situation of Middle Eastern refugees in Finland also indicates that the prime determinant of subjective wellbeing of refugees during the process of refugee settlement is not the degree of discrepancy between goals and actual conditions of settlement. Rather, their oubjective wellbeing is determined by 'the extent to which agency can be exercised in the resettlement situation', (p. 57).
23. For information on the acts of regularisation of illegal immigrants in Italy, in 1986, 1990, and 1996, and their consequences see Reyneri (1998).

4

Negotiating Continuity and Change: The Process of Recontructing Life

Negotiation between continuity and change shapes the process of reconstructing life in a new society and is central to emplacement. A complex set of contexts and variables characterising individual refugees or their specific groups determine how refugees negotiate the issue of continuity and change, how they aim to 'nest' themselves, and what type of place-making strategies they devise. Central to the process of reconstructing life and negotiation between continuity and change, as discussed in Chapter 1, are webs of interpersonal relationships established at different levels of societal communication. Different types of social networks and links, those within and outside ethnic boundaries, have different roles, significance and meaning for the 'nesting' of refugees in specific contexts and at particular points in time.

The establishment of co-ethnic networks in receiving societies, as pointed out in Chapter 1, is important for emplacement, as they enable maintenance of links with the native culture and country. In this sense, they contribute to individual and group feelings of 'rootedness'. However, the increasingly transnational and global character of co-ethnic links and networks of people living way away from home, as will be discussed in Chapter 5, reveal that continuity and the sense of belonging to a community are reconstructed in a variety of ways, many of which correspond to neither local/national borders nor policies which reflect notions of territorial and sited identities. Moreover, given that ethnic boundaries are not fixed but flexible, the process of 'nesting' is characterised by contextual shifts of demarcation lines between 'us' and 'them' in new sociocultural environments, as the discussion in this chapter will demonstrate. In other words, ethnicity may be seen as 'not always the most appropriate principle around which social activity or identity may be organized. In some situations it has so little relevance that participants may simply set it aside, acting without reference to their 'ethnic' affiliations.' (Wallman 1979: x).[1]

Problems occur, however, when the policies of receiving societies expect ethnic associations of minority groups and refugees coming from the same country of origin to 'voice' their needs and interests within the multicultural milieu of the receiving society. Although aimed at 'managing diversity', such policies often tend to intensify ethnic tension and divisions among people fleeing conflict. Furthermore, when reception and assistance systems for refugees fleeing wars constructed as ethnic strife are set up so that cross-ethnic coexistence among compatriots is not essential for the process of regaining control over one's life, ethnic tensions and divisions tend to be carried over, transplanted or even intensified within the new context. As a consequence, ethnic divisions not only create displacement, but remain central to the experiences of emplacement.

It is also believed that allowing minority populations to 'voice' their group needs and interests through the realisation of their cultural (group) rights will help create a sense of belonging to the receiving society and increase cooperation and trust between the refugees/minority and the majority groups. The development of trust between minority and majority groups in the receiving society is however a process that only partially depends on a set of rights that can be granted to the 'ethnic' or minority members of the society. It importantly depends on the possibility of establishing a complex set of interpersonal relationships between those belonging to 'ethnic' and majority groups. These contacts occurring at the micro-level of society are an important element of meaningful changes occurring in the process of emplacement, forging new identities, loyalties and notions of belonging, as already emphasised in Chapter 1. These informal, interpersonal relationships established at the micro-level are of different nature than those occurring at the institutional, structural level of the receiving society.

As discussion in this chapter will show, experiences of inclusion based on informal, interpersonal contacts and ties with the local populations are critical for how individuals and groups feel about their location in the receiving society. Sociability, as Wellman (1981: 184) points out, affirms self-worth and continued network membership, regardless of the fact that such ties may not provide supportive resources directly. In this sense, experiences of belonging based on this type of informal, micro-level inclusionary mechanism are central to becoming and feeling 'of place'. Formal ties established through citizenship rights do not necessarily bring about such attachments. While there is no doubt that formal ties affirm a condition of 'being in', they do not automatically translate into a feeling of 'being of' place.[2] In the following pages, I explore the social ties of refugees I met in Rome and Amsterdam. In so doing, I examine the role and meaning of co-ethnic, cross-ethnic (among compatriots) and minority–majority social networks they established in the process of their 'nesting' in these two different settlement contexts.

Bonding Networks and the Emplacement of Refugees in Rome and Amsterdam

Recreating Cross-Ethnic Links among Compatriots in Rome

In Italy, co-ethnic networks are critical alternative service providers, as pointed out in the previous chapter, because its system of reception and settlement rests upon the assumption (and expectation) that refugees and other newcomers will be assisted through self-help groups they form. However, the policy framework at the time of this research did not specifically encourage the formation of formal community associations. Consequently, although immigrant or refugee organizations existed in Italy and Rome, they were not numerous or evenly spread over the country, well-established and funded. This is in contrast to some EU countries, such as the UK, where state institutions create spaces for the recognition of groups rather than individuals (Joly 1996). Hence, intra-group ties and networks among the people I met in Rome were primarily informal and formed spontaneously to facilitate the fulfilment of their pressing existential needs.

These links were also almost exclusively formed by the newly arrived, rather than incorporating both new and old immigrant networks. This was due partially to the fact that the group of old immigrants from Yugoslavia in Rome, and Italy, is negligible and consequently their links and ties are underdeveloped.[3] More importantly, however, the people in my Roman study did not find the experiences and aspirations of those who came earlier and under different circumstances compatible with their own. Furthermore, almost all of the people I met were sceptical about networks formed by old immigrants. Their presence and visibility in Rome and Italy was perceived as primarily linked to their campaigns for winning the 'hearts and minds' of the Italian public for their 'nationalist cause'. Their activism was thus perceived as politically motivated, rather than emerging from their humanitarian concerns about the situation of refugees in Italy, as Bogdan, who fled Croatia, put it. Consequently, almost all of the people I met in Rome were unmotivated to establish links with groups formed by old immigrants, because they perceived them as engaged in identity politics within which ethnic origin had become articulated and constructed as the means of achieving political ends.[4] The people in this study, however, fled their places of origin not because of their involvement in a political project, but because they felt forced by political circumstances. They perceived themselves as victimised by the political turmoil rather than as protagonists involved in its creation. Consequently, they did not see themselves becoming involved in a type of politics that, as they felt, forced them into decisions to flee their homes.

The spontaneous networks they formed upon arrival were not primarily co-ethnic, but mostly cross-ethnic, open and inclusive. This is in stark contrast not only to the exclusionary politics of the conflict they fled, but also to the experiences of many people from the region who fled to other countries.[5] There are several reasons for this type of connecting in Rome. These contacts and links emerged in the situation in which mutual help literally meant physical survival, as there were no ways to fulfil pressing existential needs other than cross-ethnic cooperation. As social ties within ethnic groups were weak, because most of the people I met in Rome were single and without any kinship connections in the city or Italy, they were prone to establishing diverse networks. Gurak and Cases (1992) argue that weak ties among migrant groups are important, because they unite diverse networks and increase the resources available to network members. This is because the more ramified weak ties link people to dissimilar social circles, in contrast to strong ties which link network members 'to persons of similar backgrounds who travel in the same social circles as they do' (Wellman 1981: 186).

The absence of strong, family and kinship ties among the people in my Roman study is primarily due to the policy context that did not allow family reunification and was generally unfavourable to people fleeing with families. As pointed out in the Introduction, most of them had humanitarian/ temporary status which does not permit refugees to bring in their families. Additionally, and very importantly, the lack of any kind of support for refugees in general and for those with children in particular, such as provision of housing and access to social benefits, prompted those who fled with children to move to other countries or to other parts of Italy where it was easier to find work and accommodation. Mirsad, a 25-year-old Bosniak, explained why these co-ethnic and cross-ethnic networks formed and how they have been transformed:

> During the first years [in Rome] the refugees from ex-Yugoslavia were the circle I used to socialise with. We were pretty united in these years, we stuck together, those who would and could help each other. Later, as people managed to attain some economic security, we started growing apart.

The intensive contacts across ethnic boundaries were prompted by the specific circumstances in which they took place; they did not necessarily indicate the absence of tension linked to the politics of the conflict they fled. Milena, a woman of ethnically mixed background from Bosnia-Herzegovina, clarified the character of these networks, as well as their meaning shared by many people I met in Rome:

Each of us had our own opinions about politics … We'd have disputes over that … But despite the political discussions, we'd help each other whenever we could, regardless of where we were from and what our political views were. That attitude was essential, because we needed these contacts and each other's help … As soon as I arrived here, it become clear to me that I couldn't expect any help from this state … Despite the fact that this has generally been a negative experience [settling without any organized assistance], I think it had one good and positive side. A very great positive side is that I saw for myself that people from different regions of the former Yugoslavia, despite the war in the country, could live together.

The character of the policy context in Italy has created (unintentionally) a situation in which people fleeing the deeply divided war-torn country had to re-create links and coexistence destroyed by war.

This was facilitated by additional contributing factors. In Italy, as in many other countries in Europe and beyond, the networks of old immigrants coming from Yugoslavia have been bitterly divided by the politics of war in the formerly common country. The lack of links with these networks among the people in Rome freed them from political disputes about the conflict, the causes of their flight, and other highly politically charged issues. The possibility of by-passing disputes about political issues that caused their displacement in the first place was also enhanced by the lack of encouragement to form formal associations of their own. As such associations provide links to the institutions of the country of origin they can, in specific circumstances, 'box' people into their respective ethnic groups by locking them in identity politics associated with ideologies and institutions of their countries of origin. Finally, the establishment of these cross-ethnic links and communication was also possible and successful because the people in my Roman study were mostly young, educated, from multi-ethnic urban areas, and very often themselves of ethnically mixed backgrounds. Quite a few of them, like Bojana for example, considered themselves 'Yugoslav', a category which was to them beyond ethnicity and ethnic affiliation. Bojana was twenty-nine years old when I met her in Rome, and is of mixed ethnic background, born and brought up in Bosnia-Herzegovina. She worked and lived Croatia for a few years before fleeing to Italy and Rome in 1993. Bojana said:

I was a Yugoslav and to this day, when someone asks me where I'm from I say from Yugoslavia although it does not exist anymore. I believed in that country. When they [nationalists] destroyed it, it was such a blow and disappointment for me, so I've lost the feeling of belonging. I've had it before, I felt that I belonged to a nation and a state, to a generation of young people from mixed marriages where it wouldn't matter what were their first or last names [for the purposes of determining their ethnic origin] or religion, where we never felt any kind of ethnic belonging, which has become so important now.

But regardless of whether they identified themselves as 'Yugoslavs', as Bojana did, or as belonging to one of the ethnic groups from the war-torn country, as Mirsad did, they themselves had no other experience but that of peaceful multi-ethnic coexistence and friendships before the war.

Co-ethnic and cross-ethnic networks and social ties formed in Rome were, therefore, instrumental in the process of gaining control over the lives of the people I met. In their search for a sense of stability, they sought contacts and forged social ties based upon a broadly defined common identifier: having fled the war-torn region of Yugoslavia and struggling to survive in Rome. This type of 'bonding' and association was not primarily about ethnicity, 'roots', and culture. Rather, it was linked to a kind of struggle they all shared: the struggle for physical survival in a new city and country.

Although these networks can be defined as solidarity networks in the sense that they were mobilising help quickly through the network, they were not, for the most part, based on intimate relationships and thus embedded in strong ties. Mirsad explained how although he was part of co-ethnic and cross-ethnic networks immediately after he arrived in Rome, he did not have many if any 'real friends' among them, those he would 'talk to on the phone every day' and share more personal aspects of life. Thus, for him and many others, 'it was not a problem to leave that group' once his life circumstances in the city improved and after he met locals, Italians, with whom he developed closer ties. However, contacts which remained after overcoming the initial insecurity caused by displacement were those based upon shared interests, past experiences, and meanings embedded in common life styles and sociocultural codes. Mirsad, for example, had only a couple of 'our people' with whom he was in touch regularly and whom he considered friends. Omer's account reveals a similar pattern in establishing and maintaining co-ethnic and cross-ethnic social ties among compatriots:

> At the beginning [upon his arrival in Rome] contacts with refugees from ex-Yugoslavia meant a lot to me, because I needed to share information and my experiences with our people. As time went by, however, I reduced these contacts to a small circle of our people with whom I remain friends to this day.

The initial contacts with people who fled the war-torn country were in many ways forced associations. They were based upon shared and pressing existential needs associated with acute experiences of displacement and problems of functional adjustment to a new socioeconomic and cultural environment, rather than chosen because they fulfilled any more complex desires for sociability, sharing, and identification. The selectivity with which the more stable/lasting co-ethnic relationships and cross-ethnic ties are created reveals the differences among categories of people belonging to the same ethnic group and culture. It points to the importance of the positionality of individuals and groups within the sending society. It emphasises how boundaries within boundaries are created with respect to gender, class, stage in the life cycle, etc., forming ties of sociability and identification. It was not the culture of the country of origin per se that united them in Rome, they bonded along other types of social codes and identifiers.

As this discussion demonstrates, the establishment of co-ethnic and cross-ethnic networks among people in Rome was in many ways central to regaining continuity and for their process of 'nesting' in the city. However, the establishment of such networks is neither the only, nor the most important, place-making strategy they developed, as will be discussed later in this chapter.

The Importance of Ethnic Boundaries in Amsterdam

The process of reception and settlement in the Netherlands did not require fast mobilisation of resources through co-ethnic and cross-ethnic networks of compatriots during the initial phase of adjustment of people I met in Amsterdam. The reception system in fact often suppressed that need. Refugees were 'helped' and 'cared for' in an institutionally well-supported and phased manner. This situation shaped inter-ethnic relations among the people in my Amsterdam study in many unintended ways, one being the maintenance of tension and furthering of social distance between different ethnic groups in the city and country.

Those who arrived before legal and other reception measures for people fleeing war-torn Yugoslavia were introduced, did establish a pattern of spontaneous and cross-ethnic networking similar to the one that emerged in Rome. However, these forms of networking were soon reshaped. Zenaida, a Bosniak woman, recalled how it was at the time when she arrived, in the early 1992:

> Those who came here up to early 1993 helped each other. There was nothing here [no organized assistance to those fleeing war-torn Yugoslavia] so we exchanged any bit of information we had, we helped each other with finding shelter for the newly arrived. I had a couple from Croatia, for example, for almost five months, although I'd never seen them before. It was a very tense period in terms of politics and war, and I remember arguments and tensions between some of the people I used to socialise with. But we were all in the same boat then [refugees from variety of ethnic backgrounds and from different parts of Yugoslavia], and I can't recall any serious problems or people who wouldn't help each other.

Unlike in Italy, networks of old immigrants from the region existed in the city and were well-established. However, not many of those who arrived early had any closer contacts with them. These earlier immigrants came to the

Netherlands as 'guest-workers' and consequently, the people I met in Amsterdam perceived their reasons to migrate as qualitatively different in character from their own. Unlike the old immigrants they were fleeing war. Here again, as with those in Rome, ethnic links with old migrants were not perceived as a 'natural' way of bonding and/or belonging regardless of shared language and other elements of culture.

In addition to perceiving the motivation of those who arrived in the Netherlands in the 60s and 70s as different, a majority pointed to the discrepancy between their level of education and that of the people who came before the conflict. This difference, they felt, created problems in communication and mutual understanding. Education was the main channel of social promotion in socialist Yugoslavia, and the people I met in Amsterdam, for the most part, belonged to the generation that was much better educated than the generation of working-class people who become 'guest-workers' in the West.[6] The latter group grew up in circumstances of rural poverty before, during or immediately after the Second World War. By contrast, the group I met in Amsterdam grew up not only in economically better conditions, but also in a more open society.[7] They were exposed to a value system that was increasingly becoming 'Westernised', and thus, different from the one characterising the upbringing, socialisation and education of the generation of old migrants in Amsterdam/the Netherlands.

As the war intensified and with it the number of people seeking protection in the Netherlands increased, Dutch policies changed, leaving no need for intense networking among the people fleeing the country in search of alternative ways to regain control over their lives. Their networks became primarily based on family and kinship ties and established along ethnic lines. The former characteristic of their social ties was due to their legal status, which allowed family reunification, as well as to socioeconomic conditions in the country that were favourable to people fleeing with their families. Due to the family reunification scheme a significant majority of people I met were there with their children or parents. But there were also quite a few of those who reunited with their extended families, making the family circle much more central to emplacement. Sinisa, for example, was able to bring his brother and his family from Bosnia, and his wife's parents as well as her brother and his family were also in Amsterdam. This made him feel that 'they [his wife, children, and himself] are not alone'.

The lack of cross-ethnic ties among compatriots was shaped by several interrelated factors. Some aspects of the Dutch reception system, such as prolonged periods of stay in reception centres, tend to intensify the importance of ethnic boundaries among those confined to them, my research reveals. Boris and his wife were among those who stayed in such a centre after fleeing Bosnia-Herzegovina. He, who is himself of ethnically mixed background, explained the problem:

> The situation at the centre [the reception centre] was difficult because we didn't have any information about how long the procedure [the determination procedure] was going to last. We had nothing to do, we just sat there and waited, and we became paranoid about what we could say to people and who we could trust. There were people from all nationalities [from war-torn Yugoslavia] there and tensions were inevitable because we just sat and talked about what had happened back home and why we had to leave. After a while, there was nothing left to talk about, only tension and hatred were left.

After leaving the reception centres, in many of which they experienced the build up of ethnic tension, the people I met in Amsterdam found themselves in a city and country in which they had hardly any contacts. In overcoming their social isolation after leaving the centres and in fulfilling their need for sociability and 'nesting' they had to turn to their immediate family members, to associations of immigrants from the Yugoslav successor states in the Netherlands, and in some cases to people they met while in the centres. Smilja's social contacts, for example, were at the time of this research and after almost five years in the Netherlands almost entirely limited to 'a few people' she met while she and her son Kemo were at the reception centre. For others, the few contacts they had with people they met at the reception centres were the only social contacts they had for 'quite a while', as Cica and her husband Boris said, after they moved out of the centres and into their own accommodation.

Immigrant associations of people from Yugoslavia who came as so-called 'guest-workers' in the 1960s and 1970s were well developed and established, as mentioned earlier. Before the war broke out in the country, the majority of them formed communities of compatriots linked to the then Yugoslav embassies and consular offices in the places of their settlement. For the most part, these communities perceived themselves as Yugoslavs. With the increase of political tensions, the armed conflict and the consequent rupture of the federal state along ethnic lines, the majority of these immigrants aligned themselves with the new states that emerged during the war, with their institutions and their politics. In so doing, many of them became actively involved in emerging forms of 'diaspora nationalism' which, as Kaldor (1999) points out, played an important role in shaping the conflicts of the 1990s. Networks of old immigrants in the Netherlands, as in some other European countries, became deeply involved in 'long distance nationalism' (Wimmer and Glick Schiller 2003) and implicated in the identity politics of war.[8]

Given the character of the reception and settlement policies in the Netherlands, the formation of refugee and other 'ethnic' associations is encouraged and funded by the government, primarily to facilitate the recognition of their group cultural needs in Dutch multicultural society. Although involved in different and useful cultural programmes and educational activities, such as mother-tongue courses for children, they have also become spaces in which the identity politics of war in the places of origin featured highly on the agendas. The latter processes transformed them into a fruitful ground for maintaining or even deepening divisions and tensions caused by the conflict. Consequently, the cultural and social events they organize, as well as daily gatherings were often marked by open and heated debates and arguments with those who 'did not belong' or more concealed tensions and animosities towards people who were not of 'the right kind'. During my relatively frequent visits to one of the so-called community associations in Amsterdam, I witnessed many such heated debates and arguments, as well as instances of less overt ways of conveying a message that some visitors 'did not belong'.

Among the people I met there were those who made a conscious effort to cross ethnic boundaries and make social connections with people associated with different ethnic associations. For the most part the experience was disappointing. Miro and his mother, who fled Bosnia-Herzegovina, went to the 'Croatian, Bosnian, and Serbian clubs' in Amsterdam, and felt that they 'didn't belong there', because the people who ran these places were the ones to whom 'nationality matters', as Miro put it. Ivana was also one of the quite a few people who tried and failed to cross ethnic boundaries imposed by some of these community associations. She is a Bosnian Serb and a single parent of two children born in an inter-ethnic marriage, which broke before the war. After she moved out of a reception centre, Ivana tried to establish contacts with people from the war-torn country in Amsterdam. She said:

> I am very disappointed because our people [from the Yugoslav successor states] are more divided here than they are back home where they fought the war. I went to all three associations [Bosnian, Croatian and Serbian] and I feel like a stranger there. These people care more about their ethnic background than anything else.

The process of ethnic boundary formation among the people in my Amsterdam study was also shaped by their war experiences. Many of them came from parts of Bosnia heavily affected by war and were themselves subjected to victimisation because of their ethnic origin. Thus, the organization of their experience of war and sense of difference shaped by their war-time victimisation made them reluctant to reestablish ties and relationships of trust across ethnic lines.

The importance of ethnic boundaries for the process of 'nesting' in Amsterdam, as shown here, represents a type of encapsulisation of the people I met within their 'ethno-national world'. However, this did not imply their self-imposed segregation, as will be discussed in the following section. The discussion so far has revealed how ethnic boundaries have been reshaped among the people I met in Rome and Amsterdam and what were the roles and meanings of co-ethnic ties and networks of compatriots in the process of their emplacement. Now, I turn to discussing the emergence, meaning and importance of minority–majority ties or bridging social networks they established, as well as the consequences of their absence.

Bridging Social Networks and the Emplacement of Refugees in Amsterdam and Rome

Socially Isolated and Not 'Of Amsterdam'

Of the people I met in Amsterdam, both those employed and unemployed enjoyed relatively good living conditions and had short and longer-term plans for their future. Despite their relatively good standard of living, enjoyment of fine public amenities and social tolerance, as well as willingness to reconstruct their lives in Amsterdam, the majority of the people I met felt that they were not 'of Amsterdam'.[9] They continued to perceive themselves as the Other and generally not accepted by the Dutch. Boris, the doctor, who was among very few who were employed in their profession, gave the following account on the type of 'otherness' he felt since in the Netherlands:

> Foreigners are extremely marginalised here, although that is officially denied. Foreigners, except the Americans who work here, are usually portrayed in the media in a very bad way ... I feel here pretty much the same as I felt in my hometown in Bosnia under the Muslim government during the war. They kept us [non-Muslims] there to show the world that they were a democratic state. It's the same thing here; they keep us here to show the world that some foreigners may be successful and 'well-integrated'.

The experience of marginalisation revealed in their accounts did not originate, for the most part, in any form of open racism or discrimination. They all emphasised their appreciation of the social tolerance of the Dutch. However, those with professional skills and university degrees did talk about tension or discrimination they experienced when searching for jobs. Sinisa was one of them. It was important for him to establish 'good relationships with the Dutch'. He took great care to nourish one such contact he made at the training course which he took soon after he had learnt the language well enough to be able to retrain and search for a professional job. At the training he 'became friends' with another trainee, a Dutch person, who 'even came into my house a few times', as he pointedly said. However, upon finishing the training course and after both of them had applied for the same job in a Dutch firm, his Dutch friend called him up to let him know that 'the World Bank has opened a position in Sarajevo' advising him to apply as he 'should return to Bosnia, because there are not enough jobs in the Netherlands for the

Dutch, let alone for the foreigners'. Sinisa was reportedly taken aback by this gesture, because he had made clear to his Dutch friend in their earlier discussions regarding 'the question of return' that he and his family did not intend to go back to Bosnia-Herzegovina once the war was over. Sinisa reminded his friend of these conversations and offered him help with local contacts if he himself decided to go to work in Bosnia. After this incident, Sinisa said, they had not been in touch.

The majority, however, did not have any 'bad experiences' in their (limited) informal communication with the Dutch, but they felt 'invisible'. Miro, who was twenty-seven years old when I met him, studying for his university degree and also working as an intern in a Dutch firm, clarified this point:

> I have a great desire to integrate, to the extent that is possible for someone who isn't Dutch. I want my life to be normal. I want to be accepted by the Dutch, but no matter how much I try, I feel invisible among my colleagues at work, for example. They are perfectly correct work-wise, but when it comes to some kind of socialising at work or after working hours, they behave as if I am not there. Then I feel excluded.

Feelings of 'otherness' were experienced and strongly felt at the micro-level of communication with the Dutch, as revealed in Boris' explanation of the roots of such feelings:

> I am employed in a Dutch medical firm, I speak the Dutch language well, my child goes to a Dutch school and soon he'll speak Dutch better than his mother tongue, but we live a parallel existence here, because we don't have real contact with Dutch society. We are neither accepted nor rejected. The biggest problem is that we don't have any friends among the Dutch here. We are left to ourselves here. I have a flat in Amsterdam, I live here, but I don't have any ties with Dutch people.

Among the people I met, there were very few who reported having Dutch friends or more regular contacts with the Dutch, outside the work place (for those who were employed). Due to the limited scope and nature of their micro-level communication with the local people, almost all of these 'well-settled' people I met felt socially isolated, because they lacked any closer ties with the Dutch. Some accepted their situation by explaining it as 'normal' and as 'something to be expected' at their age and in their circumstances. It is not realistic, they claimed, to expect to develop close and meaningful social ties as they once had with people and friends in their places of origin. A few also tried to 'normalise' their situation by asserting that it is difficult to establish closer ties with the Dutch in a city as multicultural as Amsterdam, in which 'the Dutch may be actually regarded as foreigners', as Ivana remarked.

This problem did not seem self-imposed, as the refugees emphasised the importance of establishing such informal interpersonal contacts at and beyond the work place. This need for developing bridging social networks was usually accompanied by their conscious effort to establish closer social contacts and ties in their neighbourhoods, at work, and various other social settings. Although those who were younger or better educated were more prone to 'building bridges' between themselves and the new society, they were not the only ones who were proactive. Those few who shared with me their 'success stories' of meeting the Dutch did so outside the work place. Kemo, for example, developed friendships with people he met at the local dancing club of which he became a member soon after he and his mother moved into their own accommodation in Amsterdam. Although he 'socialises regularly' with some club members who were not Dutch but 'also foreigners' as he pointed out, at the club he has regular and 'friendly' contacts with the Dutch too. Belma was also one of those few who reported having Dutch friends. This 42-year-old woman from Bosnia-Herzegovina, a single parent of two, was employed in a Dutch firm when I met her. She had become friends with the refugee worker she met while at the reception centre. They were in touch 'regularly via email'; they also saw each other when her Dutch friend, who was still working with refugees at the reception centre in which they met, invited Belma to special events and celebrations she organized there. Belma felt that she could always call on her if in need of advice, support, or help of some kind and that realisation made her 'feel safe'. Sasa was yet another example of a person who was 'successful' in developing social ties with the Dutch. Within two years of his arrival in the Netherlands, where he reunited with his family, Sasa joined a chess club in his neighbourhood, on the outskirts of Amsterdam. He was sixty-three years old when I met him and his family, with a university degree and professional work experience in Bosnia-Herzegovina. After completing a very intense Dutch language course, he started searching for a job. He realised that because of his age as well as the character of his skills, he would not be able to find work in his profession. Instead, he turned to his favourite hobby – chess. Sasa was the only non-Dutch member of the local chess club, where he was 'very well accepted' and was also achieving some very good results on 'important tournaments'. Through this activity he developed closer ties with a couple of people 'of his age', with whom he exchanged a 'couple of home visits'. Still, Sasa was reluctant to refer to these contacts as 'friendships'; nevertheless, he spoke of them very proudly.

The desire to reach out and establish bridging contacts with the local population was shared by the vast majority of people I met in Amsterdam. Even those who viewed their stay in the Netherlands as 'temporary', waiting only for 'the right' moment to return, as Emir, for example, were nonetheless motivated to 'meet the Dutch'. By doing so they were actively trying to nest themselves in the new society and focusing on emplacement, although temporary. Emir, a 51-year-old man, was unemployed and volunteering at the Bosnian Association when I met him. He recalled his efforts to establish closer contact with his Dutch neighbours:

> I did try in my neighbourhood to break the ice and make friendships. The first Christmas after I moved in, in '94, I dropped a card to all my new neighbours. They seemed to like it, because I got cards from them next year, for Christmas. By the third year, they learned that I was a Muslim, and sent me cards for the New Year. They are nice people, I can't say that they are not, but our contacts don't go much further that that.

This is contrary to the generally accepted view in refugee (and migration) literature that the establishment of bridging social networks depends on the aim and objectives of migration (e.g., Robinson 1986; Bloch 2002). If refugees consider their stay as temporary, it is argued, they may be less prone to engage in creating bridging social networks and, hence, unwilling to undergo the process of adjustment necessary for their full participation in the receiving society. It is also accepted that the establishment of bridging social networks, that is, outside the group of compatriots, emerges at 'later stages' of refugee settlement, in the work place. In this sense, they are seen as primarily 'structurally embedded' in the larger structure of the receiving society, rather than voluntarily, linking people who were not otherwise likely to form a relationship (Wellman 1981).

The experiences of disconnectedness from the receiving society, which first occurred during prolonged stays in reception centres, have continued to characterise the subsequent emplacement phases during which the people I met were not successful in establishing closer informal ties with the Dutch. Without closer, informal communication with Dutch residents, many of them gradually formed a perception of a profound cultural distance between Dutch society and their societies of origin. It affected the formation of a boundary between 'us', refugees, and 'them', the Dutch. Their main micro-level social communication remained limited and based on networks developed along ethnic lines or focused on family ties.

Feeling at Home in Rome

Although initially the social communication of the people I met in Rome was primarily with their compatriots, as pointed out in the previous chapter, the process of intensive networking between them and Italians/residents of Rome emerged soon after their arrival. Most of the contacts with Italians were established in neighbourhoods where they lived, while shopping, at work, or when socialising at places such as cafés. Through these day-to-day activities they encountered many Italians who made many generous gestures of support and were willing to help. Because the social ties made through these encounters were (initially) neither egalitarian nor reciprocal, they were for the most part material-aid ties. They were in many cases essential for the people I met. Mirsada, a 37-year-old woman from Bosnia-Herzegovina, shared the experience of her family, after they arrived in Italy in 1992:

> Many people from the neighbourhood would come to see us when they found out that we had moved in. We never got any help from the Italian government, but we did get help from many Italians, ordinary people, who helped us with essential information, such as how to find schools for the children, where to shop, how and where to search for jobs. Some even offered us furniture, clothes, and you name it.

Gestures of kindness, support, and solidarity with 'a stranger in need' were important to all, but such gestures were critical for the survival of those with families, like Mirsada, as well as for men, as these were the categories of people who had particular difficulties in finding first jobs and accommodation, as discussed in the previous chapter. Stipe's account of his first days and months in Rome, after he found his first job in a restaurant through 'a Montenegrin guy', reveals the importance of contacts and connections with Italians for getting by during this difficult period filled with existential insecurities and uncertainties:

> I was very well accepted at the place I'd worked in the beginning. I had no problems at all; everyone accepted me as if I were one of their own. Everyone was terribly nice to me. No harassment, no insults, everyone was trying to be helpful. For example, the cook from the first restaurant I'd work in offered for me to stay with him as soon as I said that I had no place to stay. It was as if I'd walked into his house from the street. Who'd invite you into their house [apart from Italians]? I stayed with him for about a week, until they [friends, also refugees from war-torn Yugoslavia] found me a place to say.

The main obstacle for people in making closer social contacts with Italians during their first years in Rome was the lack of opportunity for becoming acquainted with people who were of a similar educational and social background as they were (used to be before flight). During their first years they were primarily in touch with the Italians with whom they worked. As most of them were underemployed and did work for which they were overqualified, Italians of different interests and life aspirations overwhelmingly made up their social milieu. In this respect, during their first years in Rome, men were more disadvantaged than were women. Initially, as discussed in Chapter 3, women were primarily employed in domestic service, giving them access to the social world of middle-class Italian families. Although not all the women I met developed supportive or friendly relationships with their employers, this type of work provided many of them with valuable initial contacts with Italians. In many cases these hierarchical, non-supportive ties gradually developed into supportive ones. Wellman (1981: 181) suggests that non-egalitarian and non-reciprocal social ties can be significant, because non-supportive ties often provide access to other, potentially supportive relationships. For many women in this study, therefore, contacts with Italian families they worked for developed into friendships not only with their employer, but also with their relatives and friends.

In the few families with children that stayed in Rome,[10] children were often instrumental in developing networks and friendships with Italians through their contacts with Italian children at school. Many of these contacts were critical for finding employment for their parents. Milan details how he got his first job after almost five years of unemployment:

> My wife must've told you about the difficulties we had for many years after we arrived here. There wasn't anything for us here, no help at all. My wife got a housekeeping job soon after we came here, through the contacts she had with an Italian family from the time when she was working in Rome, as a young, single woman, in the '70s. But I couldn't find a job for years. We were lucky to meet some nice Italian people who were willing and able to help us. One of our sons became friends at school with an Italian boy and they would visit each other at home. The boy told his mother that I was unemployed so she talked to a man who was the manager of the company I'm working for now. That man came to our house to meet us and told me to come and work for him. For the first two years, it was illegal work. After that, I signed a one-year contract, and this year they've given me a steady job. Now, I can even start thinking about retirement.

By the time I met them, after they had been in Rome for between seven and eight years, over a half of the group had more contacts with Italians than with people from their places of origin. These contacts were predominantly described as 'good friendships' involving regular outings, home visits, and joint vacations. While in Rome, I was invited on many occasions to outings of the people I met and their Italian friends or to some of their home visits. Occasionally, I would run into them on the street or in a café and would be invited to join them. These occasions were filled with a lot of friendly banter and laughter, sometimes also with discussions about work, sport or politics: Italian most often, as well as international, including occasionally what may be termed 'the situation back home'.

Within this group, there were also those who had Italian partners or spouses. For those married, entering their partner's 'circle of friends' was not always a problem-free experience, as it was in some cases experienced as a loss of agency in forming social ties. Iva, who met her Italian husband four years before the war broke out in Bosnia, explained her difficulties. She fled her hometown in 1992 and came to Rome where she subsequently married her then boyfriend. Iva, who was thirty-four years old when I met her, recalled how difficult it was to adjust in the beginning. She was regularly going out with her husband and his friends, and kept seeing people whom she had not chosen herself, they were chosen for her, as she remarked. After the initial period of adjustment and after she had started looking for a job in her profession, she got to know 'different people' and was able to start choosing and creating 'her own social circle'. It was only then that she started to feel more 'rooted' in Rome.

Iva's case was indeed exceptional. Most of the other close relationships people formed with Italians started accidentally, through many spontaneous contacts they made with Italians in their neighbourhoods and other public settings while searching for information or help of some kind. Amin (2002, cited in Mumford and Power 2003: 90) argued that semi-invisible micro-links of undeclared sociability that occur through casual contacts between diverse groups of people in public spaces, help people 'rub along together' and develop a positive web of support. The pattern of change from asymmetrical, hierarchical and, for the most part, material-aid ties, which emerged soon upon their arrival, to more symmetrical, egalitarian and emotional-aid social ties revealed in this study, supports arguments that support and trust are not fixed relationships (e.g., Wellman 1981).

However, all of the people who reported more contacts with Italians than with people from their places of origin, also emphasised that they have 'a couple of' or 'a few' very close friends among 'our people' in Rome. Some, like Omer, for example, talked about 'phases' through which they went since arriving in Rome. In the beginning, for Omer and others, it was first 'our own folk phase', which was often followed by a 'purely Italian phase' during which they become better adjusted to Italy and Rome in particular. Quite a few pointed out that they 'insisted on socialising with Italians, because you need to adopt here', as Dragan put it. By the time of my research, they were all in a 'more mixed phase', socialising mostly with Italians, but keeping contact with carefully chosen friends from their hometowns or country. Omer explained the need for this carefully balanced mix as his need for 'deeper communication, which you cannot have even with the best of Italian friends you have here', because they do not share the same mentality, history or sense of humour.

The other half of the people in my Roman study did not express a tendency to isolate themselves from Italians or society at large, but they preferred to socialise with 'their own folk', as Mirza put it. This preference, as he explained, stemmed from his feeling that they understood each other better because they still led more 'extreme' lives than Italians do. This preference was not based on the feeling of shared ethnic 'roots', rather it was embedded in their shared experiences as people fleeing war and their still unsettled life situations in Rome. Some explained their preference for socialising with people from their own country by pointing to a 'specific view of friendship' among Italians, compared to 'us Yugos' [people from Yugoslavia]. Mirza, for example, talked about the '*legerezza* that keeps Italian friendships together'. He explained that 'there is helping each other and all [among Italians], but when an Italian needs help he'll go to his family, never to a friend'. This perceived difference in the quality and character of interpersonal relationships among Italians led some of the people I met to view Italian friendships as 'superficial', not involved in 'personal matters' as much as 'our friendships are'. For a few, this superficiality meant 'not keeping one's word', as Dragan pointed out, or friendships based on 'favours or profitability' as Misa put it, 'he does you a favour, and he expects one in return'. For these reasons, this group of people had some Italian friends, but much preferred closer contacts with 'their own'.

Indeed, many social encounters with Italians were often characterised by confrontation, misunderstanding or disappointment. But because these social encounters were spontaneous and individualised they were perceived as the process of learning and mutual adjustment. Alija, recalling many instances of confrontation or disappointment since he arrived in Rome, said: 'I've been kicked around by Italians myself during these six-seven years, but I figure it was inevitable. It was inevitable as well as normal, because you have to get to know their character.' These informal interpersonal relationships were also perceived as the way to confront bias among Italians and newcomers alike. Having Italian friends who can get to know you 'as you really are' was frequently mentioned as the best way to challenge the prejudice about immigrants in general, as well as a more specific bias in relation to the people coming from war-torn Yugoslavia. These bridging, spontaneous and individualised contacts also made many people I met cautious about labelling and judging all Italians as representatives of a 'culture' or a 'nation', as Dragan emphasised when sharing with me his critical views of 'Italian friendships'. Additionally and very importantly, the experience of the identity politics of war in Yugoslavia and the consequences of labelling they encountered made some of the people I met aware of its dangers. Marko was one of them; he said:

> I don't have a general impression of Italians, because I'm aware of what happened to us [people from war-torn Yugoslavia] when we started looking at each other in general. There are wonderful people and there are bad people. There is no general Italian characteristic that I'm specifically fond of or that drives me crazy. Every person's got characteristics of their own.

Such attitudes, as well as the scope for establishing interpersonal, spontaneous contacts with Italians, enhanced the openness of the refugees towards Italians and vice-versa. Vera's account summarises the attitude of many of the people I met in Rome:

> We're here and we must learn how to live with Italians. We must find what we have in common with them, although we're different. Many Italians managed to learn a great deal from us too, especially those who work with our people. We are more precise, for example, we're some kind of 'Germans' to Italians. Perhaps we've changed them a bit, too.

Contacts with Italians were seen not only as a way of learning about the receiving society and its culture. They also shaped their awareness that the process of learning, shifting and shaping attitudes is mutual, that it affects Italians too.

The importance they placed on and success with which they made contacts with local people meant that they did not feel threatened by their new social milieu and thus did not feel a need for 'entrenching a symbolic boundary' (Baubock 1996) between themselves and Italians. Rather, these 'bridging' social networks encouraged them to step out of 'a kind of "national scheme"' as Dragan put it. His account details the way in which many have negotiated a balance between continuity and change. Dragan said:

> Limiting yourself to what you see as your own identity prevents you from accepting whatever may be outside it. Some of us, for example, speak perfect Italian, even the *dialetto Romano*, so there's no way you can recognise them as foreigners, they're very well adapted. However, there's still a difference, which isn't bad at all. From what I've seen it's not a disadvantage and I'd like to keep that distinctive quality.

This outward thinking and attitude fostered by social communication outside their ethnic groups not only helped them understand the new culture and the 'rules' of the new society. It also helped them incorporate many changes in their way of life, attitudes, expectations, and skills, as meaningful, helping them to restore a sense of continuity in their lives in Rome.

Social links and connections with Italians were also important in overcoming often divisive tendencies found among compatriots. Many pointed out that they 'feel better among Italians', as Omer put it, because in socialising with them they avoid being sucked into political debates concerning 'absolute truth' about the war in their place(s) of origin. Milan, for example, explains why he and his family prefer socialising with Italians to contacts with people from the Yugoslav successor states:

> I thought that socialising with our people and talking about our problems and politics would only give me a headache. It's better to be with Italians, especially if they're such wonderful people as the ones we know.

Spontaneous contacts with Italians not only strengthened people's adaptability to the new environment, and encouraged their openness to differences between cultures and people. They also enabled them to deal better with the mechanisms of exclusion at the state institutional level. The experiences of inclusion at micro-level were central to their general satisfaction with their situation in Italy. They felt 'good and safe', because most Italians they knew were 'good and emotional', despite existing xenophobia in Italy, which is an issue that 'politicians keep up their sleeve when they need someone to blame', as Lepa put it. The discrepancy between the experiences of inclusion at one level, and exclusion at the other, shaped the notions of belonging among the people I met in Rome. Dule explained the way he felt in Rome:

> I feel at home in Rome. The only time I don't feel at home is prior to the expiry date of my residence permit to stay. Then I really feel a foreigner. Otherwise, I feel at home. My social contacts have always been almost entirely with Italians, except that my partner is also from Bosnia. I feel that I belong here in many ways and Italians accept me as such. But when I am faced with state institutions, I feel humiliated and that is when I feel that I don't belong here.

Successful social interaction and close contacts with local people enhance the feeling of social inclusion at the micro-level and may counterbalance the experience of exclusion at the level of state institutions and the wider public. For some, the possibility of having this type of social contact and the opportunity for widening their social world was one of the ways in which they measured their success and satisfaction with their new home. Goca, who first fled to Germany before joining her boyfriend in Italy,[11] said: 'I'm sure I'm better off here than in Germany. German's don't make friends with foreigners at all and here we've [she and her partner] many friends among Italians.' Her partner Dule, who often goes to Sweden to visit his brother and his family who are refugees there, pointed out that:

> Italians are quite sociable, while in Sweden everything seems to be more or less confined to family circles. It's another thing of course, that Sweden gives you social security – accommodation, food and other things. However, I don't find their way of life interesting at all.

They were open and positive about Italians and Italy, often perceiving the 'Italian way of life' or Italians and 'their character closer to us from ex-Yugoslavia'. Italians would, as Dule explained, 'help you even if they don't know you', they would 'lend you money though they are not sure they'll get it back'.

Nonetheless, they were often also critical of Italian society and way of life. This criticism was best summarised by Alija's account of the situation in Italy:

Everything's 'maybe' in this country. In other countries it's either black or white – there's no grey in between. Well, everything is grey around here, that's for sure. Even if the law of this country guarantees you something, you still have to fight for it. You have to be prepared, to be well informed and in the end when you get there [to a state institution] you have to have someone backing you.

Most were, however, pragmatic in how they negotiated their criticism of Italian society and 'its ways' and their attachment to Rome, which they viewed as their new home. Mirsad's account illustrates how most of the people I met approached the problem:

There is no point in complaining about Italy and Italians, because this is their country. There's fifty-seven million of them here. There's room, of course, for constructive criticism but things aren't that bad at all. They aren't one hundred per cent bad. You feel like a foreigner as much as you wish to feel as a foreigner. I socialise with Italians and I make an effort to understand their mentality. The more nations and cultures you get to know, the richer you are. Besides, many Italians managed to learn something from us, too.

Others, who were less ready to acknowledge the acceptance of difference as an asset in life, still felt that they 'adapted nicely' to Italian society, as Misa put it. 'Intimately', he said:

I don't accept their way of thinking, because I was brought up in a different way … But in day-to-day contacts with Italians, at work, I behave just like them. That's normal … I learnt a lot from them.

The scope and quality of social contacts made with the majority community contributed to a subjective feeling of refugees that the wider society was not an alien and closed community, beyond reach. This subjective feeling played a positive role in assessing their individual situation in Italy. It tended to counterbalance their dissatisfaction with the quality of their participation in the labour market as well as their objectively undervalued social role. It also helped to deal with uncertainties of their temporary (legal) status.

Social Networks and Emplacement: The Process of Becoming 'of Place'

The discussion in this chapter has examined the lived experience of refugees by exploring how they went about reconstructing their lives in two different sociocultural locations and policy settings. It revealed the centrality of the role of various micro-level social interactions in how refugees adjust to and perceive their new social environment. There is no doubt that bonding social links among co-ethnics are in many cases critical for 'getting by' in new urban settings, as discussed in Chapter 3. They can be indeed instrumental for the development of individual and group survival strategies and for the creation of livelihoods. These links are also central to the process of 'getting on' with life, because they provide a link with past lives of refugees, helping them to maintain a sense of continuity. By keeping their language and elements of culture alive as well as some connection to their past roles and identities, co-ethnic contacts are often central to the well-being of people whose lives have been severely disrupted and identities challenged. Some authors argue that this type of connecting represents a protective strategy, because ethnic networks can represent safe havens for socially and culturally excluded immigrant groups (e.g. Barnes 2001; Reinsch 2001). However, as discussion in this chapter has pointed out, bridging networks of relations can also be vital for the process of regaining control over the lives of people experiencing dislocation.

If bridging links with majority groups are established early on these contacts help refugees to 'get by' and 'ahead' with their lives by providing vital information, contacts, and by enhancing the use of the considerable human capital they bring to new urban settings. Very importantly, bridging contacts are also central to the process of 'getting inside' and the feeling 'of place'. This is because bridging links and networks not only channel information and provide access to resources, they also interpret information and articulate meaning, and in this sense they serve as a 'dictionary' to local settings as well as wider society and culture.

While co-ethnic ties and cross-ethnic networks of compatriots are central to the notion of continuity, because they provide links to self-ascribed identities embedded in shared sociocultural codes, minority–majority connections or bridging social networks play an important role in the process of change. This is because interpersonal contacts with the majority groups are central to how refugees understand the codes and meanings underpinning social structures and everyday life in the receiving society.

Both the notion of continuity and the process of change are critical for how refugees reconstruct their lives in exile, and how they negotiate their sense of belonging. By seeking to establish bonding and bridging contacts and networks, they actively search for and develop place-making strategies through which they can negotiate their sense of belonging in a meaningful way. The refugees themselves identified bridging social networks or ties with the majority groups at a micro-level as an important element of emplacement. They did not think that this type of social link was linked to attempts to assimilate and lose their distinct sense of identity and culture, as indicated in my research. They strongly placed value upon interpersonal contacts with the majority groups, because these social interactions and exchange made them feel included and part of the social fabric of life. As such they were central to their notion of being 'of' the place to which they fled. In this sense, bridging networks are perceived as a two-way communication central to the process of mutual adjustment and change that is the sine qua non to developing diversity. However, a desire and strategies to achieve this type of two-way communication are very often blocked by visible and invisible walls confronting people struggling to nest themselves in unfamiliar sociocultural settings. Policy systems and approaches are just one of numerous walls surrounding newcomers in receiving societies.

The refugees whose place-making strategies are presented in this book experienced different levels of success in establishing bridging social networks and in achieving this important goal of their emplacement. The analysis has shown how micro-level social interaction outside ethnic boundaries, as well as that along and across ethnic lines, was to a certain extent shaped by the settlement policy, or the lack of it, in the two settlement contexts examined. It is important to add here that the relative success or failure of the refugees to establish bridging social networks in Amsterdam and Rome cannot be attributed solely to the character of the policy and reception system in the Netherlands and Italy. Indeed, the compatibility of cultures and lifestyles in the receiving and sending societies play a role in establishing closer social ties between the refugees and the local populations. Unlike in my Amsterdam study, refugees in Rome perceived the 'Italian life-style' as similar to that in their countries of origin. Some aspects of interpersonal communication, 'café culture', some values and traditions among Italians in Rome, were found to be familiar if not identical; and were helpful in forming a positive attitude towards the receiving society. However, despite the role that different levels of compatibility of cultures may have, this study strongly suggests that the formation of bridging networks is shaped by a wider settlement policy context. The lack of a developed reception system in Rome was conducive to the creation of spontaneous and non-institutionalised links between individual people, refugees and locals, rather than linking groups of newcomers to different service providers. Two-way communication between the group I studied and citizens of Rome occurred because of the efforts of refugees to do so and their strategies to achieve such communication. This type of communication was also possible because there are many locals (Italians) open to engage with individual people and approach them as 'a stranger in need'. Openness and engagement characterising these contacts go beyond stereotypes, biases and labels constructed about specific groups defined by their ethnicity, culture or type of migration. The establishment of these contacts was facilitated by demographic and other characteristics of the refugees in my study making them a 'tolerable' if not a 'desirable' Other.

This is not to argue that structural and institutional support for refugee needs can be replaced by generosity and a 'good heart' of the local people. Rather, it is to emphasise that legal and other policy measures alone cannot solve the problems of (in)equality and inclusion. Therefore, leaving space for individual involvement and initiative is paramount, as is the need for raising awareness and knowledge among local populations about who are refugees.

In this sense, the process of 'nesting' goes beyond the acquisition of a set of formal rights and at times the process of emplacement can be meaningful even when some important citizenship rights are denied, as the discussion of the experiences of people in Rome in this chapter has demonstrated. Emplacement outcomes, therefore, importantly include the existence, quality and strength of bridging social networks. If and when such informal interpersonal contacts occur, they are perceived as a 'two-way' communication between the newcomers/minority and the majority groups. They are not perceived as threatening ethnic 'roots' and identities of refugees. This further implies that the need to form bridging social networks as a sign of willingness and need to open up to new sociocultural influences is not necessarily linked to a weakening of prior cultural alliances. Although transformed through these changes and adjustments, the past attachments can and often do remain significant markers of continuity in one's life. Moreover, a change if perceived as meaningful can be incorporated as restoration of continuity.

The desire to reconstruct one's life and become 'of place' by developing 'bridging social networks', discussed here, should not be understood as an expression of yearning to become 'rooted' into a territory of a single nation-state. Rather, it is an expression of the importance of attachment to multiple places or localities, which is a consequence of the processes of emplacement and the multiple meanings of belonging they construct. The processes of emplacement, as the next chapter will reveal, have some important local as well as transnational and global dimensions. In this sense, their place-making strategies reflect the fact that refugees are increasingly living in a 'glocalized' (Robertson 1995) social reality characterised by the interrelation between local and global systems and structures in which they are attempting to emplace themselves.

Notes

1. This argument is in contrast to the arguments made by other authors in the refugee field who claim that the origin of refugees is central to their identity (e.g., Joly 1996)
2. Bowman (2002) refers to the condition of 'being in' but not necessarily 'of' a place in his discussion of the situation of refugees in refugee camps. He argues that their existence is as one of extraterritoriality, a condition of 'being "in" but not "of" the space they physically occupy' (ibid.: 344).
3. Communities of nationals from socialist Yugoslavia consist mostly of people who settled there in the aftermath of the Second World War. Only a minority arrived

in the '70s and '80s in search of (mostly professional) jobs. Additionally, a relatively large number of people had links with Italy through seasonal work, mainly in the northern parts of the country, and some of them stayed, illegally at first, before their stay was legalised through one of the amnesties granted by the government.

4. For more on the meaning of identity politics see Hill and Wilson (2003: 2).

5. Eastmond's (1998) study of the situation of Bosnian refugees in Sweden, for example, paints a different picture concerning inter-ethnic ties among the people there.

6. The emphasis on education was very strong in Yugoslavia, although the educational system was actually beyond the nation's economic capabilities. In the 1970s, for example, Yugoslavia ranked eighth in the world in terms of the proportion of university students to its generation as a whole (Denitch 1972: 33).

7. On the type of the openness of the Yugoslav socialist society and its meaning see Denitch (1972: 33–34).

8. Diaspora or 'long distance nationalism' links people living in various geographic locations and motivates them for action in relation to an ancestral territory and its government (Wimmer and Glick Schiller 2003: 597).

9. I am paraphrasing here Mollenkopf's (2000: 127) view on boundaries between immigrants and the Dutch in the city.

10. The reasons why there were very few families with children in Rome are discussed in Chapter 3.

11. Goca's patter of flight and reasons for choosing Italy are discussed in Chapter 2.

5

Transnational Lives of Refugees, Questions of Citizenship, Belonging and Return

Researchers are increasingly turning their attention to practices, processes and institutions through which refugees seek to reestablish their lives across national borders, linking societies of origin and reception in a variety of ways: economic, social/familial, political, and cultural/symbolic. In this sense, sustained social contacts spanning borders (Portes et al.1999) are just one expression or form of transnationalism. They can also be an avenue of capital, a mode of cultural reproduction, a type of conciousness, a site of political engagement, as well as a reconstruction of place and locality (Vertovec 1999). With respect to the latter expression of transnationalism, it is emerging from research that the nature and meaning of 'home' or the 'place' refugees forge for themselves in receiving societies, and the sense of attachment to it, are importantly shaped by transnational ties and connections, as discussed in Chapter 1. They no longer tend to be situated within the 'national order of things' (Malkki 1992) within which 'home', identity, and belonging are defined by national borders and territories of either sending or receiving societies.

Transnational and 'Glocal' Ties: A Sense of Continuity and Belonging

Accounts of people I met in Rome and Amsterdam demonstrate that their place-making strategies often cross national borders to fulfil their complex and subtle needs of continuity. In their search for emotional aspects of home as well as symbolic or sociocultural markers of place, refugees tend to re-create them by engaging in transnational or global networking, communication and exchange. Through these activities and arrangements they piece together different dimensions of home, forge new identities and a sense of belonging. The important role of co-ethnic networks and cross-ethnic ties among compatriots in the processes of reconstructing life and 'nesting' cannot be sufficiently understood if 'the community' of people who are forcibly displaced is defined by and confined to local or national borders. As Marx (1990: 194) points out, a social world of refugees 'is not confined to a particular place or limited by territorial boundaries'. For a significant minority of people whose 'social world' revolves intensely around their associations or 'the community' in Amsterdam, continuity is situated within the 'national order of things', and identities and belonging defined by national borders and territories. In their effort to maintain their identities and nurture their sense of belonging they keep not only transnational links to their places of origin, family and friends left behind, but also develop and rely on close ties with one another, their 'community' in the Netherlands. I met some of them during my visits to the Bosnian Community Association in the city. They, all men, were always there, primarily 'to socialise' and 'make contacts with our people', 'to listen to Bosnian music and drink Bosnian coffee', as they explained. Women would be there, in passing, on a 'hairdresser's day' when a hairstylist, also a refugee from Bosnia, came to do their hair. On regular days, with no special events scheduled, it was usually very quiet, with a few groups of men reading Bosnian papers or watching satellite TV programme from Bosnia and talking; sometimes there would be a couple or two playing chess. Emir, who was always among them, explained how they were 'more oriented towards Bosnia and what is happening *there*' than to what is 'happening *here*' in Amsterdam and the Netherlands.

The majority of people I met in Rome and Amsterdam, however, were part of communities that were importantly transnational as well as global in character. Through these networks criss-crossing national borders they not only share their experiences of life way away from home with people left behind, in their places of origin, or exchange information about the settlement 'rules' in different receiving countries. They also develop and maintain links with those who are, like themselves, refugees in other countries. In this sense, some of these networks spanning borders are actually global in character. For the majority of people I met in both Rome and Amsterdam their links and visits to the places they came from lead them to more intensive search and development of global ones. Most of the people I met could not go to their home areas for at least four years, in many cases even longer. These visits made most of them feel 'like foreigners', because these places were no longer the towns or cities they left, they were hardly recognisable, not only or necessarily in physical terms, but primarily in terms of atmosphere and its sociocultural and political underpinnings. Marko, for example, recalling his first visit to his home city explained why he felt like foreigner there: 'It is no more that city, no more that language, no more those people.' Because they could no longer recognise and identify with dominant political and sociocultural codes or find people they once knew and were friends with they experienced acute feelings of 'otherness'. For a few, their only remaining link was 'their elderly parents' and/or 'a few remaining family members'. Hence, these transnational links make most of them feel that they do not belong to any place in particular, but could easily adjust to 'any urban centre' and 'any normal city life' 'anywhere in the world, as long as it's a metropolis' as Mirza explained. For a few whom I met in Rome, first visits to their home areas brought about a more intense feeling of belonging to Rome, as the place where their home was 'at the moment', as Alija put it.

Their links spanning borders of different states and continents with their friends and relatives scattered around the world have been fulfilling a range of complex and subtle needs of continuity relating to emotional, symbolic, and specific sociocultural aspects of place and emplacement. They regularly 'meet' in cyberspace or keep 'in touch' over the phone with friends who are also refugees, 'in England, America, and who knows where', as Suada, whom I met in Rome, put it. Many of them also go to or organize reunions with family or friends in countries across Europe and beyond. These reestablished ties with friends from their places of origin fill in lost or missing dimensions of 'home' in the places where they now live. Although these connections and exchanges gain a new quality and character, the change is perceived as meaningful and consequently helps restore a sense of continuity and belonging. At the time of my fieldwork in Rome, for example, Marko was involved in co-organising a gathering of friends from his hometown in Bosnia, who were at the time scattered over Europe, North America and Australia. The reunion was to take place in Turkey. Similarly, Branka at the time I met her in Rome, had just returned from an (extended) family reunion in Norway. Nikica, in yet another example, returned from one such reunion with friends in Canada, just a few months before I met him in Amsterdam. Through these transnational contacts and activities they were actively searching for continuity and meaning linked to their past roles, status and identities; through these they were actively 'nesting' in transnational and global spaces. A few of the people I met in Amsterdam also happened to belong to networks involving some of the people whom I met while doing my research in Rome. By actively seeking and maintaining these contacts they were regaining a sense of continuity of their lives in Italy and the Netherlands as well as recreating a sense of belonging, which was no longer defined in local, territorial or national terms. As a result, many of them feel like 'citizens of the world', describing their sense of belonging in global, rather than local terms.

For many people I met, transnational and global links are the only way to maintain a sense of family life and thus to regain a very important aspect of continuity and stability. Not only that most of the people I met had their parents or sometimes siblings left behind; some had their families split because of the war, and family members living in different countries. Tanja's family, for example, were divided between Bosnia, Denmark, and Italy, with her farther and brother living 'back home', her mother in Denmark, while she lives in Rome. Her regular visits to Denmark and her frequent phone communication with her father and brother in Bosnia cobble together her transnational family life into one social field and experience. This gives her a sense of continuity, despite the changed character of her family life and relations. Although it has not always been easy for Tanja to be 'the link' keeping her 'disintegrated family together', her transnational ties with her family fulfil a missing dimension and aspect of her life in Rome. These types of engagement and action of the people in my study represent some of their place-making strategies through which they create a meaningful place for themselves in Rome and Amsterdam.

These and other similar transnational and global contacts have been enhancing a sense of continuity by re-creating familiar forms of sociability and exchange according to their self-ascribed cognitive reality and identity.[1] By the same token, this type of connection and link is also an important corrective to the often forced association with compatriots or 'ethnics' living in the same town/city/country, who are not necessarily perceived as 'the community'. In this sense, the notion of belonging to a community gains an important transnational and global dimension in the process of emplacement as refugees search for continuity of meanings and identities.

Although their lives are localised in some important ways, because people do live in concrete localities characterised by their own social structures, cultures and mechanisms of inclusion and exclusion, as this book has demonstrated, they also form transnational ties and global connections in their attempt to emplace themselves and reconstruct a 'sense of place'. Thus, the search for continuity through local, transnational and global 'ethnic' networks is central to their processes of emplacement. Their dialectic relationship is continually negotiated in particular contexts and at specific points in time. Often, this negotiation results in transnational lives which are increasingly being developed as a strategy of survival and betterment, as will be further discussed in this chapter.

Transnational Strategies of Survival and Betterment

Transnationalism and transnational lives in themselves are increasingly becoming a strategy of survival and betterment (Faist 2000).Transnational links across borders of receiving and sending countries play a critical role in addressing insecurities, uncertainties and dilemmas about life projects of refugees and their families in specific locations and at particular points in time. Many of the refugees I met in Rome and Amsterdam were compelled to help financially their parents and families left behind. For many years after they fled, very few of them sent remittance regularly (i.e., monthly). They were themselves in dire need of money and financial security or it was difficult to send money to their home areas, because of the conflict. However, by now practically all of them were helping their loved ones 'back home'. As much as they were themselves financially insecure, very often their families left behind experienced similar or even greater problems. Milena and Bojana, two sisters who fled to Rome separately, one from Bosnia-Herzegovina, the other from Croatia, and were reunited in Rome, talked about struggling to survive while making sure that they could send money to their parents left behind in Bosnia, who were 'left without their savings' and without a salary or a pension for 'many months during the war.' In some cases, and at some points in time, the commitment to help family back home shaped their shorter-term employment strategies. This was particularly the case with those in Rome during the early years of their life there and at the time when the war in many parts of Yugoslavia was still raging. As they did not receive any financial help, they were often forced into decisions to postpone the continuation of their education or retraining and continue working long hours in their low-paying jobs in order to earn enough to live on and send back home. Sending remittances, therefore, was widespread among the people I met and was, at times, burdensome for many.

Transnational practices and links to the sending societies are not always limiting or demanding, though. They may often facilitate betterment of those who fled; not only their survival or the survival of those left behind. When economic and other circumstances in the receiving society do not permit refugees to reestablish their lives in a way they themselves see as desirable, the establishment of transnational lives spanning borders of sending and receiving states may become the strategy refugees opt for. These emerging forms of transnationalism among people I met in Rome and Amsterdam are discussed in the following section. Also, as research demonstrates, when refugees do not want to accept underemployment or loss of social status, they increasingly opt for the establishment of transnational families and households; by doing so they are renegotiating their goals and redefining their life projects to fit their aims and expectations (Eastmond 2006).

The creation of transnational households and engagement in transnational family life may also be a way of tackling the dilemma of return. Refugees who flee their countries of origin with a shared collective project of return often find their original commitment to return to the places they came from reshaped both by circumstances in the country of origin and their own experiences in the countries of settlement. This is because both the experiences of refugeehood and the situation in a sending country are evolving at various levels: individual, community, societal, cultural, and state. A complex interplay of these changes, it has been long argued, often affects decisions about return (Zetter 1988). As a result, people who once shared a collective project and determination to return are often prompted to renegotiate their individual, family, and group goals, and redefine their life plans and projects. They may, as many Chileans in the US did (Eastmond 2006), opt for transnational strategies in addressing the question of return: parents usually return, while they keep regular contacts with their children who remain in the place of settlement.

In both scenarios of transnational life arrangements created to better the life prospects and situations of refugees mentioned here, those who decide to return keep links and multiple connections across borders. Engagement in this type of active maintenance of links across borders of sending and receiving societies among refugees has been made possible by their residence or citizenship status in the receiving society. This type of transnational life also requires a renegotiation of conceptions of home in response to both the conditions in the country of origin and the receiving country. Transnationalism and increasing possibilities of transnational emplacement arrangements and place-making strategies should be, therefore, added to the factors influencing the decisions about return. They also reshape the very notion of return. Therefore, it is not only economic migrants who devise transnational strategies to better their life prospects, migrants who come initially for other than economic reasons tend to do that too.

Transnationalism and the Changing Notion of Return

Transnational practices reveal that settlement, resettlement, and return are not definite or irreversible decisions (Faist 2000). Rather, they should be seen as processes, commonly long-term ones and consisting of stages that frequently overlap. Refugees I met in Amsterdam and Rome often devised transnational place-making strategies, as mentioned earlier, tending to 'nest' themselves in transnational spaces in their search for (to them) a meaningful social, familial, cultural and symbolic context of emplacement: one in which a sense of belonging to both their new and former homes is redefined to express the significance of both of their 'homes' for how they reconstruct their lives. Their multi-site place-making strategies also blur the boundaries between exile/settlement and return, transforming the notions of belonging and the meaning of citizenship. These processes, as we shall see, challenge the dominant conceptions of membership, integration and belonging, as well as notions of 'citizen', 'refugee', and 'returnee'. These notions are all linked to a single unitary realm of nation-state and are embedded within notions of sited identities. In discussing the implications of 'transnationalisation of migrants' lives', de Hass (2005: 6) notes that:

> [C]lear-cut dichotomies of 'origin' or 'destination' and categories such as 'permanent', 'temporary', and 'return' migration seem increasingly difficult to sustain in a world in which the lives of migrants seem increasingly characterised by circulation and simultaneous commitment to two societies.

Increased involvement of all migrants in transnational practices, thus, fosters multiple loyalties, and challenges the still prevailing political construct of the nation-state and citizenship. The emergence of multiple loyalties also leads to the formation of a type of cosmopolitanism which does not necessarily imply the absence of belonging, but a possibility of belonging to more than one sociocultural context or locale simultaneously.[2] In this sense, the notion of national expands into the transnational.

The Emergence of Transnational Place-making Strategies in Amsterdam

A majority of people I met in Amsterdam saw their future tied to the Netherlands in some important ways. Many of them were however contemplating transnational life arrangements based on the establishment of transnational households and involving active maintenance of links with both the Netherlands and their places of origin. Some of these transnational strategies were in the making at the time I met them, because their newly acquired citizenship rights opened more options and choices on where to live and how to make a place for themselves. In this sense, citizenship was not unequivocally seen as an 'anchor' tying them deeply to the territory of the Dutch state or indeed as a marker of belonging and identity. Rather, formal citizenship was in many cases facilitating different forms of strategising return or yet another move (secondary migration). As Sinisa explained: 'I no longer have any problem in thinking about moving on and going where I think it is going to be better for me and my family'. The actual realisation of their transnational plans depended on their individual circumstances, ranging from outcomes of their property claims in the places in which they lived before coming to Amsterdam, or the circumstances and life plans of their grown-up children or elderly parents who were also in the Netherlands, as will be discussed later in this chapter.

Younger people who were studying or working, and those middle-aged people who were employed, did not think about returning in a straightforward way. A majority of them shared the 'migration plans' and the attitude of Belma, a 42-year old woman, who explained:

> Since I arrived here [in 1993], I suppressed any thoughts about going back. I think that I've changed a lot, as well as the people I knew in Bosnia. It's a big gap between us now, and there's no way of bridging it. So, I am focused on my life here and I want to stay.

Nonetheless, many of them did not think that these decisions were irreversible. Rather, they viewed them as processes and thus flexible and changing. They were aware or were just starting to become aware that their life circumstances and thus their life projects may change.

Such was the case of Zenaida, for example, who has married and had a child since she fled Bosnia-Herzegovina and arrived in Amsterdam. After becoming a mother, this 30-year old Bosniak woman has begun to view her initial idea of living permanently in Amsterdam/the Netherlands in a different light. Her life project became importantly shaped by thoughts about her child's upbringing and how she wanted her daughter 'to be raised'. Zenaida was not entirely sure if she would be happy to do it 'the Dutch way'. She was contemplating various transnational strategies which would allow her family to spend a prolonged period of time possibly in Croatia, where both she and her husband, a refugee from Croatia, may be able to secure consulting contracts and live for a while, leaving her mother, also a refugee, in Amsterdam. She was hoping that this kind of transnational socialisation would provide her daughter with the opportunity to learn about and grow up in two different cultural milieus, enhancing her well-being and prospects for the future. In devising this strategy, Zenaida was joining an increasing number of migrants and their families in which socialisation and social reproduction occur transnationally (Levitt and Glick Schiller 2004: 1017).

This kind of strategising and negotiating did not mean, however, that Zenaida, as well as the majority of others, was not actively involved in reconstructing her life in Amsterdam, aiming at making a meaningful place for herself there. Rather, she was actively searching for ways of reconstructing life across (national) borders to create a meaningful social, familial, cultural and symbolic context for her emplacement. The realisation of her transnational strategy of place-making importantly depends, for example, on the professional experience she has been able to gain since she found a job in her profession in Amsterdam. Only this type of professional experience can open employment/consulting opportunities for her in Croatia.

Miro's emerging ideas about multi-site place-making is yet another example of the importance of the link between professional experience gained in the Netherlands and a possibility of developing some form of professional links with Croatia. Although Miro was one of those who was doing his best to adjust as much as possible 'for a foreigner', as pointed out in Chapter 4, at the time I met him in Amsterdam he begun toying with the idea of 'finding consulting opportunities in Croatia' and spending some time there. Miro saw this as an opportunity for transferring the knowledge he had gained through his studies and subsequent work experience with 'green' building materials and engineering. He did not consider this possibility as 'going back for good', but as a way of overcoming the problem of being 'invisible' among the Dutch, as he explained.

In this sense it is indeed the case that those who are 'successfully integrated' will have grater capacity, both financially and skills wise, to engage economically and socially in their places of origin (de Haas 2005: 8). Therefore, as de Haas points out, it is 'factually incorrect to automatically interpret migrants' commitment towards their countries of origin as a consequence of their inability or unwillingness to integrate' (ibid.). He argues, thus, that transnationality is not incompatible with integration per se, although he allows the possibility of it being a sign of refusal or inability of individual migrants to become members of the receiving society in specific circumstances (de Haas 2005: 8). Indeed, for most people I met in Amsterdam, the transnational practices they were engaged in or strategies they had just started to devise were not about their unwillingness to integrate. Rather, as in Zenaida's case, they were the expression of their multi-site place-making through which they aimed to link aspects of their new and former homes into one social field and experience.

Troubles with the Notion of Permanent Return: 'Go and See' Schemes in the Netherlands

The people I met in Amsterdam all appeared to be relatively 'well settled'. None had definite plans to return to Bosnia-Herzegovina, though some of those who were older and unemployed did not entirely give up the dream of going 'back home for good'. However, none of them contemplated signing up for the state-assisted programme for return. This programme, funded by the Dutch government, included, at the time, some financial incentives for those who decide to return to their places/countries of origin, but would also automatically withdraw residence/citizenship.[3]

The character of this and similar policy initiatives indicates that the policy makers do not fully understand the reality and meanings of transnational practices in the lives of many refugees. Nor do they recognize how such practices impinge upon the meaning of return by transforming it into a less acute, divisive, either-or question. Regardless of the acknowledgement that 'refugee problems are by definition transnational problems' (UNHCR 1995: 49), (voluntary) return is still seen as a permanent solution, as well as a non-reversible process.

So-called 'Go and See' schemes, introduced by some European governments, aim at enhancing voluntary return of refugees, and they also reflect some degree of recognition that transnational practices shape the realities of lives of refugees. Nonetheless, they still remain within the framework of old paradigms of membership, citizenship, and belonging. These policy initiatives allow refugees to go back to their countries of origin (for up to one month), and see/experience for themselves the situation in their home towns or villages and in the country at large. These visits are financially assisted and do not jeopardise refugees' legal status.

Such schemes may be seen as an indication, as Van Hear (2003: 13) argues, that policy makers have gradually started to move away from 'compartmentalisation of locations' by recognising the inter-relation between the situation in the receiving and sending society. However, this interpretation may be reading much more into these policy initiatives than they actually have to offer, because what they effectively do or proffer as an opportunity is more time and a kind of 'preparatory' phase in making *definite* decisions about return. These initiatives primarily indicate some level of awareness that decisions about settlement and/or return, and the development of appropriate place-making strategies, are most often long-term processes involving a preparatory phase. Consequently, it is important to emphasise that however encouraging these policies may seem there is no indication that these programmes introduced by governments of receiving societies have helped increase the number of people returning in any significant way.[4]

Losing the right to return to the receiving society is not only important to refugees, nor does it only shape the migratory plans and life projects of forced migrants.[5] Weil (2002 cited in de Haas 2005: 10) has pointed out that this is also the case with immigrants who come primarily for economic reasons. Restrictive policies cause a fear of losing the right to return, inhibiting immigrants from investing in and returning temporarily to the sending country.

This study indicates that there is a considerable gap between the goals, aims and ideals of policy-makers, and the actual experiences of refugees. This is why many refugees in Amsterdam opted for phased, unassisted return, gradually forming transnational families and households, which were beginning to emerge or were fully realised only after they became Dutch citizens.[6] These findings show how when policies pertaining to (forced) migration do not reflect the transnational reality of lives of refugees, they, as social actors, attempt to modify them. They devise (transnational) strategies enabling them to move away from the territorial notions of life and belonging that such policies entail.

A tiny minority of people in Amsterdam who were toying with the idea of going back 'for good', but at their own pace and without giving up their Dutch citizenship, as mentioned earlier, wanted to return as soon as their children were 'up on their feet and independent', as Emir, a 51-year-old intended to do. This would provide them with a sense of security or guarantee that they would be able to visit and stay with their children any time they wanted. The sense of security linked to Dutch citizenship was also importantly associated with the type of conflict they fled. They were aware that the past violence and forcible migratory movements undermined the very fabric of life in their places of origin and caused the break-up of local communities. As Warner (1994: 162) pointed out, voluntary repatriation is more than return to the territory that is associated with a political entity, it is return to a community. Those who contemplated the idea of going back knew that if they were to decide to return any time soon, they would be going back to a post-conflict society characterised by problematic and/or fragile societal relationships and political arrangements.

This type of caution is understandable if one acknowledges the types and character of destruction caused by wars that emerged in the 1990s, which were ethnically structured. The primary targets of the logic and political economy of this type of conflict are social networks, social systems and the social fabric of life in the community. Orchestrated insecurity and violence deployed by warring parties aim to destroy the very relations that form the foundations of conventional society. The destruction, thus, is not only physical and material, but social, civil and political. The costs of such destruction are immense. The conflict in Yugoslavia eroded the subsistence, human resource and skill base of the region. Not only did it result in growing displacement and impoverishment, but also in the loss of skilled and educated populations causing problems in reconstructing civil, public and political institutions, as well as the economy. This inevitably raises questions of reconciliation, post-conflict reconstruction and the return of people forced to leave their homes.[7]

Consequently, returning will always have a ring of uncertainty attached to it, because as Nadan, a 59-year-old man from Bosnia said: 'War destroyed not only houses, but also relationships and ties among people' After experiencing not only existential insecurity for years, but also painful break-ups of meaningful social ties, they did not want to find themselves in a similar situation again.[8] People I met in Amsterdam all talked about their friends or family being 'scattered around the world' and therefore of their places of origin being irreversibly destroyed by war. Consequently, instead of thinking about a possibility of permanent return, they were devising transnational strategies which would provide a possibility of combining and linking receiving and sending places in innovative and meaningful ways. For many middle-aged and older people I met, that meant dividing time up between Amsterdam and one of the Yugoslav successor states, but not necessarily their home town or even the part of Yugoslavia they originally came from. Having a physical home to return to, many of which were successfully regained through housing restitution, enhanced the possibilities of regular visits for the people I met. However, in many cases this was not the only or indeed the most important reason for them to contemplate transnational life. In this sense, while this research indicates that property repossessions support and enhance the development of transnational place-making strategies, my findings also support studies arguing that the relationship between housing restitution and return of refugees to postwar Bosnia is not straightforward (Stefansson 2006). Decisions to return permanently or indeed to engage in some form of transnational life are importantly shaped not only by the material condition and availability of the 'small home', to borrow from Stefansson (2006). They are also and very importantly influenced by the situation in the 'big home', that is, the process of normalisation of sociopolitical structures at the local and national level (ibid.).

In contemplating return or some form of transnational life, women who had children were more inclined than men/fathers to root their attitudes towards return or transnational place-making in the lives and futures of their children. Larija, a 58-year-old woman, for example, explained how her decision not to return to Bosnia permanently was linked to the life plans of her daughter and son. She said: 'As it seems now, they [the children] will stay here and so, I don't see any reason to return.' This tendency, in turn, shaped women's notions of 'home' and, hence, their place-making strategies. Laria, therefore, felt that her home was in Amsterdam and the Netherlands in many ways, and would be especially so once her children became parents and she became a grandmother. However, she also felt the need for links to people, places and some aspects of life she had in her former home. As they were all more or less settled in Amsterdam, children employed and one also married, she and her husband were contemplating 'going back for prolonged periods of time'. Although Laria's family was successful in regaining their flat in their home town in Bosnia-Herzegovina, she pointed out that she and her husband did it 'because of the children', for them to 'have some roots there'. She and her husband, however, were considering 'returning' to either Croatia, where Laria has family and friends, or to the village in Bosnia where her husband grew up.

Men in this study were more inclined to think as Emir did, that once their children were 'independent', they would have no further reason to stay in the Netherlands. Although this distinction did not apply to all those with children, it indicates that parenthood in its intersection with gender is a factor influencing the process of negotiation of return in refugees with children. Because of traditionally constructed gender roles, women are still prevailingly regarded as care givers and emotional providers for their children. Consequently, they tend to centre their lives and expectations on their parenting role. This socially constructed notion of women as responsible and involved in creating and maintaining a 'nest' for their children corresponds to a construction of the prevailing image of 'home' understood as 'locality', 'the site of everyday lived experience', as Brah (1996: 4) reminds us. Home here connotes, she points out, the networks of family, kin and other 'significant others' (ibid.). Because of these social constructs, women are more prone to relate to the social and psychic geography of space called 'home' that translates at a functional level into building their 'home' where their children are.

Regardless of these differences and attitudes towards return, everyone I met in Amsterdam was involved in some form of transnational activity involving their places of origin or the region they came from. In this sense, and unlike it has been indicated in some other studies (e.g., Al-Ali et al. 2001: 583), my research did not provide any significant indication that unemployment or language difficulties in the places of settlement had a negative impact on the capabilities to get involved in transnational activities with their places of origin. Obviously, financial factors were important in making decisions about how often people could go and visit places they came from, and in that sense those unemployed obviously had more difficulties than those employed. However, those with jobs could not afford time to go often regardless of their financial capabilities. Further, those few who toyed with the idea of returning were actually unemployed, but they nonetheless kept links and contacts with their places of origin constantly alive and 'buzzing'. They wanted to be continuously updated on the latest sociopolitical and economic developments in sending countries in order to make an informed decision about their return. This indicates that financial insecurity and unemployment are not a barrier to getting involved in transnational activities, although they may shape their forms.

No Right to Stay Permanently in Rome and the Changing Notion of Return

The lack of permanent residence rights and/or citizenship among those who were in Rome, and the frustration it caused, was aggravated by the fact that Italy has an inflexible naturalisation policy. Consequently, almost none of the people I met in Rome envisaged that they would be able to obtain Italian citizenship in the foreseeable future. This also meant that they could not properly plan for their future. Nonetheless, many of them had ideas and preferences concerning their future life projects including the question of return. As with those in Amsterdam, most of the people in Rome acknowledged that their attitudes towards staying or returning to their places of origin may change over time and that any decisions were not irreversible. Bogdan, a 53-year-old man who fled Croatia explained:

> Amongst ourselves [within his family] we openly speak about not going back, but it doesn't necessarily mean that we won't. Things change, and I hope that one day they'll change enough to bring about a change in our attitude about going back as well.

Most importantly, however, and as in my Amsterdam study, transnational strategies were emerging as desirable options for many. Omer's account reveals the process of change that has occurred since he first came to Rome:

> During my first years here I was totally convinced that I'd never go back to Bosnia. Today, I don't rule out the possibility of going back some day. And if I go back, I have a fear of being nostalgic for Italy. So I've got used to the idea that I'll always be between two worlds. You can handle that kind of situation only if one world is kind of 'next door' to the other.

Thus, Omer and many other people I met were thinking of 'rooting' their lives in transnational arrangements that they may want to pursue once their legal status and stay in Italy becomes permanent, permitting them to engage in some type of transnational life strategy. Given the geographical proximity of Rome/Italy to their places of origin, many were envisaging different work/business strategies, for example, which would link these places, enabling them to live 'permanently' in one and keep economic and other links to the other. When sending and receiving countries are 'next door' to one another, this and other similar types of transnational links and strategies are indeed conceivable.

Special proximity and distance play a role in how people develop transnational place-making strategies. The 'tyranny of distance' encourages different forms of transnationalism and calls for new conceptualisations (Colic-Peisker, 2008). Colic-Peisker (ibid.) points to the importance of spatial proximity in practicing and engaging in some forms of transnationalism; for example, it is less expected to find much travelling back and forth by ethnic entrepreneurs and even less so by seasonal workers between Australia and Europe.[9]

The situation among those few with children also mirrored the attitudes of those in Amsterdam. Women who were mothers were inclined to link the issue of return to the plans of their children. Milka, a 45-year-old mother of two said:

> I want to stay here because I have children who will marry and have their families here. I'm looking forward to watching my grandchildren grow. When you have children, I think that all plans should have to do with their lives.

Her husband, though, was toying with the idea of 'going back to Bosnia for good', once their sons become independent. Besides women being more prone to building their 'home' where their children are, as has been mentioned above, gender-sensitive analyses of refugee repatriation point to other, additional reasons for gender differences here.

The very possibility of return is always associated with the complex process of decision making, which is in itself gendered and affected by refugee experiences, both those linked to the conditions in the specific country of origin, as well as to the social place which refugees have been able to create for themselves in exile (McSpadden and Moussa 1996: 216). Differences in how refugees, as women and as men, develop life strategies in exile and bring about meaning to their 'new' lives, as this and other studies show, affect their decisions about and/or attitudes towards returning to their countries of origin. Milka, for example, apart from wanting to live where their children were, was also not keen on returning because it was in Rome that she experienced a radical shift of power within her family and the household, a change which brought about a more egalitarian relationship with her husband. She felt that this change reflected the fact that they no longer lived with her in-laws, as was 'customary back home',[10] and was also related to her being 'the breadwinner' for the family during the years her husband was unemployed. The experience of being unemployed undermined her husband's patriarchal understanding of family responsibilities, which was gradually changed to include responsibilities traditionally associated with women's roles. Milka feared that if they were to go back to their home town her family life and her marriage would return to how it was before flight, because of the sociocultural pressures to conceptualise social power within the framework of patriarchal notions of masculinity and femininity, and the corresponding 'natural' roles of men and women.

Many studies emphasise that displacement affects gender relations and power structure within the family and the community in substantial ways. Many women start working outside the household for the first time once they reach the receiving societies; in such cases men often find this type of women's work and their resulting independence threatening to their traditional image of the male as provider. This loss in status and the experience of marginality experienced by most men in exile, may, and often does, erupt into violence directed against women and children. However, in many cases, as in the case of Milka and her husband, women's greater sense of autonomy results in their increased participation in family decision making, as well as in relationships of solidarity and mutual support forged in settlement conditions.[11] This type of situation only reaffirms the importance and the power of transformative experiences of emplacement.

Citizenship: A Status or a Practice?

Conventional understandings of citizenship are multiple, and the concept is often disputed. The concept may refer to modes of legal status, right and duties, participation, and identity/affiliation.[12] Formal citizenship was primarily viewed by people I met in Amsterdam and Rome as access to freedom of travel and movement, in the strict sense of the word, or in many cases as opening up opportunities for the development of multi-site place-making strategies, as pointed out earlier in this chapter. In neither of the contexts was it perceived as signifying any closer 'bond' to Dutch or Italian society in the sense of belonging and identity. Also, rather than being seen as a means of fostering their active participation in Dutch or Italian society and their legal and political structures, citizenship was regarded as a status primarily valued because it meant the legal right to live/reside permanently in Amsterdam or Rome. Participation in the political arena and democratic processes by voting, for example, was not perceived as an important indicator of being included, even after almost ten years in both countries/cities.

Those very few I met in Amsterdam who voted after acquiring the right to do so, did it out of a sense of 'duty towards the country that accepted them', as Emir explained his voting behaviour, rather than because they felt that this particular form of political participation was significant in constituting themselves as members of the polity. It is worth reiterating here that Emir (fifty-one years old, unemployed) was, in fact, among those who contemplated a possibility of 'going back for good'. More importantly, he was among those who were much more concerned with what was happening 'there' (in Bosnia) than what was happening 'here' (in the Netherlands), as discussed earlier in this chapter. Yet he was one of the very few people I met who voted. This indicates that the idea of temporariness of the stay is not necessarily the barrier to different forms of participation, both social and political. It also points to the strength of indebtedness that may be created among refugees by the humanitarian approaches to refugee assistance, as already discussed in the Introduction, and the type of agency it engenders.

A majority, however, emphasised that they 'no longer have any illusions about democracy or voting', as Sinisa, a 40-year-old man from Bosnia put it, and therefore they were not interested 'in that crap'. These rather cynical views were, on the one hand, embedded in their experience of the first 'democratic' multi-party elections in Yugoslavia when nationalist parties came into power, which was very disappointing for many. On the other hand, many felt even more disappointed by what 'democracy' actually is in the 'democratic world'. Miro's account points to some of the reasons for this latter type of cynicism:

> After I came here I realised that all that talk about democracy, human rights and liberties is actually crap. I saw with my own eyes how violently the police dealt with anti-EU protesters at a peaceful demonstration here in Amsterdam. Besides, not many people vote here, anyway.[13]

Clearly, participation in the formal local or national political arena was not perceived as crucial for feeling and being 'of place' for the people in my Amsterdam study. It represented only a small part of their individual and group efforts to become members of the polity.

It is important to acknowledge here, however, that for disadvantaged and marginalised groups such as refugees, active political participation can also be defined in terms of participation in informal politics. Negotiation with welfare state institutions, for example, may be a much more pertinent practice of political engagement to these groups than participation in mainstream politics (Anthias 2002). With this in mind, it is important to emphasise that the diverse group of people I met in Amsterdam could find neither a niche for themselves within the context of (ethnic minority) group politics in the Netherlands, nor could they see themselves as an integral part of the mainstream political arena.

In their efforts to 'nest' themselves and to feel 'of place' they struggled to overcome social isolation primarily at the micro-level of social interactions, and not through any type of political (group) mobilisation. In doing so they strongly placed the value upon interpersonal, informal contacts with the Dutch, characterised by acts of sociability or some type of minimal exchange, as the way out of social isolation and marginalisation. Without such contacts, citizenship had very little meaning to them, beyond its practical, formal status aspects.

A telling example of the importance of 'bridging social networks' with the Dutch, and the consequences of feeling socially isolated and therefore detached from Dutch society, is a sense of insecurity concerning their legal status and newly acquired citizenship rights. Although the vast majority of those I met had Dutch citizenship, quite a few of them expressed a degree of uneasiness or even fear of a possibility of their citizenship being revoked if the political situation in the Netherlands was to change and somehow was to turn all non-native Dutch into undesired aliens. Wallman's (1979) argument that a social boundary has two kinds of meaning, structural or organizational, and subjective, based on the experience of participants, helps explain this seemingly paradoxical situation. She suggests that: 'Because a social boundary is about the organization of society no more and no less than it is about the organization of experience, neither element has more or less reality than the other. Both the difference and the *sense* of difference count' (1979: 7). Among the people in my Amsterdam study, the social distance from the Dutch was translated into doubts concerning equality of citizenship rights between the two groups.[14] In the context of the Dutch 'integration model' to which they have been subjected, citizenship was perceived as yet another way of state control rather than a guarantee of equality and full participation. Therefore, if the acquisition of formal citizenship rights to inclusion and equality are not accompanied by bridging social networks in the receiving society, the organization of experience of refugees will remain strongly shaped by their feelings of 'otherness', perceptions of inequality and exclusion. Such experiences of exclusion cannot be overcome or changed by acquisition of formal citizenship rights.

The existence of such social ties or bridging social networks between the people I met in Rome and the locals/Italians, helped them to deal with the uncertainties of their temporary status, as pointed out in Chapter 4. These networks are not a 'natural' consequence of citizenship or minority rights and they do not develop at the institutional, structural level of the receiving society. Rather, they develop at the micro-level, through informal bridging social ties with the majority groups, and they are instrumental for forging new identities, loyalties and notions of belonging. This is why such contacts and networks were also important 'bonding experiences' that made them feel 'of Rome'.

The attitude of the people I met in Rome towards citizenship can be best summarised by the following account of Mirsad, who had been in Rome since the summer of 1993, and who still had a temporary status (permit) to stay in Italy at the time I met him, in 2000. He explained his attitude towards a (distant) possibility of becoming an Italian citizen and the meaning of that citizenship for him: 'To what state I belong now [after the experience of displacement] is a purely practical matter. I don't feel that I belong to any state but I have to have someone's passport.' Although they felt 'of Rome' in some important ways, their links with Italy were defined in terms of locality, not in relation to a nation-state or the nation. They perceived and valued citizenship as a status rather than as a practice.[15]

Because citizenship was valued in terms of securing formal membership and rights, most importantly the right to remain permanently in Italy, the lack of it was regarded as not only limiting their options and future life plans, but also as a 'humiliating' and 'degrading' experience. The latter was linked to the negative public notions associated with people who do 'not belong'. Ana, from Croatia, was a 24-year-old student in Rome when I met her; she articulated these feelings in the following way:

> I'm *extra-comunitari* here [a non-EU citizen]. That has this unpleasant ring to it – as if you've just climbed down a tree or as if you're some kind of criminal, who came here in a *gommone* [rubber dinghy] at night. That feeling and the constant reminder of it bothers me very much.

However, this type of bitterness and the sense of humiliation caused by exclusionary mechanisms imposed by the state and its systems were effectively counterbalanced by their feelings of social inclusion at the micro-level, as discussed in Chapter 4.

While the lack of formal right to remain permanently in Italy was experienced as discrimination, the lack of right to vote and participate in the formal political arena was not perceived as marginalisation, inequality or any significant exclusionary experience. Quite similarly to the people in Amsterdam, those in Rome did not place any important value on this type of participation. As those in Amsterdam, they too overwhelmingly belonged to the generation of people brought up in an undemocratic political system which shaped their perception of politics and political participation as a 'dirty business'. This conviction, shared by all, was only strengthened by their experiences of the first 'democratic', multi-party political elections in Yugoslavia, in 1990. As in Amsterdam, they found the experience deeply disappointing. Lepa's account reveals how these events shaped her attitude: 'I have no interest in taking part in that "game" [participation in politics by voting], not after what had happened in our country'. Their subsequent experiences of the formal political scene in Italy did not change their attitudes. Alija explained his stance in the following way:

> I was never interested in politics, like very many people of my generation back home, because I thought that no politician there ever deserved my vote. I've kept that opinion regarding the political situation in Italy as well, because there's no such thing as an honest politician.

Hence, this type of participation, or a lack of it, was not seen as significant for their process of emplacement or for feeling at 'home' in Rome and Italy.

New Meanings of Citizenship, Belonging and Emplacement

Transnationalism and the possibilities of transnational life strategies, as demonstrated in this chapter, challenge the dominant conception of membership, integration and belonging linked to a single unitary realm of nation-state. Transnationalism increasingly allows for emplacement that entails multi-layered forms of membership and incorporation that reach across the borders of multiple states, placing different dimensions of home in 'transnational social spaces' (Faist 2000). By allowing this, transnationalism also challenges the conventional understanding of citizenship, which links rights and loyalties exclusively to a single (nation) state.[16]

Meanings of state membership are changing, as evident from the provision of dual-state membership by an increasing number of (northern) states. Moreover, the endorsement of human rights principles governed by universal discourses embedded in international agreements and nation-states' constitutions, rather than the principle of sovereignty, are also affecting meanings of citizenship. Refugees and other migrants, as Faist (2000: 207) points out, are taking advantage of this growing tendency and the opportunities it creates to move around and make a place for themselves.

Through these transnational practices, some authors have argued, nation-states have become 'deterritorialized' (Basch et al.1994). Others claim, more convincingly, that the very concept of citizenship is changing. The international human rights regimes that transcend the jurisdiction of individual nation-states, political practices associated with so-called global civil society, as well as solidarity and identity shaped by transnational practices have all been indicators of the process of denationalising of citizenship (Bosniak 2001: 242–43). However sound these and other arguments about postnational citizenship are, one has to remember that the potential of human rights discourse for refugees and other migrants is still limited. For them, to create a space and a possibility of having a home outside their homelands or to locate it in transnational social space is undermined by the fact that human rights discourse is still interpreted and enforced by nation-states (Xenos 1996: 243–44). In this sense, states still dictate migration rules, although the logic and forms of transnational mobility may increasingly not fit them. Moreover, some (European) states have been recently attempting to counteract the transnational orientation of migrants by proposing the abolishment of dual nationality for third-generation migrants, and by discouraging dual nationality in general (de Haas 2005).[17] For all these reasons, it would be obviously premature to claim that the logic of transnationalism has completely superseded national logic (Castles 2004: 212). Also, as the discussion in this chapter revealed, transnationalism and transnational networks are always importantly connected to specific localities within nation-states.

With these points of caution in mind, and with an acknowledgement of how the sovereign powers of nation-states can affect the lives of individual refugees and often the entire groups of refugees originating from specific countries, the accounts of people presented here strongly indicate that for many refugees it is actually the possibility of moving and not that of becoming 'rooted' in a particular place that is central to their place-making strategies and the complex process of emplacement in exile. In this sense, and in spite of the continuous importance of the nation-state, transnationalism, transnational links and strategies have deconstructed its notion in some important ways, making citizenship no longer the main locus of identity for many refugees and other immigrants. Formal citizenship rights, specifically the right to indefinite residence, that is, to unconditional return, are making such place-making strategies possible, and are enhancing the process of emplacement of refugees.

While the acquisition of formal citizenship rights is sine qua non for the establishment of transnational place-making strategies, citizenship as a status appears to be less central to the complex realm of belonging, and matters associated with becoming and being 'of place'. As the discussion presented in this chapter revealed, as well as the accounts in Chapter 4, if refugees are not successful in establishing bridging social networks and ties in their places of exile, citizenship will have very little meaning and consequence for their experiences of inclusion and the sense of belonging. It remains a goal to be desired for its practical aspects, such as freedom of movement/travel and the formal right to establish a 'home'. The meaning and nature of 'home', however, is to be negotiated within the various specific contexts – those pertaining to individual refugees, to localities and societies they come from as well as in which they struggle to settle.

Emplacement: A Process of Pluralisation

The experiences of creating home in new sociocultural settings presented in this book point to the processes of pluralisation of identities, solidarities and membership forms among refugees during their emplacement. Approaching refugees as agents enables us to move away from the state-centred understandings of immigrant and refugee incorporation. Viewed through this lens it becomes apparent that emplacement of refugees is a complex process of negotiation of the need for continuity and change that goes beyond the powers of the nation-states to influence social relations. Although the state still has the power to influence what is legitimate and by extension what is acceptable or possible, it is the refugees as individual and group agents who struggle to emplace themselves in what is for *them* a meaningful way. In the process, they often reshape meanings and transgress boundaries of 'integration rules' set by the receiving states. They often also have to adjust their lives and plans, or their 'ways of being', in ways that accommodate the most pressing and rigid rules imposed on them in receiving societies. In so doing they, as social actors, make choices and adjustments which help them to cope with their (and their families') unfulfilled needs, uncertain plans, and unmet expectations at any given moment of their process of emplacement. This process is by no means smooth, problem-free or even entirely rational, that is, based on a process of assessing and weighting all of the available options opened to them.

The complexity of this process through which they struggle to define their status and regain power based on their specific trajectories of displacement, as well as histories and identities, cannot be properly understood through binaries commonly used in studying the incorporation of refugees and other immigrants. Country of origin versus receiving country, acculturation versus persistence of cultural alliances – these are some of the binary approaches to studying and understanding refugee incorporation. The rigidity of these and other binaries limit the possibility of capturing the complexity of social relations shaping the interplay between the need for continuity and change which is central to the process of refugee emplacement. As such binaries are commonly accompanied by essentialist notions of culture, unitary understandings of community and society, as well as the overemphasis on centrality of origin, past and experiences of loss, our understanding of the situation of refugees moves often even further away from the realities of their lived-in worlds.

The discussion in this book suggests that the social relations and connections that refugees make, become part of, or strive for, occur both as localising processes, thus within a nation-state, as well as transnational processes, hence spanning state borders. The process of emplacement of refugees is characterised by the dialectic relationship of these connections. The nature of the interrelationship of these processes will always be contextual and relational. However, it will always also lead to some level of pluralisation of identities, solidarities and membership forms.

Notes

1. Knudsen (1991: 24) talks about similar processes in camp dwellers in the South, who resist ascribed collective identity as refugees by searching for social contacts with people who are familiar with their past status, roles and identities.
2. The other type of cosmopolitanism is associated with the 'cultural citizen' who travels frequently, feels at home everywhere and nowhere, and is thus detached, avoiding any fixed boundaries (Urry 1995). This type of cosmopolitanism is usually associated with high-profile professionals, people who travel frequently, in other words, with elites, perceived as very different from refugees, seen as individuals and groups encapsulated in their ethnicised and culturally circumscribed worlds. Werbner (1999) disputes this connection and argues that there are multiple modalities of cosmopolitanism and ways in which people of different class 'engage with the Other'.
3. Information provided by the Netherlands Institute of Migration, Utrecht, December 2000. Interviews revealed that the programme did not increase the number or voluntary returnees in any significant way.
4. There is no indication that forced repatriation schemes introduced by governments of some receiving states are very successful either. In Germany, for example, the country which took the largest intake of refugee from Bosnia and which introduced a programme of their (forcible) return after the Dayton Peace Agreement, signed in November 1995, more than a half of those 'destined' to return were still in the country in July 1999 (Al-Ali 2002: 85).
5. Al-Ali et al. (2001) also point to the importance of legal status for refugees to engage in transnational lives.
6. A similar tendency was revealed in Eastmond's (2006) research among refugees in Sweden.
7. Duffield (1997), among others, talks about these issues.
8. Al-Ali et al. (2001: 583) also point out that war experiences may decrease the willingness of people to reestablish links with their places of origin, let alone to

return. By the same token, they further argue, traumatic experiences of war that transform specific groups into a victimized ethnic group, as was the case with Bosniaks, 'might constitute a powerful impetus to maintain strong links' with people of their ethnic background who live in their newly established state (ibid.).

9. Although a transnational phenomenon of 'astronaut families' has been detected in Australia and New Zealand among migrants from Hong Kong and Taiwan. They, after taking up residence, return to their country of origin to work or do business, spending lengthy periods out of Australia or New Zealand, while leaving their spouses and children behind (Colic-Peisker, 2008).

10. In most parts of socialist Yugoslavia extended family living arrangements, that is, living with one's husband's family, were customary; in some areas such arrangements were seen as almost obligatory. The practice is characteristic of rural and semi-urban settings in which it is associated with traditional/patriarchal notions of the family and household. In urban centres these types of living arrangements, when they occur, are more a consequence of scarce housing or a sign of the economic hardship of a newly married couple who cannot afford to live on their own.

11. Matsuoka and Sorenson's (1999) research among Eritrean and Ethiopian refugees in Canada, and Al-Ali's (2002) study of Bosnian refugees in the Netherlands and UK, reveal similar experiences of individual refugees, women and men, and their family life in exile.

12. Authors propose different approaches or dimensions of citizenship. Kymlicka and Norman (1994), for example, distinguish between citizenship-as-rights, citizenship-as-activity, and citizenship-as identity. These dimensions of citizenship they contrast to citizenship as legal status, which they do not discuss. Carnes (1996–1997), in yet another example, emphasises the legal, psychological and political dimensions of citizenship. Finally, Heater (1990) points to 'the feeling of citizenship', 'the status of citizenship', and 'political citizenship'.

13. Miro refers here to anti-EU demonstrations of the 1990s.

14. An additional factor in shaping their insecurity was also a heated political debate, initiated by several political parties in the Netherlands, about the right of Convention refugees from Bosnia to remain in the Netherlands and eventually become Dutch citizens. During 2001, many political parties in the Dutch parliament were challenging this status granted to Bosnian refugees, because, as they claimed, Bosnia had become a safe place to return to. The debate received significant press coverage and triggered a wide public debate, causing Bosnian refugees, with or without Dutch citizenship, to feel unsettled.

15. Anthias (2002) distinguishes between these two aspects of citizenship in her analysis of 'the politics of location' (2002: 285).

16. Heater (1990: 211–19), however, reminds us that citizenship has not always regarded as a project of the modern nation-state. The concept originates from the classical Greek city-state.

17. De Haas refers specifically to the Dutch and Danish governments (2005: 8–9).

Appendix 1

Refugees Interviewed in Rome and Amsterdam

1.1 Rome

1. *Omer* – age 33, university degree; he fled Bosnia-Herzegovina in July 1992 and came directly to Rome. He is single, of ethnically mixed background; on a work permit since 1994.

2. *Dragan* – age 38, interrupted university education; he fled Serbia in March 1992 and came directly to Rome where he did not continue his education. He is single, Serb. He had a humanitarian status at the time of the research.

3. *Nermin* – age 31, interrupted university education, at the time of the interview he was a student in Rome. He fled Bosnia-Herzegovina in the winter of 1995 and first went to Croatia. In March of the same year he came to Rome. He is single, of ethnically mixed background. He had a humanitarian status at the time of the research.

4. *Senad* – age 42, university degree; he fled Bosnia-Herzegovina in November 1992 and came directly to Rome. He is single, Bosniak; on a work permit since 1997.

5. *Tanja* – age 22, student in Rome; she fled Bosnia-Herzegovina in March 1993 and first went to Denmark where she obtained convention refugee status. She is single, of ethnically mixed background, in Rome since 1998.

6. *Stipe* – age 24, interrupted high school education; he completed a course for barmen in Rome. He fled Bosnia-Herzegovina in July 1992 and came directly to Rome. He is single, of ethnically mixed background; on a work permit since 1997.

7. *Rada* – age 32, secondary school degree; she fled Serbia in November 1993 and came directly to Rome. She is single, Serb; on a work permit since 1996.

8. *Damir* – age 27, high school degree before the flight and a college degree from Rome; he fled Croatia in the summer of 1991, and came directly to Rome. He is single, Croat. He had a humanitarian status at the time of the research.

9. *Faruk* – age 23, interrupted primary education; he fled Bosnia-Herzegovina in March 1992 and first went to Croatia where he completed his primary education. In the summer of 1993 he arrived in Rome where he did not continue his education. He is single, Bosniak. He had a humanitarian status at the time of the research.

10. *Mirsad* – age 25, interrupted high school education; he obtained high school degree while in exile in Croatia. At the time of the interview he was a student in Rome. He fled Bosnia-Herzegovina in March 1992, first to Croatia. In the summer of 1993, he arrived in Rome. He is single, Bosniak. He had a humanitarian status at the time of the research.

11. *Milena* – age 33, university degree; she fled Bosnia-Herzegovina in October 1992, and first went to Croatia. In November of the same year she arrived in Rome. She is single, of ethnically mixed background. She had a humanitarian status at the time of the research.

12. *Bojana* – age 29, university degree; she fled Croatia in the autumn of 1993 and came directly to Rome. She is single, of ethnically mixed background, born end raised in Bosnia-Herzegovina. She had a humanitarian status at the time of the research.

13. *Marija* – age 32, secondary school degree; she fled Montenegro in December 1993 and came directly to Rome. She is single, Montenegrin; on a work permit since 1998.

14. *Jusuf* – age 42, secondary school degree; he fled Bosnia-Herzegovina in December 1993 and came to Rome via Croatia. He is single, Bosniak; on a work permit since the end of 1994.

15. *Jana* – age 23, interrupted her high school education; she fled Montenegro in the winter of 1995 and came directly to Rome. She is single, of ethnically mixed background; on a work permit since 1996.

16. *Vera* – age 34, university degree before the flight and a student in Rome at the time of the research; She fled Bosnia-Herzegovina in the summer of 1993 and came directly to Rome. She is single, Serb. She had a humanitarian status at the time of the research..

17. *Marko* – age 30, interrupted university education and trained as a computer specialist in Rome. He fled Bosnia-Herzegovina in April 1992 and first went to Serbia, in February 1993 he arrived in Rome. He is cohabiting, of ethnically mixed background. He had a humanitarian status at the time of the research.

18. *Vesna* – age 33, interrupted university education, and trained as a computer specialist in Rome. She fled Croatia in the summer of 1991 and first went to Serbia. In November 1992 she arrived in Rome. She is cohabiting, Serb. She had a humanitarian status at the time of the research.

19. *Goca* – age 31, interrupted university education and a student in Rome at the time of the interview; she fled Bosnia-Herzegovina in March 1992 and first went to Germany. She arrived in Italy to join her boyfriend in the summer of 1992. She is cohabiting, Serb. She had a humanitarian status at the time of the research.

20. *Dule* – age 29, interrupted his university education, and gained a university degree in Rome. He fled Bosnia-Herzegovina in March 1992 and first went Montenegro. In the spring of the same year he arrived in Italy. He is cohabiting, Serb. He had a humanitarian status at the time of the research.

21. *Branka* – age33, university degree; she fled Bosnia-Herzegovina in September 1991 first went to the Netherlands. In the winter of 1991 she arrived in Italy. She is cohabiting, of ethnically mixed background. She had a humanitarian status at the time of the research.

22. *Mirza* – age 36, secondary school degree and a course for chefs in Rome; he fled Bosnia-Herzegovina in September 1991 and first went to the Netherlands. In January 1992 he arrived in Italy. He is cohabiting, of ethnically mixed background; on a work permit since 1994.

23. *Suada* – age 29, interrupted university education and at the time of the interview a student in Rome. She fled Bosnia-Herzegovina in April 1992 and first went to Croatia. In September 1992 she arrived in Rome. She is cohabiting, Bosniak. She had a humanitarian status at the time of the research.

24. *Alija* – age 31, interrupted his university education and at the time of the interview a student in Rome. He fled Bosnia-Herzegovina in September 1993 and first went to Serbia. In November 1993 he arrived in Rome. He is cohabiting, of ethnically mixed background. He had a humanitarian status at the time of the research.

25. *Emira* – age 28, interrupted her university education and at the time of the interview a student in Rome. She fled Bosnia-Herzegovina in May 1992 and first went to Croatia. In the summer of 1992 arrived in Rome. She is cohabiting with her Italian partner. She is Bosniak. She had a humanitarian status at the time of the research.

26. *Mirsada* – age 37, university degree; She fled Bosnia-Herzegovina in October 1992 and came directly to Italy. She is cohabiting with her Italian partner. She is Bosniak; on a work permit since 1999.

27. *Milka* – age 45, secondary school degree; she fled Bosnia-Herzegovina in August 1992 and came directly to Rome. She is married with two children, Croat. She had a humanitarian status at the time of the research..

28. *Milan* – age 47, university degree, fled Bosnia-Herzegovina in August 1992 and came directly to Rome. He is married, with two children, Serb. He had a humanitarian status at the time of the research.

29. *Darko* – age 20, interrupted primary education and at the time of the interview in his final year of high school. He fled Bosnia-Herzegovina in August 1992 and came directly to Rome. He is single, of ethnically mixed background, and was living with his parents. He had a humanitarian status at the time of the research.

30. *Aca* – age 22, interrupted primary education and at the time of the interview a student in Rome. He fled Bosnia-Herzegovina in August 1992 and came directly to Rome. He is single, of ethnically mixed background, and was living with his parents. He had a humanitarian status at the time of the research.

31. *Silva* – age 41, secondary school degree; she fled Croatia in August 1991 and first went to Serbia. In the summer of 1993 she arrived in Rome. She is married, with two children. She is a Croat; on a work permit since 1998.

32. *Misa* – age 43, university degree, he fled Croatia in February 1991 and first went to Serbia. In February 1993 he arrived in Rome. He is married, with two children. He is a Serb; on a work permit since 1998.

33. *Lepa* – age 50, university degree; she fled Croatia in November 1993 and first went to Germany. In September 1994 she arrived in Italy. She is married, with one child. She is a Serb; on a work permit since 1995.

34. *Bogdan* – age 53, university degree; fled Croatia in November 1993 and first went to Germany. In September 1994 he arrived in Italy. He is married, with one child. He is a Serb. He had a humanitarian status at the time of the research.

35. *Ana* – age 24, interrupted high school education and at the time of the interview a student in Rome. She fled Croatia in the summer of 1993 and first went to Serbia. In the summer of 1995 she arrived in Rome. She is single, Serb, and was living with her parents. She had a humanitarian status at the time of the research.

36. *Nada* – age 32, university degree; she fled Serbia in 1991 and came directly to Rome. She is married, has no children. She is a Serb, and has Italian citizenship. She lives with her Italian husband.

37. *Sanja* – age 26, high school degree before the flight and at the time of the interview a student in Rome; she fled Bosnia-Herzegovina in the fall of 1992 and came directly to Rome. She is married, has no children. She is of ethnically mixed background, and has Italian citizen. She lives with her Italian husband.

38. *Iva* – age 34, university degree; she fled Bosnia-Herzegovina in the spring of 1992 and came directly to Rome. She is married, has no children. She is of ethnically mixed background, and has Italian citizenship. She lives with her Italian husband.

39. *Srdjan* – age 32, university degree; he fled Serbia in the fall of 1993 and came directly to Rome. He is married, has no children. He is a Serb, and has a sojourn permit to stay for family reasons. He lives with his Italian wife.

40. *Spomenka* – age 38, university degree; she fled Serbia in April 1993 and came directly to Rome. She is divorced, has two children. She is a Serb; on a work permit since 1999.

1.2 Amsterdam

1. *Zenaida* – age 30, from Bosnia-Herzegovina, university degree; in the Netherlands since January 1992. She is self-employed after obtaining an additional university degree in Amsterdam. She is married, has one child. She is a Bosniak, and has Dutch citizenship since 1997. She lives with her husband and child. Her mother also lives in Amsterdam.

2. *Boris* – age 35, from Bosnia-Herzegovina, university degree; in the Netherlands since April 1994. He is employed in his profession after completing additional education and training. He is married, has one child. He is of ethnically mixed background, and has Dutch citizenship since 1999. He lives with his wife and child.

3. *Kajo* – age 37, from Bosnia-Herzegovina, university degree; in the Netherlands since July 1992. He was in the process of additional education and training for his diploma recognition at the time of the research. He is single, Bosniak, has Dutch citizenship since 1997. He lives on his own.

4. *Nadan* – age 59, from Bosnia-Herzegovina, technical school degree; in the Netherlands since October 1992. He is unemployed and married, with one child. He fled his home town in the spring of 1992 and found refuge in a Bosnian town where he stayed until September 1992. He is a Bosniak, and has Dutch citizenship since 1998. He lives with his wife. His son also lives with his family in Amsterdam.

5. *Emir* – age 51, from Bosnia-Herzegovina, technical school degree; in the Netherlands since the summer of 1993. He is unemployed and married, with

three children. He is a Bosniak, and has Dutch citizenship since 1997. He lives with his wife, three children and his mother-in-law.

6. *Mira* – age 30, from Bosnia-Herzegovina, interrupted university education; in the Netherlands since April 1993. She is self-employed after gaining a university degree in Amsterdam. She fled her home town in the spring of 1992 and went to Croatia. She is single, of ethnically mixed background, and has Dutch citizenship since 1998. She lives on her own. Her parents and the brother also live in Amsterdam.

7. *Sasa* – age 63, from Bosnia-Herzegovina, university degree; in the Netherlands since February 1994. He works occasionally on short-term contracts. He fled his home town in the winter of 1994 and came directly to the Netherlands. He is married, with two children. He is a Serb, and has Dutch citizenship since 1999. He lives with his wife. His two children also live in Amsterdam.

8. *Laria* – age 58, from Bosnia-Herzegovina, university degree; in the Netherlands since November 1993. She is employed but not in her profession or adequate to her educational level. She fled her hometown in the autumn of 1992 and went first to Croatia. She is married, with two children. She is a Croat, and has Dutch citizenship since 1999. She lives with her husband. Her children also live in Amsterdam.

9. *Belma* – age 42, from Bosnia-Herzegovina, technical school degree; in the Netherlands since November 1993. She is employed after completing a vocational training. She is divorced, with two children, and has Dutch citizenship since 1998. She lives with her children. Her sister and her children are also in the Netherlands.

10. *Slavenka* – age 25, from Bosnia-Herzegovina, high school degree before coming to the Netherlands in April 1995, and a student at a university in Amsterdam. She fled her home town in mid 1994 and first went to Croatia. She is single, of ethnically mixed background, and has Dutch citizenship since 2000. She lives on her own. Her mother and brother are also in Amsterdam.

11. *Nikica* – age 34, from Bosnia-Herzegovina, interrupted university education; in the Netherlands since July 1993. He is employed after completing a vocational training course. He fled his home town in the autumn of 1992 and first went to Croatia. He is married, has no children. He is of ethnically mixed background, and has Dutch citizenship since 1998. He lives with his wife. His parents and younger sister also live in Amsterdam.

12. *Cica* – age 34, from Bosnia-Herzegovina, secondary school degree; in the Netherlands since April 1994. She is employed after completing a vocational training course. She fled her home town in December 1993. She is married, has one child. She is of ethnically mixed background, and has Dutch citizenship since 1998. She lives with her husband and son. Her brother also lives in Amsterdam.

13. *Vladan* – age 36, from Croatia, technical school degree; in the Netherlands since the summer of 1991. He is self-employed after obtaining a secondary school degree in Amsterdam. He is married, has one child. He is a Serb, and has Dutch citizenship since 1998. He lives with his wife and the child. His parents also live in Amsterdam.

14. *Zlatan* – age 50, from Bosnia-Herzegovina, technical school degree; in the Netherlands since June 1993. He is unemployed and married, with two children. He is Bosniak, and has Dutch citizenship since 1999. He lives with his wife and the children.

15. *Jelena* – age 26, from Bosnia-Herzegovina, high school degree before the flight; in the Netherlands since 1997. She is a student at a university in Amsterdam. She fled her hometown in July 1993 and first went to Germany. She is single, of ethnically mixed background, and holds a humanitarian, 'C', status. She lives with her parents. Her brother is also in the Netherlands.

16. *Kemo* – age 23, from Bosnia-Herzegovina, secondary school degree before the flight; in the Netherlands since autumn 1995. He is employed after obtaining an additional technical school degree. He fled his home town in the summer of 1995. He is single, Bosniak, and has Dutch citizenship since 2000. He lives with his mother.

17. *Miro* – age 27, from Bosnia-Herzegovina, university degree; in the Netherlands since January 1997. He is a student at a university in Amsterdam, and an intern in a Dutch firm. He is single, of ethnically mixed background, and holds a humanitarian, 'C', status. He lives on his own. His mother and brother also live in the Netherlands.

18. *Sinisa* – age 40, from Bosnia-Herzegovina, university degree; in the Netherlands since May 1993. He is employed after completing additional training. He fled his home town in April 1993. He is married, has one child. He is a Serb, and has Dutch citizenship since 1998. He lives with his wife and the child. His brother and his brother-in-law also live with their families in Amsterdam.

19. *Smilja* – age 48, from Bosnia-Herzegovina, secondary school degree; in the Netherlands since May 1995. She is unemployed, and divorced, with two children. She is a Serb, and has Dutch citizenship since 2000. She lives on her own. Her sons are also in the Netherlands.

20. *Ivana* – age 47, from Bosnia-Herzegovina, university degree; in the Netherlands since 1997. She was attending a technical/IT training at the time of the interview. She is unemployed and divorced, with two children. She is a Serb, and holds a humanitarian, 'C', status.

Appendix 2

Community Organisations of Nationals from the Yugoslav Successor States in Rome and Amsterdam

2.1 Rome

Associazione Italo-Croata
Mr Luka Krilic, President

Grupo di aiuto per la Bosnia-Erzegovina
Mr Nino Kemura, President

2.2 Amsterdam

Bosnian Community Association – Amsterdam
Vice President: Mr Besim Ibisevic

Croatian Community Association – Amsterdam
Mr J. Bonacic

Yugoslav Association in the Netherlands – Rotterdam
Mr R. Rakocevic

Appendix 3

Contacts Made with NGOs, Church Organisations, Governmental and International Organisations in Italy and the Netherlands

3.1 Italy

NGOs

The Italian Refugee Council
Director: Mr Christopher Hein
Integration coordinator: Ms Grazia Curalli
Integration project: Ms Sabina Eleonori, Ms Lucia Falchetti
Integration/health project: Ms Germana Monaldi
Legal unit: Ms Antonella de Donnado, Ms Laora Ferrari

Casa dei Diritti Sociali
Mr Manfred Bergmann, Programme Coordinator

Centro Informazione ed Educazione allo Sviluppo
Ms Zana Belic, Coordinator

Consorzio Italiano di Solidaritá
Mr Giulio Macon, President
Mr Nadan Petrovic, External Relations Officer

Forum delle Comunitá Straniere in Italia
Ms Loretta Caponi, President

Asociazione Recreativa Culturale Italiana
Ms Anja Gujak, Coordinator

Church Organisations

Caritas Rome
Ms Miriam Lani, Deputy Director

Caritas Documentation Center
Mr Franco Pittao, Director
Mr Olivier Forti, Research Officer

Chiese Evangeliche
Ms Ana Maria Dupre, Director

Comunitá S. Egidio
Ms Daniela Pompei, Programme Coordinator

Fondazione Migrantes
Padre Bruno Mioli
Mr Roberto Ragno

Jesuit Refugee Service
Padre Francesco De Luccia

Governmental Institutions

Ministry of Interio, Direzione Generale Servizi Civili
Mr Compagnucci
Mr Stefano Vincenzi

Ministry of Social Affairs
Integration Department: Ms Vaifra Palanka

International Organisations

UNHCR, Rome
Mr Salvatore Ippolito, Senior Liaison Officer

IOM, Rome
Ms Enisa Bukvich, Coordinator

International Rescue Committee, Rome
Mr Rade Korac, Senior advisor

3.2 The Netherlands

NGOs

Dutch Refugee Council, Amsterdam (National)
Director: Mr Eduard Nazarski
Integration coordinator: Ms Roswita Weiler
Documentator: Edy Philipsen

The Dutch Refugee Council, Amsterdam (Local)
Director: Ms Jacqueline van Loon
Integration coordinator: Mr Martijn Kool

Emplooi (organization facilitating integration in the labour market), Amsterdam
Ms Ruth Limpens

Home for Peace, Amsterdam
Ms Nives Rebernak

LIZE (umbrella organization for South Europeans), Utrecht
Mr Sittrop, Boudewijn
Mr Raimond de Prez

VON (umbrella organization for work with refugee community organizations), Utrecht
Director: Ms Fatma Ozgumus
Consultant: Ms Alem Desta
Coordinator for refugees from former Yugoslavia: Mr Dinko Kajmovic

UAF (University Assistance Fund), Utrecht
Head of the Office: Ms Wies Kalsbeek
Consultant: Ms Stani Maessen

E-Quality (organization on gender and ethnicity), The Hague
Ms Amalia Deekman
Ms Astrid de Vruch

Governmental Institutions

Ministry of Justice, The Hague
Senior policy officer: Mr Peter Wagenmaker
Ms Jacoba Ghrib-Van den Erde

Ministry of Interior, The Hague
Senior Officer Ethnic Minorities Policy: Mr Ben Koolen
Senior Integration Officer: Mr Van Alten
Integration Officer: Mr Thomas Hessels

Ministry of Health, Welfare and Sport, The Hague
Senior Officer: Mr Menon Hekker

IND Information and Analysis Centre (INDIAC), The Hague
Policy Officer: Mr Arjen Taselaar

National Statistics Office, The Hague
Ms Erna Hooghimstra

Municipality of Amsterdam
Policy advisor: Ms Susan Brom

Appendix 4

The Social Characteristics and Legal Status of the Refugees in Rome and Amsterdam

Table 1: Social Characteristics and Legal Status of the Interviewees in Rome

Characteristics		N	%
Age			
20 to 30		15	37.5
31 to 40		17	42.5
41 to 50		7	17.5
over 50		1	2.5
Total		40	100
Gender			
Female		21	52.5
Male		19	47.5
Total		40	100
Marital status			
Single		19	47.5
Married		10	25.0
To Italians	4		
To their compatriots	6		
Cohabiting		10	25.0
With Italians	2		
With their compatriots	8		
Divorced		1	2.5
From Italians	0		
From their compatriots	1		
Total		40	100

Parental status

Single with children	0		
Married with children	6		
Cohabiting with children	0		
Divorced with children	1		
Total	7 out of 40	or	17.5 out of 100

**Educational level acquired
in the home country**

Elementary level		0	0
High or Secondary level		7	17.5
University degree		16	40.0
Interrupted by war		17	42.5
Education continued or			
vocational training taken	13		
Did not continue	4		
Total		40	100

Time of arrival

1991	9	22.5
1992	17	42.5
1993	12	30.0
1994	0	0
1995	2	5.0
Total	40	100

Legal status

Humanitarian status	22	55.0
Work permit	13	32.5
Italian citizenship or permit to stay for family reasons	5	12.5
Total	40	100

Current labour market status

Employed	28	70
Work and study	7	17.5
Only study	5	12.5
Unemployed	0	0
Total	40	100

Table 2: Social Characteristics and Legal Status of the Interviewees in Amsterdam

Characteristics		N	%
Age			
20 to 30		6	30
31 to 40		6	30
41 to 50		4	20
over 50		4	20
Total		20	100
Gender			
Female		9	45
Male		11	55
Total		20	100
Marital status			
Single		6	30
Married		11	55
To Dutch	0		
To their compatriots	11		
Cohabiting		0	
Divorced		3	15
From Dutch	0		
From their compatriots	3		
Total		20	100
Parental status			
Single with children		0	
Married with children		11	
Cohabiting with children		0	
Divorced with children		3	
Total	14 out of 20	or	70 out of 100
Educational level acquired in the home country			
Elementary level		0	0
High or Secondary level		7	35
University degree		7	35
Interrupted by war		6	30
Education continued or vocational training taken	6		
Did not continue	0		
Total		20	100

Time of arrival

1991	1	5
1992	3	15
1993	7	35
1994	3	15
1996	3	15
1997	0	0
1998	3	15
Total	20	100

Legal status

Convention ('A') status	0	0
Humanitarian ('C') status	2	10
Provisional permit to stay ('F' status)	1	5
Dutch citizenship	17	85
Total	20	100

Current labour market status

Employed	8	40
Casual contracts	2	10
Study	5	25
Unemployed	5	25
Total	20	100

Appendix 5

The Ethnic Background of the Refugees Interviewed

Table 3: Ethnic Background of the Interviewees in Rome

Bosnia-Herzegovina	N	%
Bosniaks	7	28
Croats	1	4
Serbs	4	16
Mixed background	13	52
Total from B-H	**25**	**100**
Croatia	**N**	**%**
Croats	2	25
Serbs	5	62.5
Mixed background	1	12.5
Total from Croatia	**8**	**100**
FR Yugoslavia		
Montenegrins	1	14.3
Serbs	5	71.4
Mixed background	1	14.3
Total from FRY	**7**	**100**
Total number of interviewees	**40**	

Table 4: Ethnic Background of the Interviewees in Amsterdam

Bosnia-Herzegovina	N	%
Bosniaks	7	36.8
Croats	0	
Serbs	5	26.4
Mixed background	7	36.8
Total from B-H	**19**	**100**
Croatia		
Croats	0	
Serbs	1	100
Mixed background	0	
Total from Croatia	**1**	**100**
FR Yugoslavia	**0**	
Total number of interviewees	**40**	

Bibliography

Adelman, H. and S. McGrath. 2007. 'To Date or To Marry: That is the Question', *Journal of Refugee Studies* 20(3): 376–80.

Al-Ali, N. 2002. 'Loss of Status or New Opportunities? Gender Relations and Transnational Ties among Bosnian Refugees', in D. Bryceson and U. Vuorela (eds) *The Transnational Family: New European Frontiers and Global Networks.* Oxford: Berg.

Al-Ali, N., R. Black, K. Koser. 2001. 'The limits to "transnationalism": Bosnian and Eritrean refugees in Europe as emerging transnational communities', *Ethnic and Racial Studies* 24(4): 578–600.

Al-Rasheed, M. 1994. 'The Myth of Return: Iraqi Arab and Assyrian Refugees in London', *Journal of Refugee Studies* 7(2/3): 199–219.

Anderson, P. 2001. '"You Don't Belong Here in Germany...": On the Social Situation of Refugee Children in Germany', *Journal of Refugee Studies* 14(2): 187–199.

Anthias, F. 2001. 'New Hybridities, old concepts: the limits of 'culture'. *Ethnic and Racial Studies* 24(4): 619–41.

—— 2002. 'Beyond Feminism and Multiculturalism: Locating Difference and the Politics of Location', *Women's Studies International Forum* 25(3): 275–86.

Anthias, F. and N. Yuval-Davis, 1992. *Racialised Boundaries – Race, Nation, Gender, Colour and Class and the Anti-racist Struggle.* London: Routledge.

Appadurai, A. 1988. 'Putting Hierarchy in its Place', *Cultural Anthropology* 3(1): 36–49.

Barnes, D. 2001. 'Resettled Refugees' Attacment to their Original and Subsequent Homelands: Long-term Vietnamese Refugees in Australia', *Journal of Refugee Studies* 14(4): 395–411.

Basch, L., N. Glick-Schiller and C.S. Blank. 1994. *Nations Unbound: Transnational Projects, Post-Colonial Predicaments and Deterritorialized Nation-States.* New York: Gordon and Breach.

Bauböck, R. 1996. 'Introduction', in R. Bauböck, A. Heller and A.R. Zolberg (eds) *The Challenge of Diversity – Integration and Pluralism in Societies of Immigration.* Aldershot: Avebury.

Bauböck, R., A. Heller, and A.R. Zolberg (eds). 1996. *The Challenge of Diversity – Integration and Pluralism in Societies of Immigration.* Aldershot: Avebury.
—— 2005. 'Identity for identity's sake is a bit dodgy', *Soundings* 29(Spring): 12–20.
Bauman, Z. 2002. 'Up the Lowly Nowherevilles of Liquid Modernity: Comments on and around Agier', *Ethnography* 3(3): 343–49.
—— 2004. *Wasted Lives: Modernity and its Outcasts.* Cambridge: Polity.
Bek-Pedersen, K. and E. Montgomery. 2006. 'Narratives of the Past and Present: Young Refugees' Construction of a Family Identity in Exile', *Journal of Refugee Studies* 19(1): 94–112.
Berry, J.W. 1997. 'Immigration, Acculturation, and Adaptation', *Applied Psychology* 46(1): 1–34.
Bhabha, H. 1990. *Nation and Narration.* London: Routledge.
—— 1994. *The Location of Culture.* London: Routledge.
Bloch, A. 1999. 'Carrying Out a Survey of Refugees: Some Methodological Considerations and Guidelines', *Journal of Refugee Studies* 12(4): 367–83.
—— 2002. *The Migration and Settlement of Refugees in Britain.* London: Palgrave Macmillan.
Borjas, G.J. and Crisp J. 2005. 'Introduction', in G.J. Borjas and J. Crisp (eds) *Poverty, International Migration and Asylum.* London: Palgrave in association with the UN University.
Bosniak, L. 2001. 'Denationalizing Citizenship', in T.A. Aleinikoff and D. Klusmeyer (eds) *Citizesnhip Today: Global Perspectives and Practices.* Washington D.C.: Carnegie Endowment for International Peace.
Bourdieu, P.1984. *Distinctions: A Social Critique of the Judgement of Taste.* Cambridge: Harvard University Press.
Bousquet, G. 1991. *Behind the Bamboo Hedge: The Impact of Homeland Politics in the Parisian Vietnamese Community.* Ann Arbor: University of Michigan Press.
Brah, A. 1996. *Cartographies of Diaspora: Contesting Identities,* London: Routledge.
Brink, M.1997. 'The Labour Market Integration of Refugees in the Netherlands', in P. Muus (ed.) *Exclusion and Inclusion of Refugees in Contemporary Europe.* Utrecht: Utrecht University, ERCOMER.
Brubaker, R.W. 1992. *Citizenship and Nationhood in France and Germany.* Cambridge: Harvard University Press.
Carnes, J. 1996–1997. 'Dimensions of Citizenship and National Identity in Canada', *The Philosophical Forum* 28(1–2): 111–24.
Castles, S. 1995. 'How Nation-states Respond to Immigration and Ethnic Diversity', *New Community* 21(3): 293–308.
—— 2000. *Ethnicity and Globalization.* London: Sage.
—— 2003. 'The International Politics of Forced Migration', *Development* 46(3): 11–20.
—— 2004. 'Why Migration Policies Fail', *Ethnic and Racial Studies* 27(2): 205–27.
Castles, S. and A. Davidson. 2000. *Citizenship and Migration: Globalisation and the politics of belonging.* London: Macmillan.
Castles, S., M. Korac, E. Vasta and S. Vertovec. 2003a. *Integration: Mapping the Field.* London: Home Office. On-line Report, http://www.homeoffice.gov.uk/rds/pdfs2/rdsolr2803.doc (Accessed 15 August 2003).
Castles, S., H. Crawley and S. Loughna. 2003b. *States of Conflict: Causes and Patterns of Forced Migration to the EU and Policy Responses.* London: IPPR.

Cockburn, C. 1997. 'Dealing With Identity: Women in Cross-Ethnic Alliances', Paper presented at the Centre for Gender Studies, University of Hull, UK, March.

Cohen, R. 2007. 'Response to Hathaway', *Journal of Refugee Studies* 20(3): 370–76.

Coleman, J. S. 1990. *Foundations of Social Theory*. Cambridge: Belknap Press of Harvard University Press.

Colic-Peisker, V. 2008. *Migration, Class, and Transnational Identities: Croatians in Australia and America*. Chicago: Illinois University Press.

Cornelius, W. and T. Tsuda. 2004. 'Controlling Immigration: The Limits of Government Intervention', in W. Cornelius, T. Tsuda, P. Martin and J. Hollifield (eds) *Controlling Immigration: A Global Perspective*, 2nd edition. Stanford: Stanford University Press.

Cresswell, T. 2004. *Place: A Short Introduction*. Oxford: Blackwell.

Crisp, J. 1999. *Policy Challenges of the New Diasporas: Migrant Networks and Their Impact on Asylum Flows and Regimes*. Working Paper No. 7. Geneva: Centre for Documentation and Research, UNHCR.

Daniel, V.E. and J. C. Knudsen. 1995. *Mistrusting Refugees*. Los Angeles: University of California Press

de Haas, H. 2005. *International Migration, Remittances and Development: Myths and Facts*. Global Migration Perspectives, Paper No. 30. Geneva: Global Commission on International Migration.

De Jong, G. and R.W. Gardner. 1981. *Migration Decision Making: Multidisciplinary Approaches to Micro-level Studies in Developed and Developing Countries*. New York: Pergamon Press.

Dekker, P. and E. Uslaner. 2001. 'Introduction', in P. Dekker, and E. Uslaner (eds) *Social Capital and Participation in Everyday Life*. London: Routledge.

Denitch, B. 1972. 'Social Structure: Strengths and Stresses', in George M. Raymond (ed.) *Proceedings of the Sixth Pratt Planning Conference on Yugoslavia's Socio-Economic and Urban Planning Policies*, held 7 March 1972. Brooklyin, NYC: The Planning Department, School of Architecture, Pratt Institute.

Des Forges, A. 2002. 'Silencing the Voices of Hate in Rwanda', in M.E. Price and M. Thomson (eds) *Forging Peace: Intervention, Human Rights and the Management of Media Space*. Edinburgh: Edinburgh University Press.

DeWind, J. 2007. 'Response to Hathaway', *Journal of Refugee Studies* 20(3): 381–85.

de Voe, D.M. 1981. 'Framing Refugees as Clients', *International Migration Review* 15(1): 88–94.

Doná, G. 2007. 'The *Microphysics* of Participation in Refugee Research', *Journal of Refugee Studies* 20(2): 210–29.

Douglas, M. 1991. 'The idea of a Home: A Kind of Space', *Social Research* 58(1): 287–307.

Duffield, M. 1997. 'Ethnic War and International Humanitarian Intervention: A Broad Perspective', in David Turton (ed.) *War and Ethnicity: Global Connections and Local Violence*. Rochester: University of Rochester Press.

Eastmond, M. 1993. 'Reconstructing Life: Chilean Refugee Women and the Dilemmas of Exile', in G. Bujis (ed.) *Migrant Women: Crossing Boundaries and Changing Identities*. Oxford: Berg.

—— 1997. *The Dilemmas of Exile. Chilean Refugees in the USA*. Gothenburg: Acta Universitatis Gothenburgensis.

—— 1998. 'Bosnian Muslim Refugees in Sweden', *Journal of Refugee Studies* 11(2): 161–81.

—— 2000. 'Refugees and Health: Ethnographic Appriaches', in F.J. Ahearn Jr. (ed.) *Psychological Wellness of Refugees: Issues in Qualitative and Quantitative Research.* New York: Berghahn.

—— 2006. 'Beyond Exile: Refugee Strategies in Transnational Contexts', in F. Crépeau, D. Nakache, M. Collyer, N.H. Goetz, R. Modi, A. Nadig, S. Špoljar-Vržina and L.H.M. van Willigen (eds) *Forced Migration and Global Processes: A View from Forced Migration Studies.* Lanham: Lexington.

Edwards, R. 1993. 'An Education in Interviewing: Placing the Researcher and the Research', in C.M. Renzetti and R.M. Lee (eds) *Researching Sensitive Topics.* Newbury Park: Sage.

Essed, P., G. Frerks and J. Schrijvers (eds). 2004. *Refugees and Transformation of Societies: Agency, Policies, Ethics and Politics.* New York: Berghahn.

European Commission. 2001. *Study on the Legal Framework and Administrative Practices in the Member States of the European Communities Regarding Reception Conditions for Persons Seeking International Protection.* Final Report, DG for Justice and Home Affairs.

Faist, T. 2000.'Transnationalization in International Migration: Implications for the Study of Citizenship and Culture', *Journal of Ethnic and Racial Studies* 23(2): 189–222.

Favell, A. 2000. *Philosophies of Integration: Immigration and the Idea of Citizenship in France and Britain.* Basingstoke: Macmillan.

—— 2001. 'Integration Policy and Integration Research: A Review and Critique', in A. Aleinikoff and D. Klusmeyer (eds) *Citizenship Today: Global Perspectives and Practices.* Washington D.C.: Brookings Institute and Carnegie Endowment.

Fernández-Kelly, M.P. 1995. 'Social and Cultural Capital in the Urban Ghetto: Implications for the Economic Sociology and Immigration', in A. Portes (ed.) *The Economic Sociology of Immigration: Essays on Networks, Ethnicity and Enterpreneurship.* New York: Russell Sage Foundation.

Freire, M. 1995. 'The Latin American Exile Experience from a Gender Perspective: A Psychodynamic Assessment', *Refuge* 14(8): 20–25.

Fuglerud, Ø. 1999. *Life on the Outside. The Tamil Diaspora and Long Distance Nationalism.* London: Pluto Press

Giddens, A. 1984. *The Constitution of Society: An Outline of the Theory of Structuration.* Cambridge: Polity Press.

—— 1987. *Social Theory and Modern Society.* Cambridge: Polity Press.

Glick-Schiller, N. 1997. 'The Situation of Transnational Studies', *Identities* 4(2): 155–66.

Glick-Schiller, N., L. Basch, and C. Szanton Blanc (eds). 1992. *Towards a Transnational Perspective on Migration: Race, Class, Ethnicity and Nationalism Reconsidered.* New York: New York Academy of Sciences.

Gold, S. 1992. *Refugee Communities: A Comparative Field Study.* London: Sage.

Goldberg, D. 1993. *Racist Culture.* Oxford: Blackwell.

Goodhand, J. and D. Hulme. 1999. 'From Wars to Complex Political Emergencies: Understanding Conflict and Peace-building in the New World Disorder', *Third World Quarterly* 20(1): 15–26.

Gorst-Unsworth, C. and E. Goldenberg. 1998. 'Psychological Sequelae of Torture and Organized Violence Suffered by Refugees from Iraq', *British Journal of Psychiatry* 172: 90–94.

Graham, M and S. Khosravi, 1997. 'Home is Where You Make It: Repatriation and Diaspora Culture among Iranians in Sweden', *Journal of Refugee Studies* 10(2): 115–33.

—— 2002. 'Reordering Public and Private in Iranian Cyberspace: Identity, Politics, and Mobilization', *Identities: Global Studies in Culture and Power* 9(2): 219–46.

Granovetter, M. 1973. 'The strength of weak ties', *American Journal of Sociology* 78(6): 1360–80.

—— 1985. 'Economic Action and Social Structure: The Problem of Embeddedness', *American Journal of Sociology* 91(3): 481–510.

Griffiths, D.J. 2000. 'Fragmentation and Consolidation: The Contrasting Cases of Somali and Kurdish refugees in London', *Journal of Refugee Studies* 13(3): 281–302.

Griffiths, D., N. Sigona and R. Zetter. 2005. *Refugee Community Organizations and Dispersal: Networks, Resources and Social Capital.* Bristol: The Policy Press.

—— 2006. 'Integrative Paradigms, Marginal Reality: Refugee Community Organizations and Dispersal in Britain', *Journal of Ethnic and Migration Studies* 32(5): 881–98

Gurak, D.T. and F. Caces. 1992. 'Migration Networks and the Shaping of Migration Systems', in M. Kritz, L. Lim, and H. Zlotnik (eds) *International Migration Systems: A Global Approach.* New York: Oxford University Press.

Habib, N. 1996. 'The Search for Home', *Journal of Refugee Studies* 9(1): 96–102.

Hannerz, U. 1992. *Cultural Complexity: Studies in the Social Organization of Meaning.* New York: Columbia University Press.

Harding, S. 1987. 'Introduction: Is There a Feminist Method?' in S. Harding (ed.) *Feminism and Methodology.* Bloomington: Indiana University Press.

Harrell-Bond, B. 1986. *Imposing Aid: Emergency Assistance to Refugees.* Oxford: Oxford University Press.

—— 1999. 'The Experience of Refugees as Recipients of Aid', in A. Ager (ed.) *Refugees: Perspectives on the Experience of Forced Migration.* London: Pinter.

Hathaway, J.C. 2007a. "Forced Migration Studies: Could We Agree Just to 'Date'?", *Journal of Refugee Studies* 20(3): 349–69.

—— 2007b. 'Rejoinder', *Journal of Refugee Studies* 20(3): 385–90.

Heater, D. 1990. *Citizenship: The Civic Ideal in World History, Politics and Education.* London: Longman.

Hill, J.D. and T.M. Wilson. 2003. 'Identity Politics and Politics of Identity', *Identities: Global Studies in Culture and Power* 10(1): 1–8.

Hollands, M. 2001. 'Upon Closer Acquaintance: The Impact of Direct Contact with Refugees on Dutch Hosts', *Journal of Refugee Studies* 14(3): 295–314.

Hopkins, G. 2006. 'Somali Community Organizations in London and Toronto: Collaboration and Effectiveness', *Journal of Refugee Studies* 19(3): 361–80.

Horenczyk, G. 1997. 'Immigrants' Perceptions of Host Attitudes and Their Reconnections of Cultural Groups', *Applied Psychology* 46(1): 34–38.

Hyndman, J. 2000. *Managing Displacement: Refugees and the Politics of Humanitarianism.* Minneapolis: University of Minnesota Press.

Indra, D. 1993. 'Some Feminist Contributions to Refugee Studies', Paper presented at conference on *Gender Issues and Refugees: Development Implications*, York University, Toronto, Canada, 9–11 May. Toronto: Centre for Refugee Studies, York University.

Jacobs, J. 1961. *The Death and Life of Great American Cities*. New York: Random House.

Jancar, B. 1985. 'The New Feminism in Yugoslavia', in P. Ramet (ed.) *Yugoslavia in the 1980s*. Boulder: Westview.

Joly, D. 1996. *Haven or Hell? Asylum Policies and Refugees in Europe*. Basingstoke: Macmillan.

—— 2002. 'Odyssean and Rubicon Refugees: Toward a Typology of Refugees in the Land of Exile', *International Migration* 40(6): 1–21.

Kaldor, M. 1999. *New and Old Wars*. Cambridge: Polity Press.

Kelly, L. 2003. 'Bosnian *Refugees* in Britain: Questioning Community', *Sociology* 37(1): 35–51

—— 2004. 'A Community Empowerment? The Bosnian Project in the UK', in P. Essed, G. Frerks and J.Schrijvers (eds) *Refugees and Transformation of Societies: Agency, Policies, Ethics and Politics*. New York: Berghahn.

Kibreab, G. 1999. 'Revisiting the Debate on People, Place, Identity and Displacement', *Journal of Refugee Studies* 12(4): 384–410

Klarin, M. 1995. 'Raseljeno pet miliona Jugoslovena: cetvorogodisnji bilans etnickog ciscenja' [Five million Yugoslavs uprooted: the result of four years of ethnic cleansing], *Nasa Borba*, 10 August, (p.5).

Knudsen, J.C. 1991. 'Therapeutic Strategies and Strategies for Refugee Coping', *Journal of Refugee Studies* 4(1): 21–38.

Kofman, E., A. Phizacklea, P. Raghuram and R. Sales 2000. *Gender and International Migration in Europe: Employment, Welfare and Politics*. London: Routledge.

Kohler Riessman, C. 1989. 'When Gender is Not Enough: Women Interviewing Women', *Gender & Society* 1 (2):172–207.

Korac, M. 1998. 'The Power of Gender in the Transition from State Socialism to Ethnic Nationalism, Militarization, and War: The Case of Post Yugoslav States', PhD thesis, York University, Canada.

—— 2003a. 'Women Organising against Nationalism and War in the Post-Yugoslav States', in W. Giles, M. de Alwis, E. Klain, N. Silva, M. Korac, D. Knezevic and Z. Papic (eds) *Feminists Under Fire: Exchanges Across War Zones*. Toronto: Between the Lines.

—— 2003b. 'The Lack of Integration Policy and Experiences of Integration: A Case Study of Refugees in Rome', *Journal of Refugee Studies* 16(4): 398–421

—— 2004. 'War, Flight and Exile: Gendered Violence among Refugee Women from Post-Yugoslav States', in W. Giles and J. Hyndman (eds) *Sites of Violence: Gender and Conflict Zones*. Berkeley: University of California Press.

—— 2005. 'The Role of Bridging Social Networks in Refugee Settlement: A Case of Italy and the Netherlands', in P. Waxman and V. Colic-Peisker (eds) *Homeland Wanted: Interdisciplinary Perspective on Refugee Resettlement in the West*. New York: Nova Science Publishers.

—— 2006. 'Gender, Conflict and Peace-Building: Lessons from the Conflict in the Former Yugoslavia', *Women's Studies International Forum*, Special Issue on 'Framing Gender Identities: Local Conflict/Global Violence', 29(5): 510–20.

—— forthcoming. 'Creative cultural dialogue and agency: The *sine qua non* for inclusion and equality', *Mondi Migranti* (May–June 2009)

Koser, K. 1997. 'Social Networks and the Asylum Cycle: The Case of Iranians in the Netherlands', *International Migration Review* 31(3): 591–611.

Kushner, T. and K. Knox. 2001. *Refugees in an Age of Genocide.* London: Frank Cass.

Kundera, M. 2003. *Ignorance.* New York: Harper Collins.

Kunz, E.F. 1973. 'The Refugee in Flight: Kinetic Models and Forms of Displacement', *International Migration Review* 7(2): 125–146.

Kymlicka, W. 1995. *Multicultural Citizenship: A Liberal Theory of Minority Rights.* Oxford: Clarendon Press.

Kymlicka, W. and W. Norman. 1994. 'Return to the Citizen: A Survey on Recent Work on Citizenship Theory', *Ethics* 104(2): 352–81.

Lavik, N.J., E. Hauff, A. Skrondal and Ø. Solberg. 1996. 'Mental Disorder among Refugees and the Impact of Persecution and Exile: Some Findings from an Out-Patient Population', *British Journal of Psychiatry* 169: 726–32.

Lazarus, R.S. 1997. 'Acculturation Isn't Everything', *Applied Psychology* 46(1): 39–43.

Lechner, F.J. 2000. *Managing Others: Minorities Policy and National Identity in the Netherlands.* Atlanta: Claus M. Halle Institute for Global Learning, Emory University.

Levitt, P. and N. Glick Schiller. 2004. 'Conceptualizing Simultaneity: A Transnational Social Field Perspective on Society', *International Migration Review* 38(3): 1002–39.

Long, N. 1992. 'From Paradigm Lost to Paradigm Regained? The Case of an Actor-oriented Sociology of Development', in N. Long and A. Long (eds) *Battlefields of Knowledge: The Interlocking of Theory and Practice in Social Research and Development.* London: Routledge.

—— 2001. *Development Sociology: Actor Perspective.* London: Routledge.

Losi, N. 1994. *Future Plans of Displaced Former-Yugoslavs Hosted in Reception Centres in Italy.* Rome: International Organization for Migration.

Malkki, L.H. 1992. 'National Geographic: The Rooting of Peoples and the Territorialization of National Identity Among Scholars and Refugees', *Cultural Anthropology* 7(1): 24–44.

—— 1995. 'Refugees and Exile: From 'Refugee Studies' to the National Order of Things', *Annual Review of Anthropology* 24: 495–523.

—— 1996. 'Speechless Emissaries: Refugees, Humanitarianism and Dehistoricization', *Cultural Anthropology* 11(3): 377–404.

Malvern, L. 2002. 'Missing the Story: The Media and the Rwanda Genocide', in C. McInnes and N.J. Wheeler (eds) *Dimensions of Military Intervention.* London: Frank Cass.

Mamgain, V., in collaboration with K. Collins. 2003. 'Off the Boat, Now Off to Work: Refugees in the Labour Market in Portland, Maine', *Journal of Refugee Studies* 16(2): 113–46.

Marfleet, P. 2006. *Refugees in a Global Era.* Basingstoke: Palgrave.

Martin, B. and C.T. Mohanty. 1986. 'Feminist Politics: What's Home Got to Do with It?' in T. de Lauretis (ed.) *Feminist Studies/Cultural Studies.* Bloomington: Indiana University Press.

Marx, E. 1990. 'The Social World of Refugees: A Conceptual Framework', *Journal of Refugee Studies* 3 (3): 189–203.

Massey, D. 1997. 'A Global Sense of Place', in T. Barnes and D. Gregory (eds) *Reading Human Geography*. London: Arnold.

Matsuoka, A. and J. Sorenson. 1999. 'Eritrean Canadian Refugees Households As Sites of Gender Renegotiation', in D. Indra (ed.) *Engendering Forced Migration – Theory and Practice*. New York: Berghahn.

McSpadden, L.A. 1999. 'Negotiating Masculinity in the Reconstruction of Social Place: Eritrean and Ethiopian Refugees in the United States and Sweden', in D. Indra (ed.) *Engendering Forced Migration – Theory and Practice*. New York: Berghahn.

McSpadden, L.A. and H. Moussa. 1996. 'Returning "Home"? The Decision-making Processes of Eritrean Women and Men', in W. Giles, H. Moussa and P. Van Esterik (eds) *Development & Diaspora: Gender and the Refugee Experience*. Toronto: Artemis Enterprises.

Migdal, J. 1988. *Strong Societies and Weak States: State-Society Relations and State Capabilities in the Third World*. Princeton: Princeton University Press.

Milic, A. 1993. 'Women and Nationalism in the Former Yugoslavia', in N. Funk and M. Mueller (eds) *Gender Politics and Post-Communism*. New York: Routledge.

Mollenkopf, J. 2000. 'Assimilating Immigrants in Amsterdam: A Perspective from New York', *The Netherlands' Journal of Social Sciences* 36(2): 126–45.

Morokvasic-Müller, M. 2004. 'From Pillars of Yugoslavism to Targets of Violence: Interethnic Marriages in the Former Yugoslavia and Thereafter', in W. Giles and J. Hyndman (eds) *Sites of Violence: Gender and Conflict Zones*. Berkeley: University of California Press.

Moussa, H. 1993. *Storm and Sanctuary – The Journey of Ethiopian and Eritrean Women Refugees*. Toronto: Artemis Enterprises.

Muggeridge, H. and G. Dona. 2006. 'Back Home? Refugees' Experiences of their First Visit back to their Country of Origin', *Journal of Refugee Studies* 19(4): 416–32.

Mumford, K. and A. Power. 2003. *East Enders: Family and Community in East London*. Bristol: The Policy Press.

Muus, P. 1998. 'Integration Policy in the Netherlands', in *Europe of Strangers: Integration Policy in a Comparative Perspective*. Copenhagen: The Danish Refugee Council and the Danish Cultural Institute.

Nafziger, E.W., F. Stewart and R. Väyrynen (eds). 2000. *War, Hunger, and Displacement: The Origins of Humanitarian Emergencies*, Volume 1. Oxford: Oxford University Press.

Parin. P. 1994. 'Open Wounds: Ethnopsychoanalytic Reflections of the Wars in the Former Yugoslavia', in A. Stiglmayer (ed.) *Mass Rape: The War Against Women in Bosnia-Herzegovina*. Lincoln: University of Nebraska Press.

Penninx, R. 2003. 'Integration: The Role of Communities, Institutions, and the State', *Migration Information Source*, Special Issue (October): Integration & Immigrants. Washington: Migration Policy Institute. http://migrationinformation.org/ Feature/ (Accessed 3 June 2005).

Penninx, R., K. Kraal, M. Martiniello and S. Vertovec. 2004. *Citizenship in European Cities: Immigrants, Local Policies and Integration Policies*. Aldershot: Ashgate.

—— 2004a. *Integration of Migrants: Economic, Social, Cultural and Political Dimensions*. Background paper for the UNECE conference, session on 'International

Migration: Promoting Management and Integration', Geneva, 12–14 January. http://www.unece.org/pau/epf/penninx.pdf (Accessed 3 June 2005).

—— 2004b. *The Logic of Integration Policies: An Exercise in Policy Thinking.* Lecture at CEDEM, University of Liège. 29 January. http://www.cedem.ulg.ac.be/m/wp/22.pdf (Accessed 3 June 2005).

Petrovic, R. 1985. *Etnicki mesoviti brakovi u Jugoslaviji* [Ethnically Mixed Marriages in Yugoslavia]. Beograd: Institut za socioloska istrazivanja Filozoskog fakulteta u Beogradu.

Pilkington, H. and M. Flynn. 1999. 'From "Refugee" to "Repatriate": Russian Repatriation Discourse in the Making', in R. Black and K. Koser (eds) *The End of the Refugee Cycle: Refugee Repatriation and Reconstruction.* New York: Berghahn.

Pittau, F. (ed.). 1999. *Immigrazione alle soglie del 2000.* Rome: Sinnos editrice.

Portes, A., L. Guarnizo and P. Landholt. 1999. 'Introduction: Pitfalls and Promises of an Emergent Research Field', *Ethnic and Racial Studies* 22(2): 217–37.

Putnam, R.D. 1993. *Making Democracy Work: Civic Traditions in Modern Italy.* Princeton: Princeton University Press.

—— 2000. *Bowling Alone: The Collapse and Revival of American Community.* New York: Simon & Schuster.

Reinsch, P. 2001. *Measuring Immigrant Integration: Diversity in a European City.* Aldershot: Ashgate.

Reyneri, E. 1998. 'The Role of the Underground Economy in Irregular Migration to Italy: Cause or Effect?', *Journal of Ethnic and Migration Studies* 24(2): 313–31.

Richmond, A.H. 1993. 'Reactive Migration: Sociological Perspectives on Refugee Movements', *Journal of Refugee Studies* 6(1): 5–24.

—— 1994. *Global Apartheid.* Oxford: Oxford University Press.

Robertson, R. 1995. 'Glocalization – time-space and homogeneity-heterogeneity', in M. Featherstone, S. Lash and R. Robertson (eds) *Global Modernities.* London: Sage.

Robinson, V. 1996. *Transients, Settlers and Refugees: Asians in Britain.* Oxford: Clarendon Press.

—— 1998. 'Defining and measuring successful refugee integration', Report of Conference on *Integration of Refugees in Europe*, Antwerp, 12–14 November. Brussels: European Council on Refugees and Exiles.

Said, E. 1984. The Mind of Winter: Reflections on Life in Exile', *Harper's Magazine* 269 (September): 49–55.

—— 2000 [1993]. 'Intellectual Exile: Expatriates and Marginals', in M. Bayoumi and A. Rubin (eds) *The Edward Said Reader.* London: Granta Books.

Salinas, M., D. Pritchard and A. Kibedi. 1987. 'Refugee Based Organizations: Their Functions and Importance for The Refugee in Britain', *Working Papers on Refugees*, No. 3. Oxford/London: Refugee Studies Programme and British Refugee Council.

Sam, D. and J.W. Berry, (eds). 2006. *Cambridge Handbook of Acculturation Psychology*, Cambridge: Cambridge University Press.

Schulz, H.L. with J. Hammer. 2003. *The Palestinian Diaspora: Formation of Identities and Politics of Homeland.* New York: Routledge.

Shukla, S. 1997. 'Building Diaspora and Nation: The 1991 "Cultural Festival of India"', *Cultural Studies* 2(2): 296–315.

Sigona, N. 2003. "'How Can a 'Nomad' be a 'Refugee'? Kosovo Roma and Labelling Policy in Italy", *Sociology* 37(1): 69–79.

Soysal, Y.N. 1994. *Limits of Citizenship: Migrants and Postnational Membership in Europe*. Chicago: Chicago University Press.

Stefansson, A.H. 2006. 'Homes in the Making: Property Restitution, Refugee Return and Senses of Belonging in a Post-war Bosnian Town', *International Migration* 44(3): 115–39.

Stepputat, F. 1999. 'Dead Horses? Response to Kibreab', *Journal of Refugee Studies* 12(4): 416–19.

Stoetzler, M. and N. Yuval-Davis. 2002. 'Standpoint Theory, Situated Knowledge, and the Situated Imagination', *Feminist Theory* 3(3): 315–34.

Tabboni, S. 1995. 'The Stranger and Modernity: From Equality of Rights to Recognition of Differences', *Thesis Eleven* 43(1): 17–27.

Turner, J.H. 1988. *A Theory of Social Interaction*. Stanford: Stanford University Press.

Turner, V.W. 1967. *The Forest of Symbols: Aspects of Ndembu Ritual*. Ithaca: Cornell University Press.

Turton, D. 2003. *Conceptualising Forced Migration*. RSC Working Paper No. 12. Oxford: Refugee Studies Centre.

—— (2005). 'The Meaning of Place in a World of Movement: Lessons from Long-term Field Research in Southern Ethiopia', *Journal of Refugee Studies*, 18(3): 258–280.

UNHCR. 1995. *The State of the World's Refugees 1995. In Search of Solutions*. Oxford: Oxford University Press.

Urry, J. 1995. *Consuming Places*. London: Routledge.

Valtonen, K. 1998. 'Resettlement of Middle Eastern Refugees in Finland: The Elusiveness of Integration', *Journal of Refugee Studies* 11(1): 38–60.

Van Hear, N. 1998. *New Diasporas: The Mass Exodus, Dispersal and Regrouping of Migrant Communities*. London: UCL Press.

—— 2003. *From Durable Solutions to Transnational Relations: Home and Exile among Refugee Diasporas*. Working paper No. 83. Geneva: Centre for Documentation and Research, UNHCR.

Vertovec, S. 1999. 'Conceiving and Researching Transnationalism', *Ethnic and Racial Studies* 22(2): 447–62.

Wahlbeck, Ö. 1999. *Kurdish Diasporas: A Comparative Study of Kurdish Refugee Communities*. London: Macmillan.

—— 2002. 'The Concept of Disapora as an Analytical Tool in the Study of Refugee Communities', *Journal of Ethnic and Migration Studies* 28 (2): 221–38.

Walby, S. 1992. 'Woman and Nation', *International Journal of Comparative Sociology* 32(1–2): 81–100.

Wallman, S. 1979. 'Introduction: The Scope for Ethnicity', in S. Wallman (ed.) *Ethnicity at Work*. London: Macmillan

—— 1986. 'Ethnicity and the Boundary Process in Context', in J. Rex and D. Mason (eds) *Theories of Race and Ethnic Relations*. Cambridge: Cambridge University Press.

Wallman, S. in association with Ian Buchanan. 1982. *Living in South London: Perspectives on Battersea 1971– 1981*. Aldershot: Gower, for the London School of Economics and Political Science.

Warner, D. 1994. 'Voluntary Repatriation and the Meaning of Return to Home: A Critique of Liberal Mathematics', *Journal of Refugee Studies* 7(2/3): 160–85.

Wellman, B. 1981. 'Applying Network Analysis to the Study of Support', in B.H. Gottlieb (ed.) *Social Networks and Social Support*. London: Sage.

Werbner, P. 1999. 'Global pathways: Working Class Cosmopolitans and the Creation of Transnational Ethnic Worlds', *Cultural Anthropology* 7(1): 17–35.

Williams, L. 2006. 'Social Networks of Refugees in the United Kingdom: Tradition, Tactics and New Community Spaces', *Journal of Ethnic and Migration Studies* 32(5): 865–79.

Wimmer, A. 2004. 'Does Ethnicity Matter? Everyday Group Formation in Three Swiss Immigrant Neighbourhoods', *Ethnic and Racial Studies* 27(1): 1–36.

Wimmer, A. and N. Glick Schiller. 2003. 'Methodological Nationalism, the Social Sciences, and the Study of Migration: An Essay in Historical Epistemology', *International Migration Review* 37(3): 576–610.

Wolpert, J. 1965. 'Behavioural Aspects of the Decision to Migrate', *Papers of the Regional Science Association*, No. 19: 159–69.

Woodward, S. 1995. *Balkan Tragedy: Chaos and Dissolution after the Cold War*. Washington D.C.: Brookings Institution.

Xenos, N. 1996. 'Refugees: The Modern Political Condition', in M.J. Shapiro and H.R. Alker (eds) *Challenging Boundaries: Global Flows, Territorial Identities*. Minneapolis: University of Minnesota Press.

Yuval-Davis, N. 1997. *Gender and Nation*, London: Sage.

Yuval-Davis, N. and F. Anthias (eds). 1989. *Women-Nation-State*. London: Macmillan.

Zetter, R. 1988. 'Refugees, Repatriation, and Root Causes', *Journal of Refugee Studies* 1(2): 99–106.

—— 1991. 'Labelling Refugees: Forming and Transforming a Bureaucratic Identity', *Journal of Refugee Studies* 4(1): 39–62.

—— 2007. 'More Labels, Fewer Refugees: Remaking the Refugee Label in an Era of Globalisation', *Journal of Refugee Studies* 20(2): 172–92.

Zolberg, A.R., A. Suhrke and S. Aguayo. 1989. *Escape From Violence: Conflict and the Refugee Crisis in the Developing World*. New York: Oxford University Press.

Zukin, S. 1975. *Beyond Marx and Tito: Theory and Practice of Yugoslav Socialism*. Cambridge: Cambridge University Press.

Žarkov, D. 2007. *The Body of War: Media, Ethnicity, and Gender in the Break-up of Yugoslavia*. Durham: Duke University Press

Žmegač, J.Č. 2005. 'Ethnically Privileged Migrants in Their New Homeland', *Journal of Refugee Studies*, 18(2): 199–215.

Index